Cardiovascular therapeutics

« *Médecine et Preuves* » *Collection*

By the same authors and the same publisher:

*Les Grands Essais Cliniques
en Thérapeutique Cardiovasculaire,*
Volumes I (1991) et II (1996)

*These books were awarded
the Jean Di Matteo prize
by the Académie Nationale de Médecine
on 9 december 1997.*

Designer: Bernard Van Geet

© 1999 Éditions Frison-Roche, 18, rue Dauphine, Paris.

2-87671-334-9

(2-87671-335-7 spanish edition)
(2-87671-336-5 italian edition)
ISBN 2-87671-285-7 (1ˢᵗ French edition)
ISBN 2-87671-325-X (2ⁿᵈ French edition)

ROBERT HAÏAT

Head of the Cardiology Department
Saint-Germain-en-Laye Hospital
Associate Professor
at the Collège de Médecine
des Hôpitaux de Paris

GÉRARD LEROY

Hospital Practitioner
Cardiology Department
Saint-Germain-en-Laye Hospital
Ancien Chef de Clinique-
Assistant des Hopitaux de Paris

Cardiovascular therapeutics

Cross-sectional analysis
of major clinical trials

Translated from French by
Dr Anthony Saul

Preface by
Professor Claude Guérot

ÉDITIONS FRISON-ROCHE

To Brigitte and Claude, our wives,
To Caroline and Emmanuel
and Adrien and Magalie, our children,
who, once again, accompanied us
throughout this fascinating adventure

Preface

Is there a future for the conventional press?

This is a legitimate question in view of the extraordinary progress in computerized communication. It is now easier to access, often from home, all of the bibliographic search engines, rather than go to a library. The Internet therefore competes with books and periodicals, particularly as it is a medium which changes our way of thinking, skimming of the article, looking for the main facts, and contenting ourselves with a summary. We no longer have the time, or no longer want to take the time, to read the details which nevertheless often provide a more refined, subtle complexity, corresponding more closely to reality.

The rapid progress made in medicine is possibly simply an excuse to explain this change of mentality, which gives greater credit to the most recently published article than to all those which came before.

But no, the future of publishing is not really threatened by the age of computers, as these two modalities are actually complementary. Computers have provided infinite research possibilities, while, within a finite space, a book provides rapid and complete information, while also satisfying the thinking that, even today, the human mind is superior to the machine: it is faster to turn a page than click on a mouse.

Books have obviously evolved in order to continue to provide the best possible information, and this will certainly be the conclusion reached by the reader consulting this new book by Robert Haïat and Gérard Leroy. Transmission of knowledge is endlessly changing and therapeutic trends are continually accelerating, to provide, clinical trial after clinical trial, new demonstrations of evidence on which our prescriptions must be based. However, they actually constitute therapeutic trends rather than established therapeutic progress, as, after having read many articles, one feels nevertheless that the situation has still not been fully elucidated.

We are therefore grateful to Robert Haïat, currently the President of the Société Française de Cardiologie, and Gérard Leroy, for undertaking this review. With their two previous books, they have acquired an unquestionable reputation in this field of evidence-based therapeutic research, by clearly and concisely presenting and discussing the results of cardiovascular trials, which already carries a certain weight. Twenty-five years ago, on the other side of the Atlantic, certain medical prescriptions for a patient were already justified by a bibliographical reference to the latest article published in the leading journal on the subject. In this book on cardiovascular therapy, treatment recommendations are no longer based on the most recent article, but on the whole body of literature, allowing us to precisely define the current state of knowledge by distinguishing what is known from what is probable and what still remains unknown. The main conclusions of the major trials are therefore placed in context, giving a more solid basis to our knowledge.

This book is not designed to impose a universal decision tree for each situation, as the authors are well aware of the complexity of medicine and therapeutics. They simply propose an evaluation of the various treatments in the light of clinical trials. Each practitioner, faced with a particular clinical case, will be able to make best use of this clearly presented and accessible encyclopedic review of this theoretical knowledge.

The format of this book suggests that every intern will keep a copy in his or her pocket and that every cardiologist will keep it at his or her fingertips.

Professor Claude Guérot,
Professor at the Necker-Enfants Malades Faculty of Medicine, Paris
Head of the Department of Cardiology, Hôpital Boucicaut
Past-President of the Société Française de Cardiologie

Contents

Unstable angina

Acute myocardial infarction

Ventricular tachycardia and ventricular fibrillation

Venous thromboembolism

Heart valve prostheses and anticoagulants

Foreword

*"Truth is not whatever claims to be true. If orange
trees develop solid roots and bear abundant fruit
in one field rather than another, then the truth
concerning orange trees is situated in that field."*
A. de Saint-Exupéry,
Terre des Hommes

*Although this new book is the logical sequel to our two previous volumes
of* Major Clinical Trials in Cardiovascular Therapeutics, *it is based on a different concept, with particular emphasis on synthesis, and its form has been
deliberately adapted to practical teaching. However, it does not constitute a
set of ready-to-use recipes.*

*No, this book has a very different purpose. Its aim is to highlight the main
points of the major clinical trials, at the very heart of their essential truth,
which must be understood, transmitted, and then applied to everyday clinical practice. We have felt this approach to be necessary for a long time.*

*When we completed the analysis of the 400 or so major clinical trials
which constitute the body of our two previous books, it became clearly apparent that trial-after-trial analysis (which could be described as a sequential analysis) very rapidly reached its own limits. However useful it may be,
such an analysis, on its own, by revealing more or less significant and sometimes contradictory results, cannot define the subtle and often transient
boundaries which differentiate patiently acquired certainties from only
probable data and as-yet unresolved questions.*

*It therefore seemed necessary to go one step further: from sequential anal-
ysis of the major clinical trials to what we have called cross-sectional, i.e. synthetic analysis, and this exercise was particularly beneficial because we constantly had to keep a certain distance when discussing the different topics
we chose to review.*

*We decided to construct each chapter of this book according to the model
of a tree: with its trunk, in which we have classified, first of all, the demonstrated and therefore generally accepted data, followed by those which appear to be only likely, and finally the as-yet unresolved questions; its branches,
corresponding to discussion of certain particular points, which we consider*

deserve a more detailed presentation; and finally its leaves, represented by tables, largely used to lighten the main body of the text or to highlight important information. Finally, to reduce the number of pages and facilitate the reading, we decided to insert the references in the very body of the text.

In line with scientific progress, we have included in this book most of the clinical trials and meta-analyses presented or published until December 31, 1998. Despite their exponential growth, we have also tried to collect data on the ongoing studies, with no illusions about the degree of exhaustiveness that we had achieved.

Once again, the task was very difficult, and the difficulties encountered during the writing of this book were of the same magnitude as the undoubtedly ambitious objective that we have set ourselves. It is therefore not surprising that some people will contest some of our choices and some of our proposals; others may be disappointed not to have found the information they were looking for; while others may point out an omission or imperfection. We are very aware of these problems: no text or book can ever be unanimously accepted.

Nevertheless, in this book, we have explored a new approach and have tried to help clinicians in their treatment options. Although they will sometimes find that this book confirms what they already knew, they will also discover that certain elements, which they thought they were alone in not knowing, are actually a problem for the entire cardiological community. We hope that clinicians will appreciate this book, which, in a way, provides an instant snapshot of current therapeutic practice, whose changing aspects are constantly modified along with the incessant publication of new large scale studies. This book is therefore resolutely situated both in the present and in the future, which is why we would like to dedicate it, not only to today's clinicians, but also to all students, general practitioners, and trainee specialists, who will develop the tomorrow's medicine.

Robert Haïat,
Gérard Leroy,

Hypertension

Hypertension is a risk factor for direct mechanical complications and indirect complications, related to atherosclerosis, the development of which is promoted by hypertension.

Direct complications include hemorrhagic cerebrovascular accident, left ventricular hypertrophy, heart failure, nephrosclerosis, and aortic dissection.

Atherosclerosis, an indirect complication of hypertension, is responsible for coronary insufficiency, ischemic cerebrovascular accidents, and occlusive arterial disease of the lower extremities.

Current state of knowledge

 Hypertension increases the annual incidence of cardiovascular events, in both sexes.

It is now known that SBP is a better indicator of cardiovascular risk than DBP (*Circulation* 1996;93:697-703 and *J Am Coll Cardiol* 1997;29:1407-1413).

Benetos (*Hypertension* 1997;30:1410-1415 and *Hypertension* 1998;32:560-564) in a study conducted in 19,083 men, aged 40 to 69 years, with a mean follow-up of 19.5 years, also clearly demonstrated that pulse pressure (characterized by elevation of SBP and lowering of DBP reflecting loss of arterial elasticity) is an independent predictive index for long-term cardiovascular mortality, especially coronary mortality.

 Treatment improves the medium-term and long-term prognosis of hypertension.

In the **HDFP** study (*JAMA* 1979;242:2562-2571 and *JAMA* 1988; 259:2113-2122), conducted in 10,940 hypertensive patients with DBP > 89 mm Hg, a therapeutic strategy conducted in a specialized center in order to obtain strict blood pressure control, vs a less intensive therapeutic strategy, with a 5-year follow-up, controlled DBP in 50% of patients and significantly reduced all cause mortality by 17% (*p* < 0.01) and cardiovascular mortality by 19%.

In the **Framingham** study (*Circulation* 1996;93:697-703), long-term follow-up (1950-1990) of a population of unselected hypertensive patients of both sexes confirmed the medium-term results obtained in large-scale clinical trials: antihypertensive treatment significantly reduces cardiovascular mortality in males and females.

 Treatment improves the prognosis proportionally to the reduction of blood pressure figures.

 Treatment improves the prognosis regardless of the severity of hypertension.

Treatment improves the prognosis of malignant hypertension, severe hypertension, and mild-to-moderate hypertension.

● **Malignant hypertension**

Malignant hypertension is defined as DBP > 140 mm Hg associated with a neurological and/or cardiac and/or renal lesion and/or ocular fundus lesions.

Once installed, malignant hypertension is a serious disease whose prognosis has been clearly improved by antihypertensive treatment, as the 5-year survival rate was practically zero at the beginning of the 1950s, 30% to 40% at the beginning of the 1960s (*Am J Cardiol* 1960;6:858-863), and is now 74% (*J Hypertens* 1995;13: 915-924). The increasingly widespread treatment of hypertension also ensures prevention of malignant hypertension, whose incidence has considerably decreased.

● **Severe hypertension**

Treatment improves the prognosis of severe hypertension, as demonstrated, after the first controlled study by **Hamilton** (*Lancet* 1964;1:235-238), by the **Veterans** studies (*JAMA* 1967;202:1028-1034 and 1970;213:1143-1152), conducted in 143 hypertensive patients with DBP between 115 and 129 mm Hg. Drug treatment comprising hydrochlorothiazide, reserpine, and hydralazine, vs placebo, significantly decreased the cardiovascular morbidity and mortality, with a follow-up of 1.5, and 3.3 years.

● **Mild-to-moderate hypertension**

Mild-to-moderate hypertension is frequent, as it affects 70% of hypertensive patients and 60% of the mortality attributable to hypertension concerns patients with a DBP between 90 and 104 mm Hg.

Treatment improves the prognosis of mild-to-moderate hypertension.

The meta-analysis by **Collins** (*Lancet* 1990;335:827-838), based on 14 trials including almost 37,000 patients most of whom (90%) had a DBP < 115 mm Hg and were essentially treated with diuretics and/or beta-blockers, showed that a 5- to 6-mm Hg reduction of DBP significantly decreased the incidence of cerebrovascular accidents by 42% and the incidence of coronary events and coronary mortality by 14%, with a follow-up of 5 years.

⑤ Treatment improves the prognosis of all forms of hypertension in elderly subjects (> 60 years).

Eight major trials [**EWPHE** (*Lancet* 1985;1:1349-1354), **SHEP** (*JAMA* 1991;265:3255-3264), **STOP-Hypertension** (*Lancet* 1991; 338:1281-1285), **MRC-Older** (*BMJ* 1992;304:405-412), **CASTEL** (*Jpn Heart J.* 1994;35:589-600), **STONE** (*J Hypertens* 1996;14: 1237-1245), **SYST-EUR** (*Lancet* 1997;350:757-764), and **SYST-China** (*J Hypertens* 1998;16:1823-1829)], based on several thousand patients, with a follow-up of 2.2 years (**SYST-China**) to 5.8 years (**MRC-Older**), showed that the treatment of hypertension allowed a reduction of blood pressure figures with a low incidence of adverse effects and also improved the prognosis of the disease. In these studies, hypertension was essentially systolic and diastolic, but some studies also included cases of isolated systolic hypertension (**SHEP**, **SYST-EUR**, and **SYST-China** studies). Treatment was essentially based on diuretics and/or beta-blockers, except in the **STONE** (nifedipine SR), **SYST-EUR**, and **SYST-China** studies (nitrendipine), which were conducted with a calcium channel blocker.

A meta-analysis by **Mac Mahon** and **Rodgers** (*Clin Exp Hypertens* 1993;15:967-978), based on 5 randomized trials including a total of 14,283 patients over the age of 60 years with a follow-up of 5 years, showed that antihypertensive treatment decreased SBP by 12 to 14 mm Hg and DBP by 5 to 6 mm Hg and significantly reduced vascular mortality by 23% ($2p < 0.001$), the incidence of cerebrovascular accidents by 34% ($2p < 0.0001$), and coronary morbidity and mortality by 19% ($2p < 0.05$).

A meta-analysis by **Insua** (*Ann Intern Med* 1994;121:355-362), based on 9 trials including 15,559 hypertensive patients over the age of 60 years, showed that treatment significantly decreased all cause mortality by about 12% (p = 0.009), coronary mortality by 25% (p < 0.001), and mortality due to cerebrovascular accident by 36% (p < 0.001). It also reduced coronary morbidity by 15% (p = 0.036) and morbidity secondary to cerebrovascular accidents by 35% (p < 0.001).

A meta-analysis by **Pearce** (*Arch Intern Med* 1995;4:943-950), based on 8 trials including 15,990 hypertensive patients over the age of 60 years and treated for an average of 4.6 years, showed that treatment reduced: the relative risk of major fatal or nonfatal coronary events by 18% (RR: 0.82; 95% CI: 0.73 to 0.92, p = 0.001, i.e. an absolute reduction of coronary events of 3 per 1,000 patient/years); the relative risk of fatal or nonfatal cerebrovascular accidents by 35% (RR: 0.65; 95% CI: 0.57 to 0.75, p< 0.001; i.e. an absolute reduction of 5.4 cerebrovascular accidents per 1,000 patient/years); the overall mortality by 15% (RR: 0.85; 95% CI: 0.78 to 0.92, p= 0.007, i.e. in absolute terms, 4.3 deaths prevented per 1,000 patient/years).

A more recent meta-analysis by **Gueyffier** (*J Hum Hypertens* 1996;10:1-8), showed that antihypertensive treatment in patients over the age of 60 prevented 9 cerebrovascular accidents and 4 major coronary events every 1,000 patient-years. Lastly, it should be noted (**SHEP, STOP-Hypertension** studies) that the effect of treatment decreases with age, especially above the age of 80 years (*Ann Intern Med* 1994;121:355-362).

6 **In hypertensive patients over the age of 60, long-term treatment with thiazide diuretics (chlorthalidone 12.5 to 25 mg daily) only slightly modified the main metabolic constants and electrolytes.**

This was demonstrated by retrospective analysis (*Arch Intern Med* 1998;158:741-751) of patients recruited in the **SHEP** study. With a follow-up of 3 years, no significant difference was observed between active treatment and placebo for the incidence of diabetes (8.6% new cases vs 7.5%, p = 0.25) but the diuretic slightly modified the blood glucose level (+0.036 mg/L, i.e. +0.20 mmol/L, p < 0.01), total serum cholesterol (+0.035 g/L, i.e. +0.09 mmol/L, p < 0.01), serum HDL-C (-0.007 g/L, i.e. -0.02 mmol/L, p < 0.01), and serum creatinine (+0.003 g/L, i.e. +2.8 µmol/L, p < 0.001). A slightly greater alteration was observed for triglycerides (+0.017 g/L, i.e. +0.09 mmol/L, p < 0.001), serum uric acid (+0.006 g/L, i.e. +35 µmol/L, p < 0.001), and serum potassium (-0.3 mmol/L, p < 0.001).

Antihypertensive treatment is equally beneficial in males and females.

This was demonstrated by a meta-analysis by **Gueyffier** (*Ann Intern Med* 1997;126:761-767), based on 7 randomized studies including a total of 19,975 men and 20,802 women, essentially treated by beta-blockers and thiazide diuretics. In both sexes, antihypertensive treatment induced a similar reduction of the relative risk of cerebrovascular and coronary accidents and the risk of death from any cause and from cardiovascular disease.

8 Treatment of hypertension allows regression of left ventricular hypertrophy.

This was demonstrated by the meta-analysis by **Dalhöf** (*Am J Hypertens* 1992;5:95-110) and applies to the main therapeutic categories studied: diuretics, beta-blockers, calcium channel blockers, and angiotensin-converting enzyme inhibitors.

According to a meta-analysis by **Schmieder** (*JAMA* 1996;275: 1507-1513), based on 39 trials, the reduction of left ventricular mass evaluated in 1,205 patients treated for an average of 19 weeks increased in proportion to the reduction of SBP ($p < 0.001$) [and to a lesser degree DBP ($p = 0.08$)] and the duration of treatment ($p < 0.01$).

These two meta-analyses suggest that ACE-inhibitors induce a more marked regression of left ventricular mass than other therapeutic categories.

This statement will probably be slightly modified and refined over the next few years, following the development of a more rigorous methodology based on randomized, blinded, centralized reading of echocardiograms. This approach improves quantification and avoids overestimation of left ventricular hypertrophy; this methodology was adopted in the **LIVE** and **PRESERVE** studies, whose results tend to modify certain opinions that previously appeared to be well established.

In the European multicenter **LIVE** study (18th Journées de L'Hypertension Artérielle, 1998), conducted on 505 hypertensive patients with left ventricular hypertrophy, indapamide SR (1.5 mg daily) vs enalapril (20 mg daily), administered for 12 months, significantly decreased the left ventricular mass index to a greater degree, for a statistically equivalent reduction of blood pressure, mainly by reducing the thickness of the posterior wall and septum.

In the **PRESERVE** study (*Circulation* 1998;98 suppl. I:I-29), conducted in 291 hypertensive patients with left ventricular hypertrophy, enalapril was compared to nifedipine SR. Overall, antihypertensive treatment significantly decreased blood pressure and left ventricular mass at the 6th month, but no difference was observed between the effects of enalapril and nifedipine on this last parameter.

Regardless of the medication used to achieve it, reduction of left ventricular hypertrophy is clinically relevant, as increased ventricular mass *per se* is known to be a risk factor which increases cardiovascular morbidity and mortality (as it increases the incidence of atrial and ventricular arrhythmias, accentuates myocardial ischemia, and decreases left ventricular relaxation and compliance), especially when left ventricular mass is > 125 g/m^2.

According to the **Framingham** study (*N Engl J Med* 1990;322: 1561-1566), any increase in left ventricular mass by 50 g/m^2 over a 4-year period is accompanied by an increase of the relative risk of cardiovascular mortality of 2.21 in females and 1.73 in males.

 However, no controlled study has demonstrated that regression of left ventricular hypertrophy provides an additional benefit to that provided by simple reduction of blood pressure (*J Hypertens* 1996;14 suppl. 2:S95-S102).

This finding still remains valid, although some isolated data have demonstrated that regression of electrocardiographic signs of left ventricular hypertrophy was associated with reduction of the risk of developing a cardiovascular event (*Circulation* 1994;90:1786-1793).

 Non-pharmacological treatment of hypertension can reduce blood pressure.

● Non-pharmacological treatment consists of a series of health and dietary measures: weight loss in the case of obesity, reduction of daily salt and alcohol intake, and increased physical exercise.

The **TAIM** study (*Arch Intern Med* 1992;152:131-136), conducted in 529 overweight patients with mild hypertension (DBP between 90 and 100 mm Hg) showed that weight loss was more effective than sodium restriction and stress management: weight loss of 4 kg decreased DBP by an average of 2.3 mm Hg and SBP by an average of 2.9 mm Hg. It also potentiated the effect of antihypertensive treatment.

The **DASH** study (*N Engl J Med* 1997;336:1117-1124), conducted in 459 patients with mild hypertension (SBP < 160 mm Hg and DBP between 80 and 95 mm Hg) showed that a diet rich in vegetables, fruit, and low-fat dairy products, but containing little fat, especially saturated fats, prescribed for 3 weeks, significantly lowered blood pressure figures.

● However, compliance with non-pharmacological treatment tends to decline over time. The **TOMHS** study (*JAMA* 1993;270:713-724), conducted in 902 patients with mild hypertension (DBP between 90 and 99 mm Hg) clearly showed that, after one year, monotherapy drug treatment proved to be more effective than health and dietary measures alone to prevent cardiovascular events.

⓫ For a long time, diuretics and beta-blockers, used as first-line treatment for primary prevention, were the only therapeutic category demonstrated by long-term studies to reduce the morbidity and mortality of hypertension (*J Hypertens* 1996;14:929-933).

Diuretics appear to be just as effective as beta-blockers on this parameter: in the **MRC** (*BMJ* 1985;291:97-104) and **HAPPHY** studies (*J Hypertens* 1987;5:571-572), they effectively reduced the morbidity and mortality related to hypertension. However, it must be stressed that these trials were not designed to demonstrate a difference of efficacy between these two therapeutic categories which, moreover, were prescribed in combination in more than one half of cases.

A meta-analysis by **Psaty** (*JAMA* 1997;277:739-745), based on 18 randomized, placebo-controlled trials including a total of 48,220 hypertensive patients with a mean follow-up of 5 years, evaluated the efficacy of first-line antihypertensive treatments. Beta-blockers and low-dose thiazides (12.5 mg to 25 mg daily of chlorthalidone or hydrochlorothiazide), vs placebo, significantly prevented cerebrovascular accidents and congestive heart failure. Low-dose thiazides also decreased the incidence of coronary events, cardiovascular mortality, and all cause mortality.

12 Diuretics are more effective than beta-blockers in the elderly.

This was demonstrated by the meta-analysis by **Messerli** (*JAMA* 1998;219:1903-1907), based on 10 trials including 16,164 hypertensive patients (isolated systolic or diastolic hypertension), over the age of 60 years, treated by first-line monotherapy. With a mean follow-up of 5 years, diuretics controlled blood pressure in two-thirds of cases (vs less than one-third of cases with beta-blockers) and decreased the relative risk of fatal and nonfatal cerebrovascular accidents by 33% (RR: 0.67), while beta-blockers only decreased the relative risk of nonfatal cerebrovascular accidents by 26% (RR: 0.74). Diuretics also significantly decreased the incidence of coronary events, cardiovascular mortality and all cause mortality, while beta-blockers had no effect on these three parameters.

13 Calcium channel blockers are currently the subject of a controversy, revived by the publication of the favorable results of the **STONE, SYST-EUR, VHAS,** and **SYST-China** studies (see p. 55) and the less favorable results of the **ABCD** study (see p. 57).

14 The efficacy of angiotensin-converting enzyme (ACE) inhibitors in primary prevention was recently demonstrated for the first time.

The **CAPPP** study (*Lancet* 1999;353:611-616) was conducted in 10,985 hypertensive patients recruited by 536 centers in Sweden and Finland, who received, under open-label conditions after randomization (**PROBE** method, see p. 31), either captopril (50 to 100 mg daily), coprescribed with a diuretic when necessary, or a beta-blocker or a diuretic (coprescribed when necessary) in order to achieve DBP $\leq$ 90 mm Hg. With a mean follow-up of 6.1 years, captopril exerted the same effect as the other treatments on the main endpoint of the study, i.e. a composite criterion combining fatal and nonfatal myocardial infarctions, fatal and nonfatal cerebrovascular accidents, and other cardiovascular mortality. Primary endpoint events occurred in 363 patients (11.1 per 1,000 patient-years) vs 335 [10.2 per 1,000 patient-years;RR 1.05 (95% CI: 0.90 to 1.22),p = 0.52] ; cardiovascular mortality was lower with captopril [76 vs 95 events; RR 0.77 (95% CI: 0.57 to 1.04),p = 0.092]. The rate of fatal and nonfatal myocardial infarction was similar (162 vs 161), but fatal and nonfatal stroke were more common with captopril [189 vs 148; RR 1.25 (95% CI: 1.01 to 1.55),p = 0.044].

In hypertensive diabetics, tight blood pressure control reduces the complications and mortality related to diabetes.

This was demonstrated by the **UKPDS 38** study (*BMJ* 1998;317: 703-713), which compared two approaches to blood pressure control in 1,148 hypertensive patients (mean blood pressure: 160/94 mm Hg) with type 2 diabetes: tight control (758 patients) mainly based on the use of captopril (25 to 50 mg bid) or atenolol (50 to 100 mg daily) designed to achieve blood pressure < 150/85 mm Hg; less tight control (390 patients), avoiding the use of ACE-inhibitors or beta-blockers and designed to achieve blood pressure < 180/105 mm Hg.

With a median follow-up of 8.4 years, tight blood pressure control vs less tight blood pressure control more markedly decreased blood pressure (144/82 mm Hg vs 154/87 mm Hg, $p < 0.0001$); reduced the number of first events related to diabetes (mainly consisting of sudden death, fatal or nonfatal myocardial infarction, heart failure, angina, cerebrovascular accident, renal failure) by 24% (95% CI: 8% to 38%, $p = 0.0046$); it reduced also the number of deaths related to diabetes (sudden death, death associated with myocardial infarction, cerebrovascular accident, renal failure or peripheral arterial disease) by 32% (95% CI: 6% to 51%, $p = 0.019$); cerebrovascular accidents by 44% (95% CI: 11% to 65%, $p = 0.013$) and events related to microvascular disease by 37% (95% CI: 11% to 56%, $p = 0.0092$). It tended to decrease all cause mortality (NS); reduced the proportion of patients with deterioration of retinopathy by 34% (99% CI: 11% to 50%, $p = 0.0004$) and the proportion of patients with deterioration of visual acuity by 47% (95% CI: 7% to 70%, $p = 0.004$).

In these hypertensive diabetic patients, although tight control of blood pressure was achieved at the price of more frequent use of at least 3 antihypertensives (prescribed in 29% of patients), this therapeutic strategy has an overall lower cost than that designed to achieve less tight blood pressure control, because it more markedly decreases the complication rate, as demonstrated by the **UKPDS 40** study (*BMJ* 1998;317:720-726).

In hypertensive diabetic patients, captopril and atenolol have also been shown to be effective to decrease blood pressure figures and to reduce the cardiovascular risk related to macrovascular complications and deterioration of retinopathy.

This was demonstrated by the **UKPDS 39** study (*BMJ* 1998;317: 713-720), which did not reveal any harmful or beneficial effect of captopril compared to atenolol (the proportion of patients presenting an episode of hypoglycemia was similar in the two groups; a slightly higher weight gain was observed with atenolol), suggesting that blood pressure reduction is probably more important than the type of treatment used to obtain it.

This study therefore does not support the hypothesis that ACE-inhibitors exert a nephroprotective effect in patients with type 2 diabetes.

Blood pressure control of hypertensive patients still remains far from perfect.

From the **NAHNES II** survey (1976-1980) to the **NAHNES III** phase 1 survey (1988-91), the percentage of American subjects with known hypertension increased from 51% to 73%. Over the same period, the percentage of treated hypertensive patients increased from 31% to 55%, while the percentage of patients whose blood pressure was decreased to below 140/90 mm Hg, increased from 10% to 29% (*Hypertension* 1995;26:60-69). Bearing in mind that approximately 50 million Americans suffer from hypertension, it should be stressed that three-quarters of them have a blood pressure which remains greater than 140/90 mm Hg (*Hypertension* 1995;25:305-313).

In the study by **Berlowitz** (*N Engl J Med* 1998;339:1957-1963), conducted over 2 years in 800 male hypertensive patients with a mean age of 65 ± 9.1 years, in whom hypertension had been present for an average of 12.6 ± 5.3 years, 40% of patients had a blood pressure > 160/90 mm Hg despite more than 6 annual medical check-ups. More intensive treatment allowed significantly ($p < 0.01$) better blood pressure control, as SBP decreased by 6.3 mm Hg in this group during the 2 years of follow-up, but increased by 4.8 mm Hg in the less intensively treated patients.

It is therefore not surprising, as demonstrated by the **Glasgow Blood Pressure Clinic** study (*J Hypertens* 1986;4:141-156), that the risk of mortality (total and cardiovascular) in male and female hypertensive patients is still 5 times higher than that of the normotensive population.

Unresolved questions

● Although it is now known that SBP is a better indicator of cardiovascular risk than DBP, the dose/efficacy relationship of drugs on variations of SBP and the possible differences of efficacy between various classes of antihypertensives on this parameter have not yet been determined, as all comparative trials adapted the dosage of treatment to variations of DBP alone.

● What is the clinical significance of isolated white coat hypertension? What is the real value of ambulatory blood pressure monitoring and self-measurement in the therapeutic decisions concerning hypertensive patients?

● How far should blood pressure be lowered (see p. 47)?

● Is there a correlation between reduction of left ventricular mass and its consequences on morbidity and mortality?

● Although they decrease blood pressure, are the new antihypertensives (calcium channel blockers, angiotensin-converting enzyme inhibitors, and angiotensin II AT1 receptor inhibitors) superior to diuretics and beta-blockers in terms of cardiovascular morbidity and mortality?

● Is there any difference between the various classes of antihypertensives in terms of the reduction of cardiovascular morbidity? No published trial of either primary or secondary prevention has yet been conducted in order to demonstrate such a difference.

● Can the favorable effect reported with nitrendipine in the **SYST-EUR** and **SYST-China** studies be extrapolated to other new generation calcium channel blockers such as amlodipine or felodipine?

● What is the exact place of fixed combinations, especially low-dose combinations, in the treatment of hypertension (see p. 36)?

● When the use of hormonal contraceptives containing low-dose estrogens or progestogens only is accompanied by a blood pressure rise, is it comparable to that induced by conventional estrogen-progestogen oral contraceptives in certain women?

Classification according to organ damage
(*J Hypertens* 1993;11:905-918)

● Stage I   No signs of organ damage

● Stage II   At least one of the following signs:

Left ventricular hypertrophy (electrical, echocardiographic)

Narrow arteries on ocular fundus

Proteinuria and/or slight elevation of serum creatinine between 12 and 20 mg/L

Atheromatous plaques on the aorta, femoral, or carotid arteries

● Stage III

Heart	Angina pectoris, myocardial infarction, heart failure
Brain	Transient ischemic attack, cerebrovascular accident, hypertensive encephalopathy
Eyes	Hemorrhage or exudates with or without papilledema
Kidneys	Serum creatinine > 20 mg/L
Vessels	Aneurysm, occlusive arterial disease of the lower extremities

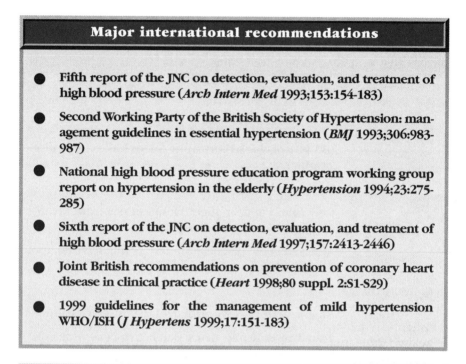

Major international recommendations

- Fifth report of the JNC on detection, evaluation, and treatment of high blood pressure (*Arch Intern Med* 1993;153:154-183)

- Second Working Party of the British Society of Hypertension: management guidelines in essential hypertension (*BMJ* 1993;306:983-987)

- National high blood pressure education program working group report on hypertension in the elderly (*Hypertension* 1994;23:275-285)

- Sixth report of the JNC on detection, evaluation, and treatment of high blood pressure (*Arch Intern Med* 1997;157:2413-2446)

- Joint British recommendations on prevention of coronary heart disease in clinical practice (*Heart* 1998;80 suppl. 2:S1-S29)

- 1999 guidelines for the management of mild hypertension WHO/ISH (*J Hypertens* 1999;17:151-183)

WHO/ISH definition
(*Hypertension* 1999;17:151-183)

Hypertension is defined as a SBP of 140 mm HG or greater and/or a DBP of 90 mm HG or greater in subjects who are not taking antihypertensive medication.

JNC-VI classification*
(*Arch Intern Med* 1997;157:2413-2446)

Category	Systolic (mm Hg)		Diastolic (mm Hg)
Optimal	< 120	and	< 80
Normal	< 130	and	< 85
High-normal	130-139	or	85-89
Hypertension	≥ 140	or	≥ 90
• Stage 1	140-159	or	90-99
• Stage 2	160-179	or	100-109
• Stage 3	≥ 180	or	≥ 110
Isolated systolic hypertension	≥ 140	and	< 90

In diabetic patients, it is recommended to lower blood pressure to below 130/85 mm Hg.

* This classification concerns adults over the age of 18.

The PROBE approach
(*Blood Press* 1992;1:113-119)

This new methodological approach constitutes a more pragmatic alternative to the classical double-blind method. It consists of strict central randomization of patients, while the study is conducted under open-label conditions. However, the results are analysed under blinded conditions by an independent expert committee only informed about the type of treatment administered after analysis of the results. This methodology, which more closely resembles routine clinical practice, allows better compliance of patients with treatment.

When should hypertension be treated?

In practice, according to the WHO, the decision to treat hypertension must not be based exclusively on the values of SBP and DBP, but also on evaluation of the overall cardiovascular risk (*J Hypertens* 1996;14:929-933).

● Treatment is required whenever SBP > 160 mm Hg or DBP > 95 mm Hg.

● When SBP is between 140 and 160 mm Hg and DBP is between 90 and 95 mm Hg (so-called borderline hypertension), the cardiovascular prognosis is good in the absence of other risk factors. In contrast, the presence of other risk factors considerably increases the absolute cardiovascular risk. Introduction of antihypertensive treatment then depends on the level of this individual absolute risk, which can easily be evaluated from predetermined tables (*Eur Heart J* 1994;15:1300-1331).

Regular follow-up may be sufficient in patients with a low risk (5% to 10% of events at 10 years). Treatment is required in patients with a higher risk (> 20% of events at 10 years) or in the presence of organ damage (cerebral, myocardial, renal, etc.), which dramatically increases the absolute risk.

Practical aspects of the treatment of hypertension

● It is essential not to treat mild-to-moderate hypertension immediately; an observation and evaluation period lasting several weeks or even several months is important to define the real blood pressure and the permanent nature of hypertension.

● Drug treatment improves the hypertensive patient's quality of life, as it decreases or eliminates a whole series of symptoms, which are therefore only retrospectively attributed to high blood pressure, which is now known to be not as asymptomatic as was previously considered.

● Placebo lowers the hypertensive patient's blood pressure; in the Veterans Comparative Study (*N Engl J Med* 1993;328:914-921), the blood pressure reduction observed at the 4th to 8th week in one third of patients was still present at 1 year in 25% of cases.

● According to the WHO (*J Hypertens* 1996;14:929-933), two- or three-agent combination therapy using various drug classes is necessary in more than 50% of hypertensive patients.

● In postmenopausal women, there is no contraindication to low-dose estrogen hormone replacement therapy, provided blood pressure is monitored more frequently (*J Hypertens* 1996;14:929-933).

Diuretics in the treatment of hypertension
(*Arch Mal Cœur Vaiss* 1996;89 suppl. 4:39-43)

● The mechanism of action of diuretics in hypertension has not been fully elucidated. They initially act by slightly decreasing blood volume and cardiac output; they subsequently lower peripheral vascular resistance by a direct action on the smooth muscle fibers of the arteriolar wall. In addition to their specific antihypertensive action, they also potentiate the effects of low-salt diet and angiotensin-converting enzyme inhibitors.

● A diuretic remains the most effective combination with most anti-hypertensives and hypertension cannot be considered to be refractory to treatment unless a diuretic has been prescribed.

● In order to be effective, diuretics must be prescribed at low doses, as the incidence of adverse effects is increased at higher doses.

● Hypertensive black subjects are particularly sensitive to diuretics.

Beta-blockers in the treatment of hypertension

- The efficacy of beta-blockers in the treatment of hypertension has been clearly demonstrated since 1964, when the antihypertensive properties of beta-blockers were discovered by **Prichard** (*BMJ* 1964;1:1227-1228), who was studying their efficacy as antianginal agents in patients with coronary heart disease. This is a class effect specific to all beta-blockers, whether they are lipophilic or hydrophilic, cardioselective or non-cardioselective, and whether or not they possess an intrinsic sympathomimetic activity.

- Cardiac output decreases immediately after administration of a beta-blocker, but blood pressure is not decreased immediately due to the reflex increase of peripheral resistance induced by the reduction of cardiac output. The therapeutic effect is observed after 24 to 48 hours: blood pressure decreases at the same time as peripheral arterial resistance and the degree of this reduction varies according to the beta-blocker (the onset of action is more rapid for cardioselective beta-blockers and for molecules with an intrinsic sympathomimetic activity).

- Regardless of the beta-blocker, the antihypertensive action, whose mechanism has still not been clearly identified, is related to a reduction in peripheral resistance, due to multiple effects: reduction of sympathetic tone, decreased release of renin and therefore decreased angiotensin production, decreased secretion of aldosterone, increased synthesis of prostacyclin and reduction of thromboxane, release of NO by endothelium, and stimulation of atrial natriuretic factor secretion.

- Some 50% of patients respond to beta-blocker treatment administered as monotherapy at the usual dosage; in the case of failure, it is generally useless to prescribe another beta-blocker.

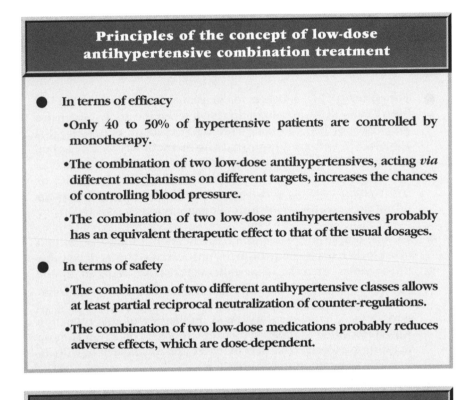

Principles of the concept of low-dose antihypertensive combination treatment

● In terms of efficacy

• Only 40 to 50% of hypertensive patients are controlled by monotherapy.

• The combination of two low-dose antihypertensives, acting *via* different mechanisms on different targets, increases the chances of controlling blood pressure.

• The combination of two low-dose antihypertensives probably has an equivalent therapeutic effect to that of the usual dosages.

● In terms of safety

• The combination of two different antihypertensive classes allows at least partial reciprocal neutralization of counter-regulations.

• The combination of two low-dose medications probably reduces adverse effects, which are dose-dependent.

Effect of increased dietary potassium intake on blood pressure

A meta-analysis by **Whelton** (*JAMA* 1997;277:1124-1132), based on 33 randomized trials including a total of 2,609 hypertensive patients, studied the effects of oral potassium supplementation on blood pressure. Potassium supplementation significantly decreased SBP and DBP by an average of 3.11 mm Hg and 1.97 mm Hg, respectively; the effect was more marked when a high sodium intake was maintained.

Effect of reduction of dietary salt intake on blood pressure

● A meta-analysis by **Midgley** (*JAMA* 1996;275:1590-1597), based on 28 randomized trials including a total of 1,131 hypertensive patients, showed that a reduction of 100 mmol of daily sodium excretion significantly decreased SBP by an average of 3.7 mm Hg and tended to decrease DBP by an average of 0.9 mm Hg. Compared to the overall hypertensive population, the response to low-salt diet was much more marked in hypertensive patients over the age of 45: a 100-mmol reduction of daily sodium excretion significantly decreased SBP and DBP by an average of 6.3 mm Hg and 2.2 mm Hg, respectively.

● These data were confirmed by the meta-analysis by **Graudal** (*JAMA* 1998;279:1383-1391). In 58 trials conducted in hypertensive patients, a reduction of salt intake, assessed by the reduction of the mean daily sodium elimination of 118 mmol, was accompanied by a 3.9 mm Hg reduction of SBP (95% CI: 3.0 to 4.8 mm Hg, $p < 0.001$) and a 1.9 mm Hg reduction of DBP (95% CI: 1.3 to 2.5 mm Hg, $p < 0.001$). In 56 trials conducted in normotensive subjects, a reduction of daily salt intake (an average of 160 mmol) decreased SBP by 1.2 mm Hg (95% CI: 0.6 to 1.8 mm Hg, $p < 0.001$) and DBP by 0.26 mm Hg (95% CI: 0.3 to 0.12 mm Hg, $p = 0.1.2$, NS). Plasma renin was multiplied by 3.6 ($p < 0.001$) and plasma aldosterone was multiplied by 3.2 ($p < 0.001$); this increase was proportional to the degree of reduction of salt intake.

These results therefore do not support recommendation of a decreased salt intake for the general population, but this measure should be reserved as adjuvant treatment for hypertensive patients.

Hypertension in children
(N Engl J Med 1996;335:1968-1973)

● The diagnosis of hypertension can only be made after confirmation by 3 successive measurements performed at 3 different consecutive examinations. The real prevalence of hypertension in children is therefore much lower than 5% and could be about 1%.

● Hypertension in children is often due to an identifiable etiology, predominantly renal or vascular disease.

● Even more than in adults, recommended treatment consists of reducing any obesity and encouraging regular physical exercise (it has not been demonstrated that children with mild-to-moderate hypertension have an increased risk of cardiovascular events during organized sports).

● First-line treatment consists of angiotensin-converting enzyme inhibitors or calcium channel blockers because they are generally effective and induce few adverse effects. However, one drug may be preferred over another and all the drugs used in adults have also been successfully used in children.

● No long-term data are available concerning the correlations between blood pressure during childhood or adolescence and cardiovascular risk in adults.

Hypertension in children is defined by SBP and DBP > 95th percentile
(*Pediatrics* 1996;98:649-658)

Age (years)	Girls' SBP/DBP 50th percentile for height	Girls' SBP/DBP 75th percentile for height	Boys' SBP/DBP 50th percentile for height	Boys' SBP/DBP 75th percentile for height
1	104/58	105/59	102/57	104/58
6	111/73	112/73	114/74	115/75
12	123/80	124/81	123/81	125/82
17	129/84	130/85	136/87	138/88

Ambulatory blood pressure monitoring
(*Ann Intern Med* 1993;118:867-882)

● Normal blood pressure is < 135/85 mm Hg while subjects are awake and < 120/75 mm Hg while subjects are asleep.
In the majority of individuals, blood pressure falls by 10% to 20% during the night.

● Blood pressure-related end-organ damage, particularly left ventricular hypertrophy, is more closely associated with ambulatory than with office blood pressure.

Self-measurement of blood pressure
(*Am J Hypertens* 1995;9:1-11 and 1997;10:409-418)

The blood pressure of persons with hypertension tends to be higher when measured in the clinic (*Lancet* 1997;349:454-457). There is no universally agreed-on upper limit of normal home blood pressure, but readings of 135/85 mm Hg or greater should be considered elevated.

Ongoing trials: diuretics or beta-blockers vs new therapeutic classes

ALLHAT   Various classes of antihypertensives (chlorthalidone, amlodipine, doxazosin, lisinopril) and a lipid-lowering drug (pravastatin vs usual treatment) in 40,000 hypertensive patients ≥ 55 years with moderate hypercholesterolemia, followed for 5 years (*Am J Hypertens* 1996;9:342-360).

ASCOT   Atenolol vs amlodipine, subsequently coprescribed with a thiazide and perindopril, respectively, in 18,000 hypertensive patients with moderate hypercholesterolemia (serum cholesterol ≤ 6.5 mmol/L, i.e. 2.5 g/L), followed for 5 years. In each arm, doxazosin GITS is associated with two-agent therapy whenever necessary. One arm of the study is also evaluating the effect of atorvastatin vs placebo (*Am J Hypertens* 1998;11:9A-10A).

CONVINCE   Verapamil vs diuretics or beta-blockers in 15,000 hypertensive patients followed for 5 years.

CPHRP   Alpha-blockers vs beta-blockers vs ACE-inhibitor vs diuretics in 5,000 hypertensive patients followed for 15 years.

INSIGHT   Diuretics vs nifedipine SR in 6,600 hypertensive patients followed for 3 years (*J Hum Hypertens* 1996;10 suppl. 3:S157-S160).

INVEST   Verapamil 240 mg daily vs atenolol 50 mg daily for 6 weeks in 27,000 hypertensive coronary patients; verapamil may then be successively combined with trandolapril 2 mg daily then 4 mg daily or hydrochlorothiazide 25 mg daily; in parallel, atenolol 50 mg daily is increased to 100 mg daily then combined with hydrochlorothiazide 25 mg daily or trandolapril 2 mg daily (*J Am Coll Cardiol* 1998;32:1228-1237).

• • •

• • •

NORDIL	Diuretics and/or beta-blockers vs diltiazem in 12,000 hypertensive patients followed for 5 years (*Blood Press* 1993;2:312-321).
STOP Hypertension 2	Conducted in 6,628 hypertensive patients over the age of 70 followed for 4 years with 3 treatment arms: 1. beta-blockers (atenolol, metoprolol or pindolol) or diuretics (hydrochlorothiazide and amiloride); 2. felodipine or isradipine; 3. enalapril or lisinopril (*Blood Press* 1993;2:136-141).

Ongoing trials: particular objectives

Prevention of cerebrovascular accidents

PROGRESS	Perindopril in the prevention of recurrent cerebrovascular accidents in 6,000 normotensive or treated hypertensive patients followed for 4 years (*J Hypertens* 1995; 13:1869-1873).

ECG signs of left ventricular hypertrophy

LIFE	Losartan vs atenolol in 8,300 hypertensive patients with ECG signs of left ventricular hypertrophy followed for 4 years (*Am J Hypertens* 1997;10:705-713).

Ongoing trials
elderly subjects, diabetics, or high-risk patients

ANBP 2   ACE-inhibitor vs diuretics in 6,000 elderly hypertensive patients followed for 5 years (*Clin Exp Pharmacol Physiol* 1997;24:188-192).

CSG   Irbesartan in type II diabetic hypertensive patients with nephropathy.

HOPE   Ramipril vs placebo in 9,541 high-risk patients followed for 5 years (*Can J Cardiol* 1996;12:127-137).

HYVET   Indapamide SR 1.5 mg daily, possibly combined with perindopril 2 mg daily or 4 mg daily in very elderly hypertensive patients ($\geq$ 80 years) (*J Hum Hypertens* 1994;8:631-632), followed for 5 years, in primary and secondary prevention of cerebrovascular accidents.

SCOPE   Candesartan vs placebo in 4,000 hypertensive patients (SBP: 160 to 179 mm Hg and/or DBP: 90 to 99 mm Hg) between the ages of 70 to 89 years, followed for 3 years.

SHELL   Lacidipine vs diuretics in 4,800 patients over the age of 60 with isolated systolic hypertension, followed for 2.5 to 5 years (*J Hypertens* 1995;13 suppl. 4:S35-S39).

VALUE   Valsartan (80-160 mg daily) vs amlodipine (5-10 mg daily) with possible addition of hydrochlorothiazide (12.5-25 mg daily) in 14,000 hypertensive patients between the ages of 50 and 85 years, also presenting hypercholesterolemia, in about 50% of cases, and diabetes, in more than 30% of cases.

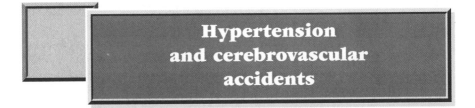

Hypertension and cerebrovascular accidents

Epidemiological studies, especially the **Framingham** *study (JAMA 1970; 214:301-310), have clearly demonstrated that blood pressure figures are correlated with the risk of cardiovascular accidents: any elevation of mean diastolic blood pressure increases the relative risk of cerebrovascular and coronary accidents.*

Primary prevention

Current state of knowledge

 The cardiovascular risk is closely correlated with SBP and DBP.

It increases regularly with SBP, and a cut-off value for normal blood pressure below which this risk no longer exists cannot be defined. The risk is therefore real even in mild hypertension (DBP: 90-104 mm Hg). It is identical in the two sexes and increases regularly with age.

 Treatment of hypertension reduces the incidence of cardiovascular events, especially cerebrovascular accidents (*JAMA* 1970; 214:301-310).

According to the meta-analysis by **Collins** (*Lancet* 1990;335:827-38) performed in mild-to-moderate hypertension, lowering DBP by 5 to 6 mm Hg decreases the rate of fatal or nonfatal cerebrovascular accidents by 42% ($p < 0.0001$) and the rate of coronary events by 14% ($p < 0.01$), at 5 years.

 The favorable effect of antihypertensive treatment has been demonstrated with diuretics, beta-blockers and, more recently, calcium channel blockers (nifedipine SR in the STONE study, nitrendipine in the SYST-EUR and SYST-China studies).

The only available results concerning ACE-inhibitors were obtained in the **CAPPP** study (see p. 24), in which captopril was found to be as effective as a beta-blocker or diuretic on lowering of blood pressure figures and for the prevention of total cardiovascular events, but nonfatal cerebrovascular accidents were more frequent with captopril. The long-term efficacy of angiotensin II AT1 receptor antagonists has not been evaluated.

 The efficacy of treatment of systolic hypertension in the elderly has now been established [SYST-EUR, SYST-China studies (see p. 19)].

Four meta-analyses [**Mac Mahon** and **Rodgers, Insua, Pearce, Gueyffier** (see pp. 19 and 20)], which each included 12,000 to 16,000 patients over the age of 60 years, all showed with a mean follow-up of 5 years, that treatment of hypertension decreased the relative risk of fatal and nonfatal cerebrovascular accidents by about 35% and coronary events by 18% to 25%, by a mean blood pressure reduction of the order of 15/6 mm Hg. Reduction of the relative risk of cerebrovascular accidents in the elderly is similar to that observed in subjects younger than 60, but the absolute reduction of the number of cerebrovascular accidents is twofold higher. According to **Gueyffier**, treatment is therefore able to prevent 10 cardiovascular events per 1,000 treated patients each year.

Unresolved questions

 The exact nature of the cerebrovascular accident complicating the course of hypertension has been poorly evaluated.

In the **Framingham** study (*JAMA* 1970;214:301-310), cerebrovascular accidents were described as hemorrhagic in 20% of cases and ischemic in 80% of cases, i.e. embolic, atherothrombotic or lacunar.

 The precise mechanism of development of cerebrovascular accident has not been elucidated.

It is simply known that hypertension: accelerates atherosclerosis; can mechanically damage vessels; is able to alter left ventricular function and decrease cerebral perfusion; increases the incidence of heart failure, coronary heart disease, electrocardiographic abnormalities, all factors correlated with an increased incidence of cerebrovascular accidents.

In practice, evaluation of the cardiovascular risk cannot be limited to simple assessment of blood pressure. This evaluation must be global and tighter control of blood pressure must be achieved when hypertension is associated with other risk factors, especially hypercholesterolemia.

Cerebrovascular accidents and serum cholesterol

Although this is a complex relationship, three concepts now appear to be established.

● According to the **Prospective Studies Collaboration** (*Lancet* 1995; 346:1647-1653), based on a cohort of 450,000 subjects followed for an average of 16 years, there is no correlation between total serum cholesterol and the development of cerebrovascular accident, after adjustment for ethnic group, gender, DBP, and history of coronary heart disease, except perhaps in subjects younger than 45. However, in the absence of data concerning the type of the various cerebrovascular accidents observed, the possibility that the global absence of correlation actually masks a positive association with ischemic cerebrovascular accidents and a negative association with hemorrhagic cerebrovascular accidents cannot be excluded.

● According to the meta-analysis by **Atkins** (*Ann Intern Med* 1993;119: 136-145), lowering of total serum cholesterol by dietary intervention alone or by lipid-lowering drugs other than statins, does not decrease the risk of cerebrovascular accidents, which even increased with clofibrate.

● According to the meta-analyses by **Hébert** (*JAMA* 1997;278:313-321) and **Bucher** (*Ann Intern Med* 1998;128:89-95), the reduction of total serum cholesterol induced by statins significantly decreases the risk of fatal and nonfatal cerebrovascular accidents. This reduction was 31% ($p = 0.003$) in the **CARE** study (see p. 82) and 20% ($p = 0.022$) in the **LIPID** study (see p. 83).

Secondary prevention

The fragmented data concerning secondary prevention are essentially derived from two studies, in which not all patients were hypertensive.

● The **INDANA** meta-analysis (*Stroke* 1997;28:2557-2562) was based on 9 very heterogeneous trials (including 6,752 patients): 2 trials included 551 hypertensive stroke survivors; 1 trial included stroke survivors, wether hypertensive or not (5665 patients), 6 trials of hypertensive patients included a small proportion of stroke survivors (536 patients). In this meta-analysis, lowering of blood pressure significantly decreased the risk of recurrence of fatal and nonfatal cerebrovascular accidents (RR: 0.72; 95% CI: 0.61 to 0.85). There was no evidence that this intervention induced serious adverse effect.

● The Chinese **PATS** study (*J Am Coll Cardiol* 1998;31 suppl. A:211A) was based on 5,665 patients with a mean age of 60 ± 8 years, with or without hypertension (mean blood pressure: 154/93 mm Hg) and presenting a history of transient ischemic attack or cerebrovascular accident. With a mean follow-up of 3 years, indapamide (2.5 mg daily) vs placebo decreased the incidence of fatal and nonfatal cerebrovascular accidents by 31% (8.2% vs 12.1%, $p < 0.001$).

The results of the **PROGRESS** study (*J Hypertens* 1995;13:869-873) are eagerly awaited

This randomized double-blind placebo-controlled in 6,000 patients with a history of transient ischemic attack or cerebrovascular accident (ischemic or hemorrhagic) is designed to determine, with a mean follow-up of 4 to 5 years, the effects of lowering blood pressure by perindopril and/or indapamide on the risk of recurrence of cerebrovascular accident.

How far should blood pressure be lowered? The J-curve

*Although the management of hypertension improved between 1960 and 1991, according to the **NAHNES III** study (Hypertension 1995;25:305-313), hypertension is controlled (SBP < 140 mm Hg and DBP < 90 mm Hg) in only 21% of cases. This figure was confirmed by the **STEPHY** study (16th session of the International Society of Hypertension, 1996), which showed that, in a population of hypertensive patients, 34% were not aware of their disease, 12% did not seek treatment; 32% received treatment, but their blood pressure remained ≥ 160 mm Hg, while blood pressure was controlled in only 22% of hypertensive patients, or in 41% of cases when only treated patients were considered. In France, the **PHARE** survey (Arch Mal Cœur Vaiss 1996;89:1075-1080), conducted by 235 representative general practitioners in 12,351 subjects, revealed that only 24% of treated hypertensive patients had a normal blood pressure; the success rate was slightly higher (28%) in patients younger than 65 compared with older subjects (21%). Under these conditions, it is not surprising that hypertensive patients have a fivefold higher risk of total and cardiovascular mortality than the normotensive population.*

As it is so difficult in practice to achieve normal blood pressure in the long term, one therefore wonders whether it is realistic or even legitimate to want to decrease it any further.

The J-curve hypothesis

In 1979, **Stewart** (*Lancet* 1979;1:861-865) showed that the relationship between cardiovascular risk and blood pressure in treated hypertensive patients also presenting myocardial ischemia was not linear, but formed a J- or U-shaped curve. The relative risk of developing myocardial infarction is therefore multiplied by 5 when antihypertensive treatment lowers DBP below 90 mm Hg. The same does not apply to patients not presenting ischemic heart disease, in whom reduction of DBP remains proportional to the decreased incidence of fatal myocardial infarction, even for DBP < 85 mm Hg. According to **Cruickshank** (*Lancet* 1987;1:581-584), these findings demonstrate the reality of a J-curve reported in certain trials, such as the study by **Coope** and **Warender** (*BMJ* 1986;293:1145-1151) and the **Göteborg** study (*JAMA* 1987;258:1768-1776), and are based on the theory of altered coronary perfusion pressure.

Altered coronary perfusion pressure

● Under normal conditions, coronary blood flow is self-regulated and is maintained constant for a large range of perfusion pressure. Coronary autoregulation is rapid (15 to 30 seconds) and is mediated by changes in the calibre of small arteries and arterioles, which contract or dilate as blood pressure increases or decreases. The mechanisms of these changes have been only partly elucidated. The term *coronary reserve* refers to the capacity of coronary arteries to dilate; this dilatation capacity can induce a fivefold increase in coronary perfusion in response to a fall in DBP.

● In hypertensives, coronary reserve decreases and eventually disappears. It raises the threshold beyond which the coronary perfusion pressure is no longer maintained; consequently, coronary perfusion is altered at a higher DBP, which means that a moderate fall in blood pressure (which would be well tolerated in a normotensive subject) can induce: myocardial ischemia, increased by the fact that myocardial oxygen extraction is already maximal at rest; increased blood viscosity and platelet adhesion, with a risk of intracoronary thrombosis; and heterogeneous perfusion, responsible for metabolic gradients which can, in turn, induce ventricular arrhythmias.

The reduction of coronary reserve in hypertensive patients is the consequence of independent disorders of the microcirculation or disorders related to left ventricular hypertrophy. It is multifactorial and depends on anatomical factors (enlargement of intercapillary spaces and rarefaction of arterioles), mechanical factors (increased tissue rigidity and wall stress), structural factors (especially proliferation of smooth muscle cells of the media, inducing a reduction of arteriolar calibre), and functional factors (alteration of endothelial function with increased vasoconstrictor reactivity).

The reduction of coronary reserve is considerably worsened by the presence of significant coronary stenoses.

Overall, the supporters of the reality of the J-curve therefore considered that it is unwise to lower the DBP of a hypertensive patient with ischemic heart disease to below 80-85 mm Hg.

The controversy

 Many authors refuse to accept the concept of the J-curve, arguing that this hypothesis is based on non-controlled, retrospective studies, none of which were designed to specifically study the level to which DBP should be lowered; that the trials to which it refers are based on a small number of deaths; that the J-curve is less clearly demonstrated in trials including a larger number of patients; that the J-curve has been demonstrated in subjects of control groups as well as the most seriously ill patients, i.e. elderly patients and patients with heart failure, diabetes, and coronary heart disease with a history of myocardial infarction; that the minimal critical level of the normotensive or hypertensive coronary patients' coronary perfusion has not been clearly defined (it could be ≤ 60 mm Hg); that the J-curve could well be not the consequence of treatment, but may simply reflect pre-existing cardiovascular dysfunction, independent of treatment.

 Furthermore, if we accept that the J-curve exists, it would raise a whole series of practical questions: is it conceivable that the lower range for which a beneficial effect can be demonstrated is really as limited as 85 to 90 mm Hg? In view of the variability of blood pressure, is it really possible to control DBP in the long term to within several millimeters of mercury? To achieve this control, should we use a standard sphygmomanometer or systematically perform ambulatory blood pressure monitoring? How many additional visits would be necessary to ensure such a precise control? Finally, if we decide not to lower DBP as much as possible, would hypertensive patients be exposed to an increased risk of cerebrovascular accidents?

Contribution of the major clinical trials

Retrospective data

● In the **IPPPSH** study (*J Hypertens* 1985;3:379-392), based on 6,357 hypertensive patients, the risk of cardiac and cerebral accidents was directly correlated with the DBP achieved during treatment. The best protection was observed for the lowest DBP (< 90 mm Hg).

● In the **MRC** study (*BMJ* 1985;291:97-104), based on 17,354 hypertensive patients, the J-curve was not demonstrated in the majority of patients with ischemic heart disease.

● In the **SOLVD** study (*N Engl J Med* 1991;325:293-302 and 1992;327: 685-691), based on 6,797 patients, most of whom presenting symptomatic or asymptomatic ischemic left ventricular dysfunction (history of myocardial infarction), enalapril decreased the mean DBP by 4 mm Hg, from 77 mm Hg to 73 mm Hg, without any harmful effects.

● In the **MRFIT** study (*JAMA* 1982;248:1465-1477), the 16-year follow-up of 5,362 men evaluated for inclusion in the study, all presenting a history of myocardial infarction, demonstrated a relationship between SBP and DBP, on the one hand, and coronary morbidity and all cause mortality, on the other, only for the first 2 years. Subsequently, however, only SBP $\geq$ 140 mm Hg (vs < 140 mm Hg) increased these two parameters by 40%, regardless of the DBP (> or $\leq$ 80 mm Hg). According to this study, therefore, the risk related to hypertension following myocardial infarction is more strongly correlated with high blood pressure than with low blood pressure.

● In the **SHEP** and **SYST-EUR** studies, performed in elderly subjects with isolated systolic hypertension and therefore normal DBP on inclusion (an average of 77 mm Hg in **SHEP** and 87 mm Hg in **SYST-EUR** studies), treatment was responsible for a moderate reduction of DBP (9 mm Hg in **SHEP** and 7.3 mm Hg in **SYST-EUR** studies), which did not appear to be harmful (the incidence of cardiovascular events was not increased).

Prospective data

Two prospective studies have tried to answer this question more directly.

 The **BBB** study (*Blood Press* 1994;3:248-254), although it failed to give a definitive answer, nevertheless provided a number of interesting elements. This Swedish multicenter study conducted in 2,127 male and female hypertensive patients with no signs of ischemic heart disease on clinical examination or electrocardiogram tried to answer the following three questions: Can DBP be more markedly lowered by intensifying treatment? Can this objective be achieved without increasing the frequency and severity of adverse effects? If so, is the additional reduction of DBP accompanied by an increased reduction of morbidity and mortality. After randomization, group A received intense medical treatment designed to achieve DBP ≤ 80 mm Hg, while, in group B, basic treatment was maintained to ensure a DBP of 90 mm Hg.

With a follow-up of 4 years, intense antihypertensive treatment, compared to basic treatment, tended to more markedly reduce SBP and DBP at the cost of a 58% increase in the number of drugs, which increased from a mean of 1.24 to 1.96 per day, and significantly reduced the adverse effect score in group A, while it remained unchanged in group B. It did not modify the total number of cardiovascular complications (myocardial infarction or cerebrovascular accident), but the power of the study was not sufficient to express a difference on this parameter.

The **HOT** study (*Lancet* 1998;351:1755-1762) provides an important element in the discussion. This open, randomized, multicenter study was conducted in 18,790 hypertensive patients with DBP between 100 and 115 mm Hg (mean: 105 mm Hg), and including 3,080 subjects (16.4%) with angina or a history of myocardial infarction. It had a dual objective 1) to determine the optimal DBP level during antihypertensive treatment by comparing the cardiovascular morbidity and mortality of patients randomized to 3 blood pressure objectives, DBP ≤ 90 mm Hg, DBP ≤ 85 mm Hg, or DBP ≤ 80 mm Hg; 2) to evaluate the effects of low-dose aspirin (75 mg daily) vs placebo on cardiovascular morbidity and mortality. It was conducted with felodipine (5 to 10 mg daily), possibly combined with a beta-blocker and/or ACE-inhibitor (low or high dose), or even hydrochlorothiazide.

With a mean follow-up of 3.8 years, DBP was decreased by 20.3 mm Hg, 22.3 mm Hg and 24.3 mm Hg in the groups in which the objective was set at DBP ≤ 90 mm Hg, ≤ 85 mm Hg and ≤ 80 mm Hg, respectively; the lowest incidence of major cardiovascular events (myocardial infarction and fatal or nonfatal cerebrovascular accidents; all other cardiovascular deaths) was observed for a mean DBP of 82.6 mm Hg, while the lowest risk of cardiovascular death was observed for a mean DBP of 86.5 mm Hg. In diabetic patients, major cardiovascular events were reduced by 51% in the DBP ≤ 80 mm Hg group vs the DBP ≤ 90 mm Hg group (p for the tendency = 0.005).

Aspirin vs placebo reduced the incidence of major cardiovascular events by 15% (p = 0.03) and myocardial infarctions by 36% (p = 0.002) without modifying the incidence of cerebrovascular accidents; it significantly increased the incidence of nonfatal serious bleeding (129 vs 70, p < 0.001) without increasing the number of fatal hemorrhages (7 cases vs 8 with placebo).

According to **Kaplan** (*Lancet* 1998;351:1748-1749), the results of the **HOT** study were a disappointment and a triumph.

● Disappointment because it failed to provide an answer to the controversy concerning the existence of the J-curve, which was its primary goal. The differences between DBP obtained in the 3 groups (≤ 80, 85 or 90 mm Hg) were only half the expected differences. Consequently, the reductions of DBP observed in each of the groups were so close that it was impossible to demonstrate a difference of protection according to the degree of lowering of blood pressure. The J-curve theory was therefore not disproved, although the **HOT** study clearly showed that any increase in mortality from coronary disease is probably not induced by the lower blood pressure but that underlying coronary disease is responsible for the lower blood pressure.

● The **HOT** study was a triumph in that:

• DBP was reduced by more than 20 mm Hg in most of the nearly 19,000 patients, far beyond the average 5-6 mm Hg reduction achieved in other controlled trials reviewed by **Collins** (see p. 19) (this difference with the other studies is probably less than it appears as the **HOT** study had no placebo group);

• it emphasized that intensive therapy is beneficial, with maximum protection attained for a blood pressure around 140/85 mm Hg; it was reassuring concerning the long-term use of calcium channel blockers; it emphasized the cardiac protection provided in the group of diabetic patients and the 3,000 patients with pre-existing ischemic heart disease, although it is preferable not to lower blood pressure below 140/85 mm Hg, as the study demonstrated no additional benefit below these figures;

• finally, it demonstrated for the first time that prescription of aspirin in hypertensive patients with well controlled blood pressure significantly reduced major cardiovascular events and especially the number of fatal and nonfatal myocardial infarctions, without increasing the number of fatal bleeds or strokes, but at the cost of significantly more nonfatal hemorrhages.

The controversy concerning calcium channel blockers

The place of calcium channel blockers in the treatment of hypertension has recently been the subject of a controversy raised by the publication of two meta-analyses.

Meta-analyses by Psaty and Furberg

● The meta-analysis by **Psaty** (*JAMA* 1995;274:620-625), based on a bank of case-controls, compared the treatment of hypertensive patients who developed a first myocardial infarction over a 7-year period with that of hypertensive patients who remained free of myocardial infarction.

First of all, the risk of developing myocardial infarction was increased by 60% in hypertensive patients treated with a calcium channel blocker (verapamil, diltiazem, nifedipine) compared with those treated with diuretics and/or beta-blockers.

This risk was significantly decreased by high-dose beta-blockers, but was increased by high-dose calcium channel blockers.

● The meta-analysis by **Furberg** (*Circulation* 1995;92:1326-1331), on the effect of nifedipine prescribed in coronary patients who presented an episode of acute myocardial ischemia showed that this calcium channel blocker increased the all cause mortality in parallel with increasing dosage. The relative risk (RR) of 1.06 for a dosage of 30 to 50 mg daily was increased to an RR of 2.83 for a dosage of 80 mg daily.

Several hypotheses, none of which have been clearly confirmed, could explain the harmful effect of nifedipine: pro-ischemic effect due to coronary steal; increased myocardial oxygen consumption secondary to a reduction of blood pressure, increased heart rate, and increased sympathetic activity; negative inotropic effect; and prohemorrhagic effect due to vasodilatation and a specific platelet aggregation inhibitor action.

However, Furberg's meta-analysis has been criticized because of the numerous methodological biases. For example, it has been noted that the patient groups were not homogeneous, with a marked variability for the date of inclusion and for the date of mortality, a wide range of treatments were used in the control group, and, finally and most importantly, all the studies analysed used rapid-acting, short-half-life nifedipine capsules [it is now preferable to use the latest generation of long half-life dihydropyridines, amlodipine, felodipine, and nifedipine GITS (pharmaceutical formulation which allows very progressive release of nifedipine in the gastrointestinal tract)].

● Regardless of the importance of the questions raised by this controversy, it must not be forgotten that according to international guidelines, calcium channel blockers are one of the drugs recommended for first-line treatment of hypertension, along with diuretics, beta-blockers, and angiotensin-converting enzyme inhibitors. Calcium channel blockers are essential in the treatment of spastic angina and remain very effective in hypertensive crisis (preferably administered *via* the IV route rather than the oral route), in some cases of pulmonary artery hypertension or severe aortic incompetence [in this last indication, they can defer surgical operation (*N Engl J Med* 1994;331:689-694)].

STONE, SYST-EUR, SYST-China, VHAS, and ABCD studies

The contradictory data of these recent studies must also be added to this controversy.

● In the **STONE** study (*J Hypertens* 1996;14:1237-1245), conducted in 1,632 hypertensive patients (SBP = 160 mm Hg and/or DBP = 96 mm Hg) between the ages of 60 and 79 years, with a mean follow-up of 36 months, nifedipine SR (10-60 mg daily), possibly combined with captopril (25-50 mg daily) and/or dichlorothiazide (25 mg daily) in order to maintain SBP between 140 and 159 mm Hg and DBP below 90 mm Hg, vs placebo, significantly decreased the morbidity after 18 months of treatment (the overall incidence of cardiovascular events was four times lower with treatment and the effect was maximal on serious arrhythmias and cerebrovascular accidents) and tended to decrease the number of deaths (NS).

• In the **SYST-EUR** study (*Lancet* 1997;350:757-764), conducted in 4,695 patients over the age of 60, presenting with isolated systolic hypertension (SBP between 160 and 210 mm Hg and DBP < 95 mm Hg) with a mean follow-up of 4 years, nitrendipine (6 to 40 mg daily), possibly combined with enalapril (5 to 20 mg daily) and hydrochlorothiazide (12.5 to 25 mg daily), to achieve SBP < 150 mm Hg or a reduction of at least 20 mm Hg, vs placebo, decreased SBP by 10.7 mm Hg and DBP by 7.3 mm Hg; significantly decreased the number of cardiovascular events by 31%, the number of nonfatal cerebrovascular accidents by 44%, the number of nonfatal cardiac events by 33%, and tended to reduce cardiovascular deaths by 27% (NS).

It should also be stressed that active treatment (1,238 patients) vs placebo (1,180 patients) in the context of a more specific study (*Lancet* 1998;352:1347-1351), conducted over 2.0 years, reduced the incidence of dementia by 50% [3.8 cases vs 7.7 for 1,000 patient/years (21 vs 11 patients, p = 0.05)]. Pharmacological treatment of 1,000 hypertensive patients for 5 years would therefore prevent 19 cases of dementia.

• In the **SYST-China** study (*J Hypertens* 1998;16:1823-1829), conducted on 2,394 patients over the age of 60, with isolated systolic hypertension (SBP ≥ 160 mm Hg and DBP< 95 mm Hg), nitrendipine (10 to 40 mg daily) possibly combined with captopril (12.5 to 50 mg daily) and/or hydrochlorothiazide (12.5 to 50 mg daily) to decrease SBP by at least 20 mm Hg or to lower it below 150 mm Hg, vs placebo, with a 2-year follow-up, reduced SBP by 20.0 mm Hg and DBP by 5.0 mm Hg and significantly decreased the total number of fatal and nonfatal cerebrovascular accidents by 38%, from 20.8 to 13.0 per 1,000 patient/years (p = 0.01); all cause mortality by 39%, from 28.4 to 17.4 per 1,000 patient/years (p = 0.003); cardiovascular mortality by 39%, from 15.2 to 9.4 per 1,000 patient/years (p = 0.03); mortality from cerebrovascular accidents by 58%, from 6.9 to 2.9 per 1,000 patient/years (p = 0.02) and the incidence of fatal or nonfatal cardiovascular events from 33.3 to 21.4 per 1,000 patient/years (p = 0.004). In practice, treatment for 5 years of 1,000 patients over the age of 60 years with isolated systolic hypertension, would prevent 55 deaths, 39 strokes or 59 major cardiovascular events.

• In the **VHAS** study (*J Hypertens* 1997;15:1337-1344), conducted in 1,414 hypertensive subjects (SBP ≥ 160 mm Hg and DBP ≥ 95 mm Hg), between the ages of 40 and 65 years, with a 2-year follow-up, verapamil SR (240 mg daily) vs chlorthalidone (25 mg daily) showed a similar efficacy on blood pressure (DBP controlled in 69.3% of cases vs 66.9%); but only verapamil SR decreased heart rate by 5.8% ($p <$ 0.01), total serum cholesterol level ($p <$ 0.01), and total serum cholesterol/serum HDL-C ratio ($p <$ 0.01). The incidence of fatal and nonfatal cardiovascular events was similar in the two groups (42 cases out of 707 vs 43 out of 707).

Valuable complementary information concerning the place of calcium channel blockers in the treatment of hypertension will soon be available following publication of the results of several ongoing clinical trials (see pp. 34, 40, and 41).

The prospective, randomized, double-blind **ABCD** study (*N Engl J Med* 1998;338:645-652), in 950 non-insulin-requiring diabetic patients who were either hypertensive (470 patients: DBP ≥ 90 mm Hg) or normotensive (480 patients: DBP between 80 and 89 mm Hg), treated with nisoldipine (10 to 60 mg daily) vs enalapril (5 to 40 mg daily), compared (main endpoint) the effects of two blood pressure levels on renal function. The secondary endpoint of the study was to compare the effects of intensive antihypertensive therapy vs moderate therapy on the incidence of retinopathy, left ventricular hypertrophy, albuminuria, and cardiovascular events (sudden death, progressive heart failure, fatal myocardial infarction, fatal arrhythmia, cerebrovascular accident, ruptured abdominal aortic aneurysm).

The objective of intensive therapy was to achieve a DBP of 75 mm Hg in hypertensive patients and a 10 mm Hg reduction of baseline DBP in normotensive patients. Moderate therapy was designed to achieve DBP between 80 and 89 mm Hg in hypertensive patients with no alteration of DBP in normotensive patients.

The study was stopped prematurely after a 5-year follow-up, as although the two medications induced a comparable reduction of blood pressure, a higher incidence of fatal and nonfatal myocardial infarction was observed with nisoldipine: 25 cases vs 5 with enalapril (RR: 9.5; 95% CI: 2.3 to 21.4). The time to onset of myocardial infarction was also longer in the enalapril arm. On the basis of the currently available data, it is unclear whether this result is related to a harmful effect of nisoldipine, a protective effect of enalapril or a combination of these two possibilities. These findings, which concern a secondary endpoint of the study, must be interpreted cautiously, and no definitive conclusions can be drawn concerning the safety or harmful effect of nisoldipine prescribed under these conditions. However, as emphasized by **Cutler** (*N Engl J Med* 1998;338:679-681), these conclusions maintain an uncertainty which will hopefully be resolved by the results of the ongoing **ALLHAT** study, based on 40,000 patients (see p. 40).

Hemorrhages and cancers

● Some retrospective or isolated studies have reported an increased risk of hemorrhages (*BMJ* 1995;310:776-777 and *Lancet* 1996;347:1061-1065) or cancers (*Lancet* 1996;348:493-497) during treatment with calcium channel blockers, but these findings are difficult to interpret. The **SYST-EUR** and **SYST-China** prospective studies, with a mean follow-up of 4 years and 2 years, respectively, did not report any difference between nitrendipine and placebo for the incidence of noncardiovascular deaths, hemorrhages, or cancers.

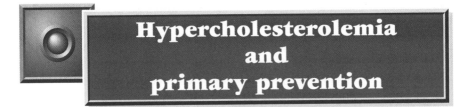

Hypercholesterolemia and primary prevention

As already suggested by epidemiological and experimental studies, primary prevention trials have confirmed the relationship between the serum cholesterol level and the incidence of ischemic heart disease; they have demonstrated that the relative reduction of the incidence of coronary heart disease was proportional to the reduction of serum cholesterol; furthermore, some studies have demonstrated a reduction of coronary mortality without, however, any significant reduction of all cause mortality.

Current state of knowledge

 A high serum cholesterol level considerably increases the risk of coronary heart disease.

Several years ago, the serum cholesterol level considered to be normal was expressed by the formula: 2 g/L with the patient's age in years in the decimal position (for example 2.30 g/L at 30 years, 2.60 g/L at 60 years).

Two studies have led to give up this concept.

The **Framingham** study (*Am J Med* 1984;76:4-12), in which the mean serum cholesterol of subjects who developed coronary heart disease was 2.44 g/L (6.3 mmol/L) vs 2.19 g/L (5.6 mmol/L) in the population without coronary heart disease.

The **MRFIT** study (*JAMA* 1990;263:1795-1800), which showed that the coronary risk, very low for serum cholesterol < 1.7 g/L (4.3 mmol/L), became significant above 2 g/L (5.1 mmol/L).

2 **The coronary risk, for the same serum cholesterol level, varies from one country to another.**

The so-called **7-country** study (*Circulation* 1970;41 suppl. I:1-211) showed that, for an equal serum cholesterol, coronary mortality was 20-fold lower in Crete than in other countries.

More recently, in the **MONICA** study (*Circulation* 1994;90:583-612), the coronary morbidity and mortality was lower in Toulouse than in Lille and Strasbourg, independently of the distribution of cardiovascular risk factors in these three cities.

 The risk is greater when hypercholesterolemia is associated with one or several other risk factors: hypertension, smoking, age > 50 years, male gender, family history, diabetes.

 Control of hypercholesterolemia reduces the coronary morbidity and mortality.

This was demonstrated by clinical trials conducted with diet alone (see p. 63), multifactorial trials designed to control several risk factors (see p. 65), and trials conducted with lipid-lowering drugs (see p. 67) administered in the case of insufficient response to diet.

A meta-analysis by **Muldoon** (*N Engl J Med* 1991;324:922-923), based on 6 primary prevention trials and a total of 24,847 men treated for an average of 4.8 years, reported that the fall in serum cholesterol obtained with lipid-lowering drugs, significantly reduced the mortality from ischemic heart disease by 14.4% ($p = 0.04$), without significantly decreasing all cause mortality.

 Control of hypercholesterolemia reduces cardiovascular morbidity and mortality when baseline serum cholesterol is high (WOSCOPS study) or only slightly raised (AFCAPS-TexCAPS study).

In the **WOSCOPS** study (*N Engl J Med* 1995;333:1301-1307), conducted in the Scottish population, which differs from the French population by the much higher risk of coronary heart disease, presenting a mean serum cholesterol of 2.72 g/L (7.0 mmol/L) and a mean serum LDL-C of 1.92 g/L (5.0 mmol/L), pravastatin (40 mg daily) significantly decreased cardiovascular mortality by 32% ($p = 0.033$), with a follow-up of 4.9 years.

In the **AFCAPS-TexCAPS** study (*JAMA* 1998;279:1615-1622), conducted in 6,605 subjects with a mean serum cholesterol of 2.21 g/L (5.6 mmol/L), a mean serum LDL-C of 1.50 g/L (3.8 mmol/L), and a mean serum HDL-C slightly lower than the normal mean values, i.e. 0.36 mg/L (0.94 mmol/L) in males and 0.40 mg/L (1.03 mmol/L) in females, lovastatin (20 to 40 mg daily), vs placebo, significantly decreased the risk of developing a first acute coronary event by 36%, with a follow-up of 5.2 years. However, the power of this study was not sufficient to demonstrate a possible effect on cardiovascular or coronary mortality (see p. 69).

 The safety of use of statins is excellent.

The **WOSCOPS** study confirmed the results of the **4S** study on secondary prevention with simvastatin, which showed that reduction of serum cholesterol was not accompanied by an excess extracar-diac mortality. This puts an end to the controversy concerning whether, in the context of primary prevention, a reduction of hypercholesterolemia decreases coronary morbidity and mortality only at the cost of increased non-cardiovascular mortality, especially from cancer and violent death.

Unresolved questions

 Control of hypercholesterolemia by statins probably reduces all cause mortality.

In the **WOSCOPS** study, pravastatin (40 mg daily) almost significantly ($p = 0.051$) decreased all cause mortality by 22%.

Such a result was not achieved with either fibrates or cholestyramine.

In the **WHO** cooperative trial (*Br Heart J* 1978;40:1069-1118), conducted in 15,745 men, aged 30 to 59 years, with serum cholesterol (mean: 2.48 g/L, i.e. 6.4 mmol/L) situated in the upper third of the serum cholesterol distribution of the overall population, and with a mean follow-up of 5.3 years, clofibrate (1.6 g daily), vs the control group, significantly reduced the incidence of a first major coronary event by 20% ($p < 0.05$), but significantly increased all cause mortality by 20% ($p < 0.05$) (see p. 67).

In the **LRC-CPPT** study (*JAMA* 1984;251:351-364 and 365-374), conducted in 3,806 men, with a mean age of 47.8 years, a mean serum cholesterol of 2.65 g/L (6.8 mmol/L), a mean serum LDL-C of 1.9 g/L (4.9 mmol/L), and a mean follow-up of 7.4 years, cholestyramine (12 g bid or 6 g qid), vs placebo, significantly decreased the coronary risk by 19% ($p < 0.05$), but only showed a tendency to reduce all cause mortality because of a non-significant 33% increase of non-cardiovascular mortality (see p. 67).

In the **Helsinki Heart Study** (*N Engl J Med* 1987;317:1237-1245), conducted in 4,081 men aged 40 to 55 years, with total serum cholesterol $\geq$ 2 g/L (5.1 mmol/L), and a mean follow-up of 5 years, gemfibrozil (600 mg bid), vs placebo, significantly reduced the cumulative incidence of cardiac events by 34% ($p < 0.02$), but had no effect on the total number of deaths (see p. 68).

● **Primary prevention and secondary prevention may coexist in high-risk subjects.**

In male subjects presenting several risk factors, coronary atherosclerosis may develop beyond a certain age, although it may initially remain mild and asymptomatic.

Conversion factors

Total serum cholesterol

mmol/L x 0.387 = g/L
g/L x 2.58 = mmol/L

Triglycerides

mmol/L x 0.875 = g/L
g/L x 1.14 = mmol/L

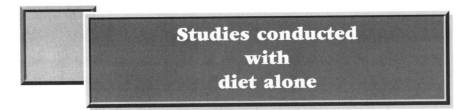

Studies conducted with diet alone

Schematically, the diets used are characterized by a high polyunsaturated fatty acid/saturated fatty acid ratio and a high fiber intake.

Three main trials

● In the **Veterans Administration** study (*Circulation* 1969;39 and 40 suppl. II:1-63), conducted in 846 men with a mean age of 65 years and moderately raised mean serum cholesterol (2.34 g/L, i.e. 6.0 mmol/L), dietary intervention (reduction of dietary serum cholesterol, increased polyunsaturated fatty acids at the expense of saturated fats, and the use of vegetable fat in the place of a large proportion of animal fat, resulting in a polyunsaturated fatty acid/saturated fatty acid ratio = 2 vs 0.9 in the control group), compared to a standard North American diet (control group), providing 40% of calories in the form of lipids, with a follow-up of 8 years, decreased serum cholesterol by 12.7%, the nonfatal myocardial infarction rate and death from ischemic heart disease by 20% and coronary mortality by 18%. This study did not demonstrate any difference in terms of all cause mortality due to an excess of deaths due to cancer and violence in the group treated by diet.

● In the **Finnish Mental Hospital Study** (*Int J Epidemiol* 1979;8:99-118), conducted in 450 mental hospital patients of both sexes, between the ages of 34 and 64 years, with a mean serum cholesterol of 2.7 g/L (6.9 mmol/L) and a follow-up of 6 years, a low cholesterol diet, vs the usual diet, decreased serum cholesterol by approximately 15%; it significantly reduced the incidence of ischemic heart disease by 44% and tended to decrease cardiovascular mortality by 50% (NS) and all cause mortality by 11% (NS).

● In the **Minnesota Coronary Survey** (*Arteriosclerosis* 1989;9:129-135) conducted in more than 9,000 subjects of both sexes with no age limit, presenting normal serum cholesterol (mean: 2.07 g/L, i.e. 5.3 mmol/L), with a follow-up of 4.5 years, a low cholesterol diet vs a stan-

Multifactorial trials

Multifactorial primary prevention trials are designed to control several risk factors; they are based on the results of epidemiological studies demonstrating the importance of combinations of risk factors in the pathogenesis of coronary heart disease.

Three main trials

- In the **Oslo** study (*Lancet* 1981;1:1303-10), conducted in 1,232 men between the ages of 40 and 49 years, presenting marked hypercholesterolemia (mean: 3.23 g/L, i.e. 8.3 mmol/L), but no hypertension, with a follow-up of 5 years, very strict dietary measures combined with cessation of smoking, vs a control group, decreased serum cholesterol by 13%, smoking by 40%, and the combined risk of nonfatal myocardial infarction and sudden death by 47% ($p < 0.05$).

- In the **WHO** cooperative trial (*Lancet* 1986;1:869-872), conducted in 60,881 men from 4 countries (Belgium, United Kingdom, Italy, and Poland), between the ages of 40 to 59 years, (the published results only concern 49,784 subjects, because of the incomplete Polish data), with practically normal serum cholesterol (mean: 2.17 g/L, i.e. 5.6 mmol/L), intervention consisting of a low cholesterol diet combined with weight reduction, reduction of tobacco consumption, and physical exercise, with a follow-up of 6 years, only slightly modified serum cholesterol vs the control group, but tended to decrease (NS) the nonfatal myocardial infarction rate by 14.8%, coronary mortality by 6.9%, all cause mortality by 5.3%, and the incidence of coronary heart disease by 10.2%. Despite a marked beneficial effect, the results of this study did not reach the limit of significance because of the poor results obtained in the British group, in whom the control of risk factors was short-lived, resulting in a slight reduction (< 4%) of the risk. In contrast, in the Belgian group, in which the multifactorial risk was decreased by 15%, the incidence of the various coronary complications was significantly decreased for the first 4 years, but was no longer decreased after 10 years.

In the **MRFIT** study (*JAMA* 1982;248:1465-1477 and *JAMA* 1990;263: 1795-800, *Circulation* 1990;82:1616-28), conducted in 12,866 men, between the ages of 35 and 57 years, presenting hypercholesterolemia (mean: 2.54 g/L, i.e. 6.5 mmol/L), smoking (mean of 22 cigarettes per day) and including 8,012 (62%) hypertensive patients (DBP > 90 mm Hg; mean DBP: 99 mm Hg), dietary advice, cessation of smoking, standard treatment of hypertension (special intervention) vs usual care:

● with a mean follow-up of 7 years, achieved a more marked reduction of the level of risk factors; tended to reduce coronary mortality by 7.1% (17.9 per 1,000 vs 19.3 per 1,000, NS), and did not modify all cause mortality (41.2 per 1,000 vs 40.4 per 1,000);

● with a mean follow-up of 10.5 years, tended to decrease coronary mortality by 15% (p = 0.19) and deaths from all causes by 11% (p = 0.13). In the subgroup of hypertensive patients with DBP ≥ 100 mm Hg, therapeutic intervention tended to decrease coronary mortality by 36% (p = 0.07) and significantly reduced all cause mortality by 50% (p = 0.0001).

In this study, the mortality of the control group receiving usual care was lower than expected, as better informed control subjects, aware of the problem of prevention, tended to reduce the level of their risk factors on their own initiative.

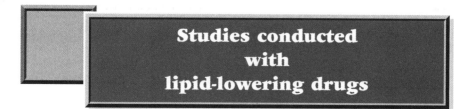

Studies conducted with lipid-lowering drugs

In practice, lipid-lowering drugs must only be administered when dietary measures, followed for several weeks, have failed to control serum lipid levels.

Five main trials

- In the **WHO** cooperative trial (*Br Heart J* 1978;40:1069-1118 and *Lancet* 1980;2:379-385), conducted in 15,745 men, between the ages of 30 and 59 years, in apparent good health, but with serum cholesterol situated in the upper third of the serum cholesterol distribution of the overall population (mean: 2.48 g/L, i.e. 6.4 mmol/L), clofibrate (1.6 g daily), vs the control group, in which olive oil capsules were administered as placebo, with a mean follow-up of 5.3 years, decreased serum cholesterol by an average of 9%, significantly reduced the incidence of a first major coronary event by 20% ($p < 0.05$), exclusively by decreasing the incidence of nonfatal myocardial infarction by 25%, without modifying the incidence of first fatal cardiac accidents. It also significantly increased all cause mortality by 20% ($p < 0.05$). Although this trial confirmed that a reduction of serum cholesterol could reduce the incidence of nonfatal myocardial infarction, it also contributed to maintaining the uncertainty about the safety of administration of lipid-lowering drugs for primary prevention, because of the increased all cause mortality.

- In the **LRC-CPPT** study (*JAMA* 1984;251:351-364 and 365-374), conducted in 3,806 men, with a mean age of 47.8 years, with no history or signs of cardiovascular disease, especially coronary heart disease, serum cholesterol ≥ 2.65 g/L (6.8 mmol/L), serum LDL-C ≥ 1.9 g/L (4.9 mmol/L), and serum triglycerides < 3 g/L (3.4 mmol/L), cholestyramine (12 g bid or 6 g qid) vs placebo, with a mean follow-up of 7.4 years, decreased: total serum cholesterol by 13.9% and serum LDL-C by 20.3% (proportionally to the dose ingested), the coronary risk by 19% ($p < 0.05$) (i.e. coronary deaths and nonfatal myocardial infarctions), the risk of developing angina by 20% ($p < 0.01$), and the risk of ischemia during a stress test by 25% (p < 0.001). It only tended to reduce all cause mortality because of a non-significant 33% increase of non-cardiovascular deaths, especially deaths due to accidents and violence in the treated group. This study demonstrated a correlation between a reduction of total serum cholesterol and serum LDL-C and a decreased incidence of coronary heart disease: a 1% reduction of total serum cholesterol decreased the coronary risk by 2%.

● In the **Helsinki Heart Study** (*N Engl J Med* 1987;317:1237-1245), conducted in 4,081 asymptomatic men with a mean age of 47.3 years and serum cholesterol ≥ 2 g/L (5.2 mmol/L), with a mean follow-up of 60.4 months, gemfibrozil (600 mg bid) vs placebo decreased total serum cholesterol by 11%, serum LDL-C by 10%, serum triglycerides by 43%, and serum HDL-C by about 10%. It significantly decreased the number of nonfatal myocardial infarctions by 37% (p < 0.05), the cumulative rate of cardiac events (i.e. deaths and fatal or nonfatal myocardial infarctions) by 34% (p < 0.02) and tended to decrease coronary mortality by 26% (NS) and increase all cause mortality by 6% (NS), without modifying the number of cancer deaths.

● In the **WOSCOPS** study (*N Engl J Med* 1995;333:1301-1307), conducted in 6,595 male subjects, with a mean age of 55.1 years, with no history of myocardial infarction (but 5% of patients included in each group suffered from stable angina), a mean serum cholesterol of 2.72 g/L (7.0 mmol/L) and a mean serum LDL-C of 1.92 g/L (5.0 mmol/L), with a follow-up of 4.9 years, pravastatin (40 mg daily) administered in addition to diet, vs placebo, decreased serum cholesterol by 20%, serum LDL-C by 26%, serum triglycerides by 12% and increased serum HDL-C by 5%. It significantly reduced the number of coronary events (i.e. the combined incidence of nonfatal myocardial infarction or coronary death) by 31% (p < 0.001), the number of coronary deaths by 33% (p = 0.042), deaths from cardiovascular disease by 32% (p = 0.033), the number of myocardial revascularization procedures by 37% (p = 0.009) and all cause mortality by 22% (p = 0.051). It had no effect on non-cardiovascular mortality and did not modify the number of cases of fatal or nonfatal cancers, suicides, or accidents.

According to the data of this study, primary prevention with pravastatin in 1,000 middle-aged male subjects with moderate hypercholesterolemia (mean: 2.70 g/L, i.e. 7.0 mmol/L) can be considered to have prevented, after 5 years: 20 nonfatal myocardial infarctions, 14 coronary angiographies, 8 revascularization procedures, 7 cardiovascular deaths, and 2 deaths due to other causes. In this study, the reduction of the relative risk of coronary events was observed in subjects younger and older than 55, in smokers and non-smokers, and in subjects with serum cholesterol less than or greater than 2.69 g/L (6.9 mmol/L), serum LDL-C less than or greater than 1.89 g/L (4.8 mmol/L), and serum triglycerides ≥ 1.48 g/L (1.68 mmol/L).

● In the **AFCAPS/TexCAPS** primary prevention study (*JAMA* 1998;279: 1615-1622), conducted in 6,505 subjects (5,608 males, 997 females) between the ages of 45 and 73 years, with no clinical signs of coronary heart disease, mean serum cholesterol of 2.21 g/L (5.6 mmol/L), mean serum LDL-C of 1.50 g/L (3.8 mmol/L), mean serum HDL-C of 0.36 g/L, i.e. slightly lower than normal, and mean triglycerides of 1.58 mg/L (1.78 mmol/L), with a follow-up of 5.2 years, lovastatin (20 mg daily and if necessary 40 mg daily to lower serum LDL-C to 1.10 g/L, i.e. 2.8 mmol/L) vs placebo decreased serum cholesterol by 18.4%, serum LDL-C by 25%, and serum triglycerides by 15% and increased serum HDL-C by 6%. Lovastatin also significantly ($p < 0.001$) decreased the relative risk of a first acute coronary event (sudden death, myocardial infarction, unstable angina, revascularization procedure) by 37%. The reduction of the risk was similar in both sexes, regardless of the age-group and serum LDL-C level. In other words, the treatment of 1,000 men and women by lovastatin for 5 years, would prevent 19 major coronary events and 17 coronary revascularizations. The mortality and fatal or nonfatal cancer rates were comparable with lovastatin and placebo, but the study did not have sufficient power to demonstrate a possible effect on cardiovascular or coronary mortality.

Hypertriglyceridemia is a cardiovascular risk factor

- On univariate statistical analysis, hypertriglyceridemia constitutes a risk factor in both sexes. On multivariate analysis, this relationship tends to be attenuated by the presence of other risk factors (hypertension, smoking, obesity, diabetes, etc.).

- The meta-analysis by **Hokanson** and **Austin** (*J Cardiovasc Risk* 1996;3:213-219), based on 17 prospective studies including a total of 46,413 men and 10,864 women followed for 8 years, showed that hypertriglyceridemia is added to the other risk factors.

- Hypertriglyceridemia is a risk factor independent of the fall in serum HDL-C that it induces (there is an inverse relationship between serum HDL and serum triglycerides).

Primary prevention by diet in children

The reduction of the dietary intake of saturated fats and serum cholesterol can be safely proposed in prepubertal children, i.e. during the active growth period, when their serum LDL-C level is between the 80th and 98th percentile. This was confirmed by the **DISC** study (*JAMA* 1995;273:1429-1435) in 663 children between the ages of 8 and 10 years, with a follow-up of 3 years. In this population, a diet in which lipids represented 28% of the caloric intake (with less than 8% of saturated fats and up to 9% of unsaturated fats and a daily serum cholesterol intake < 75 mg/kilocalorie) and for which compliance was improved by behavioral therapy sessions, vs a control group, significantly decreased total serum cholesterol by 0.033 g/L (0.08 mmol/L, p = 0.04) and serum LDL-C by 0.154 g/L (0.40 mmol/L, p = 0.02), without inducing any harmful adverse effects.

National and international recommendations

- Task Force of the European Society of Cardiology
  (*Arch Mal Cœur Vaiss* 1995;88:1493-1542)

- Secondary prevention panel
  (*Circulation* 1995;92:2-4)

- ANDEM Recommendations
  (*Et Eval Cardiovasc* 1995;12:397-428)

- 27th Conference of Bethesda
  (*J Am Coll Cardiol* 1996;27:957-1047)

- Joint British recommendations on prevention of coronary heart disease in clinical practice
  (*Heart* 1998;80 suppl. 2:S1-S29)

Primary prevention: ongoing studies

- The **FIELD** study (1st congress of the Asian-Pacific Society of Atherosclerosis and Vascular Disease, 1998) of primary (75% of subjects) and secondary prevention (25% of patients with coronary heart disease), conducted in 8,000 patients of either sex, between the ages of 50 and 75 years, presenting with non-insulin-dependent diabetes mellitus and pure or mixed hypercholesterolemia, is evaluating the effect of micronized fenofibrate (200 mg daily) vs placebo on the cardiac morbidity and mortality and all cause mortality, with a 5-year follow-up.

- The **FAME** study, conducted in 6,000 Mediterranean subjects of both sexes, aged 70 to 85 years, with no history of cardiovascular disease and serum LDL-C > 1.6 g/L (4.1 mmol/L) and triglycerides < 4 g/L (4.5 mmol/L), is evaluating, with a 5-year follow-up, the effect of a single daily dose of fluvastatin (80 mg of a modified formulation) vs placebo on the incidence of first cardiovascular event (fatal or nonfatal cerebrovascular accident, coronary event).

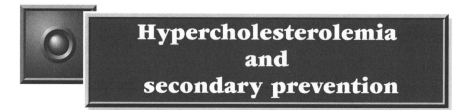

Hypercholesterolemia and secondary prevention

In secondary prevention in patients with coronary heart disease, mortality is decreased in proportion to the degree of reduction of total serum cholesterol. The efficacy of statins, in combination with dietary measures, on this parameter has now been demonstrated.

Current state of knowledge

 The reduction of serum cholesterol is almost parallel to the reduction of the incidence of cardiac events.

In the meta-analysis by **Roussouw** (*N Engl J Med* 1990;323:1112-1119), published before the **4S** (*Lancet* 1994;344:1383-1389), **CARE** (*N Engl J Med* 1996;335:1001-1009) and **LIPID** (*N Engl J Med* 1998;339:1349-1357) studies, any reduction of serum cholesterol by 10% decreases the total number of myocardial infarctions by 15%.

According to the meta-analysis by **Holme** (*Br Heart J* 1993;69 suppl. I:S42-S47), based on 19 trials before the publication of the **4S**, **CARE** and **LIPID** studies, an 8 to 9% reduction of total serum cholesterol is necessary to effectively decrease all cause mortality.

In the meta-analysis by **Gould** (*Circulation* 1995;91:2274-2282), based on 35 trials (26 of which evaluated unifactorial secondary prevention intervention), including a total of 77,000 subjects, any reduction of 10% of serum cholesterol significantly decreased coronary mortality by 13% ($p < 0.002$) and all cause mortality by 10% ($p < 0.03$).

The addition of 8 recent trials conducted with statins (*Circulation* 1998;97:946-952) allowed **Gould** to confirm his previous meta-analysis: coronary mortality was decreased by 15% ($p < 0.001$) and all cause mortality was decreased by 11% ($p < 0.001$).

 By lowering serum cholesterol and serum LDL-C by about 30%, simvastatin (4S study) and pravastatin (CARE and LIPID studies) decrease the coronary morbidity and mortality.

Simvastatin (4S study) and pravastatin (LIPID study) are currently the only statins which significantly reduce all cause mortality.

In the 4S study, simvastatin (10 to 40 mg daily) reduced all cause mortality by 30% (p = 0.0003).

In the LIPID study (see p. 83), pravastatin (40 mg daily) reduced all cause mortality by 23% (p = 0.00002).

 The reduction of mortality is essentially related to the degree of mean reduction of serum cholesterol.

In the meta-analysis by **Marchioli** (*Arch Intern Med* 1996;156: 1158-1172), based on 34 trials including 24,968 patients with coronary heart disease, a 10 to 20% reduction of baseline serum cholesterol decreased mortality by 23%, while a more marked reduction (> 20%) decreased mortality by 30%.

 The benefit related to the reduction of serum cholesterol is independent of the baseline serum cholesterol level.

In the 4S study (see p. 81), patients with a relatively low serum cholesterol level (2.12 g/L, i.e. 5.4 mmol/L) obtained the same benefit from treatment with statins as those with a high serum cholesterol level (2.70 to 2.98 g/L, i.e. 6.9 to 7.7 mmol/L).

In the CARE study (see p. 82), patients with serum cholesterol > 2.09 g/L (5.4 mmol/L) and those with serum cholesterol ≤ 2.09 g/L obtained an equal benefit from treatment.

In the LIPID study (see p. 83), the beneficial effect of pravastatin was observed both in patients with baseline serum cholesterol < 2.10 g/L (5.5 mmol/L) and in patients with baseline serum cholesterol > 2.5 g/L (6.5 mmol/L).

6 The serum LDL-C level must be lowered as much as possible.

The CARE study showed that it was probably unnecessary to try to lower serum LDL-C below 1.25 g/L (3.2 mmol/L) inasmuch as patients with baseline serum LDL-C < 1.25 g/L (3.2 mmol/L) did not obtain any benefit from treatment, in terms of reduction of the number of coronary events.

However, the **Post-CABGT** study (see pp. 94 and 103), conducted in patients who underwent coronary artery bypass graft surgery, showed that a more marked reduction of serum LDL-C, below 1.0 g/L (2.6 mmol/L), by treatment with lovastatin, significantly decreased the myocardial revascularization rate by 29% ($p = 0.03$) compared to less strict treatment which only achieved a serum LDL-C level between 1.32 and 1.36 g/L (3.4 to 3.5 mmol/L).

Similarly, in the CARS study (see p. 95), conducted in patients with coronary heart disease and virtually normal serum cholesterol [between 1.60 and 2.20 g/L (4.1 to 5.6 mmol/L)] and a mean serum LDL-C of 1.23 ± 0.24 g/L (3.17 ± 0.61 mmol/L), pravastatin (10 mg daily) vs control group, significantly decreased total serum cholesterol by 11% and serum LDL-C by 18%, reaching a value of 0.99 ± 0.21 g/L (2.55 ± 0.54 mmol/L) and reduced the percentage of patients (21% vs 49%, $p < 0.05$) with progression of coronary stenoses.

7 **The benefit of statins is observed in both sexes and in subjects over the age of 60 years.**

In the 4S (simvastatin), CARE and LIPID (pravastatin) studies, statins reduced the risk of major coronary events to a similar degree in males and females.

In the 4S study, simvastatin also induced a similar improvement of survival in patients over the age of 60.

In the CARE study, the effect of pravastatin on major coronary events was practically the same in patients between the ages of 60 and 75 years on inclusion as in those in the 24- to 59-year agegroup.

8 **The safety of use of statins is excellent.**

The remarkable efficacy of statins is combined with very good safety, as the 4S, CARE and LIPID studies eliminated any doubts concerning the long-term safety of use of this new therapeutic class. No difference between the groups (statin vs placebo) was observed in these studies, especially in terms of serious events or non-cardiovascular deaths and the incidence of cancers.

9 **The use of statins has a good cost/efficacy ratio.**

This was demonstrated by analysis of the results of the 4S study conducted with simvastatin (*Eur Heart J* 1996;17:1001-1007).

Unresolved questions

● **The effect of fibrates on cardiac morbidity and mortality is still controversial**

The **BIP** trial (*Am J Cardiol* 1993;71:909-915 and 71st Session of the American Heart Association, 1998) demonstrated not so favorable results.

This trial, conducted in 3,122 coronary patients of both sexes, with a mean age of 53.9 years, presenting moderate dyslipidemia, i.e. plasma serum cholesterol between 1.8 and 2.5 g/L (4.6 to 6.4 mmol/L), serum LDL-C ≤ 1.80 g/L (4.6 mmol/L), serum HDL-C ≤ 0.45 g/L (1.1 mmol/L), and triglycerides ≤ 3 g/L (3.4 mmol/L), bezafibrate (400 mg daily) vs placebo, with a follow-up of 5 to 7 years (average of 96 months), tended to decrease the main composite criterion, combining fatal and nonfatal myocardial infarction and sudden death, 9% (p = 0.27; NS). No significant difference was observed between the two groups in terms of all cause mortality and the incidence of adverse effects.

The **VA-HIT** trial (*Am J Cardiol* 1993;71:45-52, *Am J Cardiol* 1996;78:572-575 and 71st Session of the American Heart Association, 1998) was the first study in favor of fibrates.

This trial, conducted in 2,531 men with coronary heart disease, with a mean age of 74 years, presenting moderate dyslipidemia, i.e. serum cholesterol < 2.4 g/L (6.2 mmol/L), serum HDL-C ≤ 0.40 g/L (1.0 mmol/L), serum LDL-C ≤ 1.40 g/L (3.6 mmol/L), and triglycerides ≤ 3 g/L (3.4 mmol/L), gemfibrozil (1200 mg daily) vs placebo, with a follow-up of 5 to 7 years, increased serum HDL-C by 7.5%, decreased triglycerides by 25% (from 1.61 to 1.15 g/L, i.e. from 1.8 to 1.3 mmol/L) and did not modify serum LDL-C (with a mean value of 1.11 g/L, i.e. 2.8 mmol/L). Most importantly, gemfibrozil reduced the relative risk of coronary death or nonfatal myocardial infarction (main endpoint) by 22% (p = 0.006) and decreased the number of cerebrovascular accidents and transient ischemic attacks.

 Is it legitimate to coprescribe a statin and a fibrate?

According to **French Medical References**, it is not justified to coprescribe a statin and a fibrate because of the risk of additive adverse effects, especially muscle effects, except in the case of refractory severe hyperlipidemia associated with a high cardio-vascular risk.

● **Do different statins have different degrees of efficacy?**

In the **CURVES** study (*Am J Cardiol* 1998;81:582-587), conducted over 8 weeks in 534 patients with serum LDL-C $\geq$ 1.60 g/L (4.2 mmol/L) and triglycerides $\leq$ 4 g/L (4.5 mmol/L), serum LDL-C was decreased by 28 to 41% by simvastatin (10-40 mg daily), 18 to 34% by pravastatin (10-40 mg daily), 25 to 38% by lovastatin (20-40 mg daily), 18 to 27% by fluvastatin (20-40 mg daily), and 38 to 51% by atorvastatin (10-40 mg daily), which therefore induced a signifi-cantly greater reduction of total serum cholesterol and serum LDL-C ($p < 0.01$) than the other HMG-CoA reductase inhibitors administered at milligram-equivalent doses.

● **What is the place of antioxidant treatments?**

Their mechanism of action has not yet been completely elucidated (*N Engl J Med* 1997;337:408-416). Epidemiological studies have demonstrated an inverse relationship between the development of coronary heart disease and administration of a vitamin E (alpha-tocopherol) supplement.

In the **CHAOS** study (*Lancet* 1996;347:781-786), conducted in 2,002 patients with documented coronary heart disease, with a median follow-up of 510 days, regular administration of 400 to 800 IU of alpha-tocopherol, significantly reduced the combined risk of nonfatal myocardial infarction and cardiovascular death by 47% ($p = 0.005$). This result was essentially due to the very significant ($p = 0.005$) 77% reduction of the number of nonfatal myocardial infarctions; it was also accompanied by a non-significant increase of cardiovascular deaths, which needs to be studied more specifi-cally in subsequent studies.

In the **PART** study (*J Am Coll Cardiol* 1997;30:855-862) and **MVP** study (*N Engl J Med* 1997;337:365-372), conducted in 101 and 317 patients, respectively; in order to prevent restenosis after coronary angioplasty, probucol, a lipid-lowering drug possessing antioxidant properties, prescribed alone (**PART** study) or in com-bination with multivitamins (**MVP** study), systematically decreased the coronary restenosis rate. These results are not in agreement with those of the **PQRST** study (see p. 89), in which probucol, which has subsequently been withdrawn from the market, did not appear to exert any effect on regression of peripheral atherosclerosis.

Ongoing Studies

- The **CTT** meta-analysis (*Am J Cardiol* 1995;75:1130-1134), which will analyse all published and as yet unpublished trials studying the effects of lipid-lowering drug on all cause mortality, coronary mortality and deaths due to other causes, will recruit more than 60,000 subjects, including 12,000 women and 20,000 elderly subjects.

- The **DAIS** study (*Diabetologia* 1996;39:1655-1661), conducted in 400 dyslipidemic patients with non-insulin-dependent diabetes mellitus, is evaluating the action of fenofibrate vs placebo on regression of coronary atherosclerotic plaque, with a 3- to 5-year follow-up.

- The **HPS** study, conducted in 20,000 high-risk patients, is assessing the effect of simvastatin (40 mg daily) associated with vitamins A, E, and C, on all cause mortality.

- The **PRESERVE** study, renamed **PROSPER**, (18th International Symposium on Lipid-lowering Drugs, 30 May-3 June 1998), conducted in 5,500 patients between the ages of 70 and 82 years, at risk of or with a history of myocardial infarction or cerebrovascular accident, is evaluating the effect of pravastatin on the composite criterion composed of coronary mortality, nonfatal myocardial infarction, and fatal and nonfatal cerebrovascular accidents.

Studies conducted with diet alone

*Dietary measures are an integral part of any strategy designed to control hypercholesterolemia. The **DART** study, the **Indian** trial, and the **Lyon** study have clearly demonstrated the beneficial effect obtained with diet.*

 In the **DART** study (*Lancet* 1989;2:757-761), conducted in 2,033 men with a mean age of 56.4 years, included an average of 41 days after myocardial infarction, regular consumption, twice a week, of 300 mg of fatty fish (mackerel, herring, salmon, trout), which provides 2.5 g of eicosapentaenoic acid (bearing in mind that, by the end of the study, 22% of subjects allocated to this diet had partially or totally replaced regular fish consumption by the intake of omega-3 polyunsaturated fatty acids capsules), vs the control group, assigned to simple reduction of lipid consumption, with a 2-year follow-up, significantly reduced all cause mortality by 29% (9.3% vs 12.8%, $p < 0.05$), and also decreased mortality from ischemic heart disease (7.7% vs 11.4%, $p < 0.001$), but did not significantly modify the overall incidence of ischemic events (death from ischemic heart disease and nonfatal myocardial infarction) because nonfatal myocardial infarction occurred more frequently in these patients.

In the Indian trial by **Singh** (*Am J Cardiol* 1992;69:879-885), conducted in 406 patients included 24 to 48 hours after acute myocardial infarction, diet A (low-calorie, with increased amounts of complex carbohydrates, vegetables, fish, polyunsaturated fatty acids and therefore a higher polyunsaturated fatty acid/saturated fatty acid ratio), vs diet B (providing more calories and saturated fatty acids), with a follow-up of 6 weeks, significantly reduced total serum cholesterol and serum LDL-C and significantly decreased the overall number of cardiac events (fatal and nonfatal myocardial infarction and sudden death) by 34.5% ($p < 0.01$).

In the **Lyon** study (*Lancet* 1994;434:1454-1459), conducted in 605 patients of both sexes, with a mean age of 54 years, surviving a recent myocardial infarction (< 6 months), a Mediterranean type of diet, i.e. enriched in bread, vegetables, fruit and fish, with decreased meat, butter and cream (replaced by olive oil), vs the usual diet recommended by the American Heart Association after myocardial infarction (lipids: 30% of total energy intake, saturated fats: 10%, polyunsaturated fat/saturated fat ratio: 0.8), with a 2- to 5-year follow-up, very significantly reduced the combined risk of nonfatal myocardial infarction and cardiovascular death by 73% ($p < 0.01$) and all cause mortality (4.5% vs 18%, $p = 0.02$), while no significant difference was observed for total serum cholesterol, triglycerides, or Lp(a), but a tendency to an increase of serum HDL-C and a reduction of serum LDL-C was observed with the Mediterranean diet. This type of diet would prevent 2 to 6 accidents per year per 100 treated subjects.

The relative absence of correlation between the modest reduction of plasma serum cholesterol (varying between 0% and 13%) and the marked reduction of the cardiovascular risk has raised the hypothesis (as yet unverified) that the beneficial effect of dietary measures may be due more to a favorable action on coagulation (platelet aggregation inhibitor effect) than on a simple serum cholesterol-lowering effect.

Studies conducted with lipid-lowering drugs

Who would have imagined, before it was demonstrated for the first time in 1994 by the 4S study, and subsequently confirmed by the CARE (1996) and LIPID (1997) studies, that serum cholesterol-lowering drugs could very significantly improve the post-myocardial infarction prognosis?

Meta-analysis of Roussouw

● In the meta-analysis by **Roussouw** (*N Engl J Med* 1990;323:1112-1118), published before the **4S** and **CARE** studies and based on 8 secondary prevention studies after myocardial infarction, including a total of almost 4,000 patients, in whom hypercholesterolemia was treated by diet and/or lipid-lowering drugs (statins in more than one half of cases), treatment vs the control group: decreased serum LDL-C by an average of 25%; was accompanied twice as frequently by regression of atheroma (18% vs 9%); and significantly decreased the number of cases of progression of lesions (34% vs 50%). Clinically, lipid-lowering drugs significantly reduced the number of fatal ($p < 0.001$) and nonfatal myocardial infarctions ($p < 0.001$) and the cardiovascular mortality ($p < 0.05$), but did not modify the all cause mortality. According to this meta-analysis, an average reduction of 10% of serum cholesterol would decrease the total number of myocardial infarctions by 15%, nonfatal myocardial infarctions by 19%, and fatal myocardial infarctions by 12%.

4S and CARE studies

● The **4S** study (*Lancet* 1994;344:1383-1389) was the first secondary prevention study to demonstrate that serum cholesterol-lowering drugs could significantly lower coronary mortality and all cause mortality.

In this study, conducted in 4,444 patients of both sexes, between the ages of 35 and 70 years, presenting stable angina, a history of myocardial infarction more than 6 months previously, hypercholesterolemia between 2.10 and 3.10 g/L (5.5 to 8.0 mmol/L) and triglycerides ≤ 2.20 g/L (2.5 mmol/L), despite diet followed for 8 weeks, simvastatin (10 to 40 mg daily) vs placebo, with a median follow-up of 5.4 years, significantly decreased total serum cholesterol by 25%, serum LDL-C by 35%, and triglycerides by 10%, and increased serum HDL-C by 8%. Simvastatin also significantly reduced all cause mortality by 30% (8% vs 12%, p = 0.0003), death from coronary events by 42% without modifying the number of non-cardiovascular deaths, the incidence of one or several major coronary events 34% (19% vs 28%, p < 0.00001), and the incidence of myocardial revascularization procedures by 37% (p < 0.00001).

 The **CARE** study (*N Engl J Med* 1996;335:1001-1009) demonstrated the value of even moderate reduction of hypercholesterolemia.

In this study, conducted in 4,159 patients of both sexes, with a mean age of 59 years, all presenting a history of myocardial infarction, serum cholesterol < 2.40 g/L (6.2 mmol/L) (mean: 2.09 g/L, i.e. 5.4 mmol/L), and serum LDL-C between 1.15 and 1.74 g/L (2.9 to 4.4 mmol/L), with a mean follow-up of 5 years, pravastatin (40 mg daily) vs placebo significantly reduced the combined incidence of coronary death and nonfatal myocardial infarction by 24% (p = 0.003), the incidence of nonfatal myocardial infarction by 23% (p = 0.01), the number of myocardial revascularization procedures by 27% (p < 0.001), and the incidence of cerebrovascular accidents by 31% (p = 0.03), without significantly modifying all cause mortality and non-cardiovascular mortality.

Meta-analyses by Gould and Marchioli

 The meta-analysis by **Gould** (*Circulation* 1995;91:2274-2282), based on 35 randomized trials [31 unifactorial intervention trials of primary (5 trials) or secondary prevention (26 trials) and 4 multifactorial intervention trials of primary prevention] including a total of 77,000 subjects followed for at least 2 years, showed that:

● lowering of serum cholesterol decreased all cause mortality and coronary mortality, in proportion to the reduction of serum cholesterol: each 10% reduction of serum cholesterol significantly decreased coronary mortality by 13% (p < 0.002) and all cause mortality by 10% (p < 0.03);

● active treatment had no effect on mortality non related to ischemic heart disease;

● certain types of intervention used several years ago [especially clofibrate and hormones (dextrothyroxin, estrogens)] induced harmful effects; no harmful effects have been observed with dietary intervention, resins, niacin, and statins.

● A meta-analysis by **Marchioli** (*Arch Intern Med* 1990;156:1158-1172), based on 34 trials including a total of 24,968 patients with coronary heart disease showed that, in the context of secondary prevention, reduction of serum cholesterol by lipid-lowering drugs significantly decreased all cause mortality by 13% (12.5% during treatment vs 17.2% in the control group), coronary mortality by 16% and cardiovascular mortality by 13%. The reduction in all cause mortality was only slightly influenced by baseline serum cholesterol levels, but was more markedly influenced by the amplitude of the mean reduction of serum cholesterol. For example, a 10 to 20% reduction of serum cholesterol decreased all cause mortality by 23%, while a more marked reduction (> 20%) decreased all cause mortality by 30%. In contrast, reductions of serum cholesterol < 10% only slightly (4%) reduced mortality. It therefore appears necessary to decrease serum cholesterol by at least 10 to 20% in order to achieve a significant reduction of all cause mortality. Statins achieved the most obvious benefit in terms of reduction of the odds of death. According to these results, treatment would have to be continued for about 4 years in 110 patients to prevent one death, 96 patients to prevent a coronary death and 117 patients to prevent a cardiovascular death. Finally, it should be noted that active treatment did not have any favorable or unfavorable effects on non-cardiovascular mortality, violent deaths, or cancer mortality.

Lipid study

● In the **LIPID** study (*N Engl J Med* 1998;339:1349-1357), conducted in 9,014 coronary patients between the ages of 31 and 75 years, with a history of myocardial infarction (64%) or unstable angina (36%) and serum cholesterol between 1.55 and 2.71 g/L (4.0 to 7.0 mmol/L), with a follow-up of 6 years, pravastatin (40 mg daily) vs placebo lowered serum cholesterol by 18% and serum LDL-C by 25%; it also significantly decreased mortality from coronary heart disease (primary study outcome) (6.4% vs 8.3%) by 24% (95% CI: 12% to 35%, $p < 0.001$), the relative risk of overall mortality (11.0% vs 14.1%) by 22% (95% CI: 13% to 31%, $p < 0.001$); it decreased the incidence of all cardiovascular events, particularly myocardial infarction by 29% ($p < 0.001$), the composite risk of death from coronary heart disease or nonfatal myocardial infarction by 24% ($p < 0.001$), the risk of cerebrovascular accident by 19% ($p = 0.048$) and the risk of coronary revascularization by 20% ($p < 0.001$).

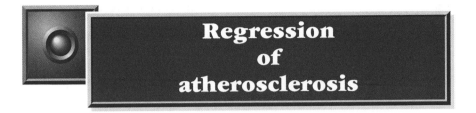

Regression of atherosclerosis

Atherosclerosis usually develops very slowly and evolves gradually over several decades; lipid striae develop over a period of 10 to 20 years, while fibrous plaques take 20 to 30 years. These lesions gradually calcify and the first clinical manifestations appear around the age of fifty. With time, the increasing thickness of the atheromatous plaque progressively accentuates the degree of arterial stenosis and eventually becomes clinically significant. The atheromatous plaque also carries a risk of numerous complications: serum cholesterol embolism, thrombosis with occlusion and risk of distal fibrin clot embolism, hematoma underneath the plaque resulting in a sudden increase in the volume of the plaque and sudden accentuation of the vascular stenosis.

Regression of the atheromatous plaque was a controversial issue for a long time. Based on the first experimental results, some authors very rapidly accepted this possibility, by considering that, in view of its plastic properties, the artery could adapt to its new condition and that atherosclerosis, which is proliferative and inflammatory for a long time, develops very slowly. Other authors rejected these arguments, asserting that myocyte proliferation is difficult to control, that atheromatous plaques are poorly accessible to medical treatment because of their poor blood supply, and that experimental results cannot be unreservedly extrapolated to man, in whom plaques contain fewer lipids, and are much more fibrous and frequently ulcerated.

In practice, what is the current situation concerning atherosclerosis regression?

Current state of knowledge

 The degree of atherosclerosis can be reliably analysed.

The degree of atherosclerosis can be reliably analysed by quantitative, computerized analysis of coronary angiography and by high resolution ultrasound examination of the carotid and femoral arteries, allowing evaluation of the intimal-medial thickness, which is now known to be well correlated with the risk of coronary artery lesions.

The reality of regression of atheromatous plaques has been demonstrated.

This was demonstrated by angiographic and/or ultrasound studies, essentially conducted in the context of secondary prevention.

 The management of hypercholesterolemia inhibits progression of atherosclerosis, prevents the appearance of new lesions or even allows regression of longstanding lesions.

These results, demonstrated on coronary, femoral, and carotid arteries, were obtained by various methods: diet combined with control of other risk factors, lipid-lowering drug treatment with agents such as cholestyramine, niacin, fibrates or, more recently, statins, or even surgical ileal bypass.

 The decreased progression or even regression of coronary atherosclerosis is only possible when serum cholesterol is reduced by 25% and serum cholesterol (LDL-C) by approximately 40% (*Arch Mal Cœur Vaiss* 1992;85 suppl. III: 47-55).

This can be achieved with statin monotherapy or drug combinations.

The CIS study (see p. 94) was the first to demonstrate a significant correlation ($p = 0.003$) between lowering of serum LDL-C and the mean reduction of the minimum lumen diameter per patient.

 Regression of coronary artery stenosis concerns stenoses ≥ as well as < 50%.

When evaluated in relation to the initial degree of coronary artery stenosis ≥ or < 50%, atherosclerosis regression was observed slightly more frequently when the baseline stenosis was ≥ 50% (**FATS, STARS, MARS, MAAS** studies), but regression was also observed for stenoses < 50% (**FATS, CCAIT, PLAC I** studies) and on diffuse lesions (**CIS** study) (see pp. 90-95 and 99-104) .

6 **Although it is significant, the amplitude of the anatomical result remains minimal (several hundredths of a millimeter), in contrast with the magnitude and rapidity of the clinical benefit reported in certain studies by the first year.**

In fact, a statistically significant reduction of the incidence of coronary or cardiovascular events was reported in the **FATS, STARS, ACAPS, PLAC I** and **II, REGRESS** studies.

In the meta-analysis by **Byington** (*Circulation* 1995;92:2019-2025), based on 4 trials (**PLAC I** and **II, REGRESS, KAPS** studies), including 1,891 subjects, with a follow-up of 2 to 3 years, pravastatin (40 mg daily) significantly decreased the incidence of fatal and nonfatal myocardial infarction by 62% ($p = 0.001$) (see pp. 86-91 and 99-104).

 Strict reduction of the serum LDL-C level (below 1.0 g/L) significantly reduced the atherosclerosis progression rate in saphenous vein coronary artery bypass grafts.

This was demonstrated by the **Post-CABGT** study (*N Engl J Med* 1997;336:153-162) conducted with lovastatin (see pp. 94 and 104).

What is probable

 All statins probably slow progression of atherosclerosis *via* a common mechanism (HMGCoA reductase inhibition).

This is illustrated by the concordant results obtained with pravastatin (**KAPS, PLAC I** and **II, REGRESS, CARS** studies), simvastatin (**MAAS, CIS** studies), lovastatin (**FATS, MARS, ACAPS, CCAIT, Post-CABGT** studies), and fluvastatin (**LCAS** study) (see pp. 86-91 and 99-104).

It is likely that statins exert their beneficial effect *via* a whole series of mechanisms other than improvement of arterial anatomy.

The slight differences observed in the course of stenoses cannot be responsible for a sufficient hemodynamic benefit to account for the improved prognosis. Other factors have therefore been suggested: reduction of the instability of a newly formed atheromatous plaque by reduction of its large lipid nucleus, reduction of platelet aggregation, resulting in a decreased risk of thrombosis, and improvement of endothelial dysfunction.

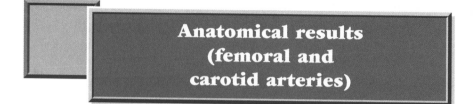

Anatomical results (femoral and carotid arteries)

Regression of carotid and femoral artery atherosclerosis was evaluated by arteriography (CLAS study) or ultrasound (ACAPS, PLAC II, KAPS studies), usually in secondary prevention studies or more exceptionally in asymptomatic patients (ACAPS, KAPS studies).

Studies based on lipid-lowering drugs

● In the **CLAS** study (*Circulation* 1991;83:438-447), conducted in 162 male normotensive, non-smoking patients (mean age: 54.5 years) with coronary heart disease, who had undergone coronary artery bypass graft at least 3 months prior to inclusion, presenting a serum cholesterol level between 1.85 and 3.50 g/L (4.7 to 9.0 mmol/L) (mean: 2.45 g/L, i.e. 6.3 mmol/L) and a mean serum LDL-C of 1.70 g/L (4.4 mmol/L), with a 2-year follow-up, colestipol (30 g daily) combined with niacin (3 to 12 g daily), vs placebo, significantly decreased the atherosclerosis progression rate of moderate lesions, especially on proximal femoral segments ($p < 0.02$) and was accompanied by more frequent regression of lesions, observed in 45% of cases vs 28% with placebo ($p = 0.02$).

● In the **ACAPS** study (*Circulation* 1994;90:1679-1687), conducted in 910 elderly subjects with a mean age of 62 years, free of any symptomatic cardiovascular disease, who, after 8 weeks of intensive diet, still had a serum LDL-C level between 1.60 and 1.89 g/L (4.1 to 4.9 mmol/L), if they presented no or only one other risk factor, or between 1.30 and 1.59 g/L (3.3 to 4.1 mmol/L) if they presented several risk factors, were randomized to 4 groups: lovastatin (20 to 40 mg daily) and warfarin placebo; warfarin (1 mg daily) and lovastatin placebo; lovastatin (20 to 40 mg daily) and warfarin (1 mg daily); double placebo. With a follow-up of 3 years, lovastatin vs placebo only tended to decrease the progression of maximal intimal-medial thickness, considered separately ($p = 0.12$, NS).

● In the **PQRST** study (*Am J Cardiol* 1994;74:875-883), conducted in 303 patients with a mean age of 55 years (17% with intermittent claudication, 24% with angina and the others were asymptomatic), presenting total serum cholesterol > 2.65 g/L (6.8 mmol/L), serum LDL-C > 1.75 g/L (4.5 mmol/L), and treated with cholestyramine (8 to 16 g daily), addition of probucol (0.5 g bid) vs placebo, with a follow-up of 3 years, was not accompanied by any significant change of the lumen of the femoral artery, did not modify irregularities of the arterial wall and therefore provided no additional benefit to cholestyramine alone.

● In the **PLAC II** study (*Am J Cardiol* 1995;75:455-459), conducted in 151 patients with coronary heart disease with a mean age of 62.7 years, presenting at least one extracranial carotid lesion defined by an intimal-medial thickness > 1.3 mm on B-mode ultrasound, triglycerides < 3.50 g/L (4.0 mmol/L) and serum LDL-C between the 60th and 90th percentiles, with a follow-up of 3 years, pravastatin (10 to 40 mg daily), vs placebo, decreased the common carotid artery atherosclerosis progression rate by 35% ($p = 0.03$), but had no significant effect in the carotid bulb or internal carotid artery.

● In the **KAPS** study (*Circulation* 1995;92:1758-1764), conducted in 447 men with a mean age of 57 years, mostly free of advanced atherosclerosis (less than 10% had had a myocardial infarction) and presenting serum LDL-C > 1.54 g/L (4.0 mmol/L) and serum cholesterol < 2.90 g/L (7.5 mmol/L) after 2.5 months of lipid-lowering diet, pravastatin (40 mg daily), vs placebo, with a 3-year follow-up, significantly decreased the annual atherosclerosis progression rate in the entire carotid artery by 45% ($p = 0.05$), but also in the carotid bulb and common carotid artery. The treatment effects were more marked in smokers, and in subjects with a greater baseline intimal-medial thickness. In contrast, no significant effect was observed on the progression of femoral artery atherosclerosis.

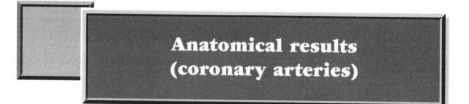

Anatomical results (coronary arteries)

Regression of coronary artery atherosclerosis was obtained by studies based on lipid-lowering drug treatment, multifactorial management, and surgical ileal bypass.

Studies based on lipid-lowering drugs

● In the **National Heart, Lung and Blood Institute** study (*Circulation* 1984;69:313-324), conducted in 116 patients with coronary heart disease, mean serum cholesterol of 3.2 g/L (8.2 mmol/L), and mean serum HDL-cholesterol of 0.39 g/L (1.0 mmol/L), with a 5-year follow-up, cholestyramine (6 g qid) combined with dietary intervention, vs placebo, tended to decrease the progression of coronary lesions observed in 25% of treated patients vs 35% with placebo. The beneficial effect of treatment was more clearly demonstrated after adjustment for differences in terms of risk factors: it significantly decreased the progression of lesions on stenoses ≥ 50%, observed in 12% of treated patients vs 33% with placebo ($p < 0.05$).

● In the **CLAS** study (*JAMA* 1987;257:3233-3240), conducted in 162 male normotensive, non-smoking patients (mean age: 54.5 years) with coronary heart disease, who had undergone coronary artery bypass graft at least 3 months before inclusion, with serum cholesterol between 1.85 and 3.50 g/L (4.7 to 9.0 mmol/L), colestipol (30 g daily) combined with niacin (3 to 12 g daily), vs placebo, with a 2-year follow-up, significantly decreased the mean number of coronary atheromatous lesions which progressed ($p < 0.03$) and the percentage of subjects who developed new lesions ($p < 0.04$) or who developed an abnormality of their coronary artery bypass graft. The 4-year follow-up of these patients (**CLAS II** study) (*JAMA* 1990;264:3013-3017) confirmed the results obtained at 2 years and proved that progression of lesions can be stopped and regression can be obtained by reducing serum lipids, even when serum cholesterol is initially < 2.40 g/L (6.2 mmol/L).

● In the **FATS** study (*N Engl J Med* 1990;323:1289-1298), conducted in 146 men over the age of 62 years presenting with coronary atherosclerosis and serum apolipoprotein B ≥ 1.25 g/L, colestipol (10 g tid) associated with niacin (4 g daily) or lovastatin (20 mg bid), vs placebo or colestipol when serum LDL-C was higher than the 90th percentile for age, with a follow-up of 30 months, significantly reduced the frequency of progression of coronary lesions (observed in 25% and 21% of treated patients vs 46% of placebo patients, respectively) and significantly increased the incidence of their regression ($p < 0.005$), observed in 32% and 39% of treated patients vs 11% of placebo patients, respectively. This significant beneficial effect was demonstrated on coronary stenoses ≥ 50% as well as < 50%.

● In the **STARS** study (*Lancet* 1992;339:563-569), conducted in 90 male patients with coronary heart disease, with a mean age of 51 years, a history of angina or myocardial infarction and serum cholesterol > 2.32 g/L (6.0 mmol/L) and a mean follow-up of 39 months, cholestyramine (8 g bid) combined with diet vs dietary intervention alone and vs usual care: significantly increased ($p < 0.05$) the mean absolute width of coronary segments by 0.103 mm compared to the group treated by diet alone (in which it increased by 0.003 mm) and compared to the group receiving usual care (in which it decreased by 0.201 mm); significantly decreased progression of coronary stenosis, observed in 12% of patients in the cholestyramine group vs 46% of patients in the usual care group and vs 15% of patients in the diet alone group; and significantly increased ($p < 0.02$) regression of lesions, observed in 33% of patients in the cholestyramine group vs 38% of patients in the diet alone group and vs 4% of patients in the usual care group. The most marked modifications of coronary stenosis diameter were observed in segments in which stenosis was > 50%.

● In the **MARS** study (*Ann Intern Med* 1993;119:969-976), conducted in 270 patients with coronary heart disease (mean age: 58 years), presenting stenosis of at least 2 coronary segments, at least one of which was ≥ 50%, and serum cholesterol between 1.90 and 2.95 g/L (4.9 to 7.6 mmol/L), with a mean follow-up of 2.2 years, lovastatin (40 mg bid) combined with diet, vs placebo, decreased the average percent diameter stenosis for lesions ≥ 50% by 4.1% (which progressed by 0.9% with placebo, $p = 0.05$) and significantly increased the number of patients in whom coronary lesions regressed ($p < 0.02$). Lovastatin also significantly decreased the mean global change score (indicating regression of coronary lesions) ($p = 0.002$), regardless of the baseline serum cholesterol level [≥ or < 2.40 g/L (6.2 mmol/L)], and decreased the number of patients presenting at least one new coronary occlusion by one-half to one-third. Lovastatin therefore slowed the progression and increased the frequency of regression in coronary artery lesions, especially in more severe stenoses (≥ 50%).

 In the **CCAIT** study (*Circulation* 1994;89:959-968), conducted in 331 patients (mean age: 52 years) with diffuse but not necessarily severe coronary atherosclerosis, fasting serum cholesterol between 2.20 and 3 g/L (5.6 to 7.7 mmol/L) and a 2-year follow-up, lovastatin (20-80 mg daily), vs placebo, significantly slowed the progression of coronary lesions (*p*= 0.03) and prevented the appearance of new lesions, which were observed in 16% of cases vs 32% with placebo (*p* = 0.001). The beneficial effect of treatment was most pronounced in the more numerous, milder lesions (< 50%) and in patients whose baseline total serum cholesterol or serum LDL-C levels were above the group median.

 In the **MAAS** study (*Lancet* 1994;344:633-638), conducted in 381 patients with coronary heart disease, with a mean age of 55 years, presenting stenosis ≥ 20% of at least 2 coronary segments and moderate hypercholesterolemia between 2.10 and 3.10 g/L (5.5 to 8 mmol/L), triglycerides < 3.5 g/L (4.0 mmol/L) and a 4-year follow-up, simvastatin (20 mg daily) administered in addition to diet, vs placebo, slowed progression of the lesions, promoted their regression (combined *p* = 0.02) and prevented the development of new lesions and new total occlusions (*p* = 0.02). Although significant, the quantitative regression of coronary atherosclerosis was only slight, with a gain of 0.06 mm for mean lumen diameter, 0.08 mm for minimum lumen diameter, and 0.17 mm for stenoses ≥ 50%.

 In the **HARP** study (*Lancet* 1994;344:1182-1186), conducted in 79 male and female patients with a mean age of 58 years, presenting with coronary heart disease and normal serum cholesterol (mean: 2.12 g/L, i.e. 5.5 mmol/L) and a follow-up of 2.5 years, active lipid-lowering drug treatment [successive administration of pravastatin (40 mg daily) then niacin (1.5 to 3 g daily), cholestyramine (8 to 16 g daily), and gemfibrozil (600 to 1200 mg daily)] in order to achieve serum cholesterol ≤ 1.58 g/L (4.1 mmol/L) and serum LDL-C/serum HDL-C ratio ≤ 2.0), vs placebo, significantly improved the blood lipid profile, but did not significantly modify coronary atherosclerosis.

● In the **PLAC I** study (*J Am Coll Cardiol* 1995;26:1133-1139), conducted in 408 patients with coronary heart disease, with a mean age of 57 years, presenting at least one coronary stenosis > 50% or a recent history of myocardial infarction or coronary angioplasty, serum LDL-C between 1.3 and 1.9 g/L (3.3 to 4.9 mmol/L) and triglycerides ≤ 3 g/L (3.9 mmol/L), with a 3-year follow-up, pravastatin (40 mg daily) combined with diet, vs placebo, decreased the incidence of new lesions (*p* ≤ 0.03) and significantly reduced, by 40%, progression of atherosclerosis, assessed on the minimum lumen diameter, which decreased annually by 0.03 mm vs 0.05 mm with placebo (*p* = 0.04), especially on stenoses < 50%.

● In the **REGRESS** study (*Circulation* 1995;91:2528-2540), conducted in 885 patients with coronary heart disease with a mean age of 56.5 years, presenting at least one coronary stenosis > 50% and serum cholesterol between 1.55 and 3.10 g/L (4.0 to 8.0 mmol/L), with a 2-year follow-up, pravastatin (40 mg daily) combined with dietary intervention, vs placebo, significantly slowed the progression of coronary atherosclerosis; in particular, the change in mean segment diameter decreased by 26% (0.06 mm with pravastatin vs 0.10 mm with placebo) (*p* = 0.019) and a similar effect was observed on the minimum obstruction diameter.

● In the **BECAIT** study (*Lancet* 1996;347:849-853), conducted in 92 male patients under the age of 45 years with coronary heart disease, following a first myocardial infarction (the number of patients included is less than that of other studies of atherosclerosis regression because this population is relatively small), serum cholesterol ≥ 2.0 g/L (5.2 mmol/L) and triglycerides ≥ 1.4 g/L (1.6 mmol/L), with a 5-year follow-up, bezafibrate (200 mg tid), vs placebo, significantly slowed progression of coronary atherosclerosis assessed on the mean minimum lumen diameter, which decreased by 0.06 mm vs 0.17 mm with placebo (*p* = 0.049). Parallel treatment effects, although not statistically significant, were observed for the secondary angiographic endpoints: mean segment diameter and percentage stenosis.

● In the **LCAS** study (*Am J Cardiol* 1997;80:278-286), conducted in 340 men and women aged 35 to 75 years, presenting at least one 30 to 75% coronary stenosis on a coronary artery not treated by coronary angioplasty and mean serum LDL-C between 1.15 and 1.90 g/L (2.9 to 4.9 mmol/L), fluvastatin (40 mg daily), possibly associated with cholestyramine when prerandomization serum LDL-C remained ≥

1.60 g/L (4.1 mmol/L), vs placebo or vs placebo and cholestyramine, was accompanied by a significantly lower reduction of minimum lumen diameter, which decreased by 0.028 ± 0.021 mm vs 0.100 ± 0.022 mm with placebo (p = 0.005). Fluvastatin also decreased the number of patients with lesion progression by 25% (29% of patients with fluvastatin vs 39% with placebo), increased the number of patients with regression of lesions by 75% (15% with fluvastatin vs 8% with placebo), and significantly decreased the number of patients who developed new lesions by 40.5% (p = 0.03) (22 with fluvastatin and 37 with placebo). A *post hoc* analysis performed in 84 patients with baseline serum LDL-C < 1.30 g/L (i.e. an average of 1.21 g/L) showed that fluvastatin induced an increase of the mean lumen diameter of 0.21 ± 0.040 mm vs a reduction of 0.062 ± 0.040 with placebo. The results of the **LCAS** study clearly indicate that coronary patients with slightly or moderately raised serum LDL-C benefit from treatment with fluvastatin [3/4 of this study population had a normal or only slightly raised serum LDL-C and 3/4 had serum cholesterol < 1.3 g/L (3.36 mmol/L), well below recommended values in patients with coronary heart disease].

● In the **Post-CABGT** study (*N Engl J Med* 1997;336:153-162), conducted in 1,351 male and female patients who had undergone coronary artery bypass surgery (1 to 11 years previously) and who had a serum LDL-C between 1.30 and 1.75 g/L (3.3 to 4.5 mmol/L), rigorous lowering of serum LDL-C below 1.0 g/L (2.6 mmol/L) (i.e. between 0.93 and 0.97 g/L) obtained with lovastatin (40 to 80 mg daily), possibly associated with cholestyramine (8 g daily), vs more moderate lowering of serum LDL-C [between 1.32 and 1.36 g/L (3.4 to 3.5 mmol/L), p < 0.001] obtained with lovastatin (2.5 mg daily), decreased atherosclerosis progression, observed in 27% of grafts during aggressive treatment vs 39% during moderate treatment (p < 0.001), with a follow-up of 4.3 years. Note that low-dose warfarin (about 1 mg daily adjusted so that the INR remained < 2), did not reduce atherosclerosis progression.

● In the **CIS** study (*Eur Heart J* 1997;18:226-234), conducted in 254 males with coronary heart disease, serum cholesterol between 2 and 3.5 g/L (5.1 to 9.0 mmol/L), and serum triglycerides < 3.30 g/L (3.7 mmol/L), with a follow-up of 2.3 years, simvastatin (40 mg daily), vs placebo, slowed atherosclerosis progression: the minimum lumen diameter decreased by 0.02 mm with simvastatin vs 0.10 mm with placebo (p = 0.002). This was the first study to demonstrate a significant correlation between lowering of serum LDL-C and mean reduction of minimum lumen diameter per patient ($p = 0.003$).

● In the **CARS** study (*Am J Cardiol* 1997;79:893-896), conducted in 90 patients with coronary heart disease, presenting at least one stenosis $\geq$ 50% of one of the main coronary arteries and with serum cholesterol between 1.60 and 2.20 g/L (4.1 to 5.6 mmol/L) and a mean serum LDL-C of 1.23 ± 0.24 g/L (3.17 ± 0.61 mmol/L) with a 2-year follow-up, pravastatin (10 mg daily), vs the control group, significantly decreased total serum cholesterol, serum LDL-C, and apoprotein B, and reduced the percentage of patients (21% vs 49%, $p < 0.05$) with progression of coronary stenoses, without modifying the percentage of patients (3% vs 2%, NS) with atherosclerosis regression.

Multifactorial management

● In the **Lifestyle Heart Trial** (*Lancet* 1990;336:129-133), conducted in 48 patients (95% males) with coronary heart disease, with a mean age of 56 years, mean serum cholesterol of 2.24 g/L (5.8 mmol/L), mean serum LDL-C of 1.51 g/L (3.9 mmol/L) and one-, two- or three-vessel disease, with a one-year follow-up, radical modification of lifestyle [combining: dietary intervention (low-fat vegetarian diet), moderate but regular physical exercise, stopping smoking, and stress management training], vs a control group which did not modify its lifestyle, significantly decreased, even for coronary stenoses > 50%, the average percentage diameter stenosis which regressed from 40% to 37.8% ($p = 0.001$), but significantly progressed from 42.7% to 46.1% ($p = 0.001$) in 53% of patients in the control group.

● In the **German** study by **Schuler** (*Circulation* 1992;86:1-11), conducted in 113 patients with coronary heart disease and stable angina, with a one-year follow-up, regular physical exercise simply combined with low-fat diet, vs a control group receiving usual care and diet, more markedly slowed progression of lesions, observed in 23% of cases vs 48% ($p < 0.05$), and promoted their regression, observed in 32% of cases vs 17%, and their stabilization, observed in 45% of cases vs 35%.

● In the **SCRIP** study (*Circulation* 1994;89:975-990), conducted in 300 patients with coronary heart disease (mean age: 56 years) with mean serum cholesterol of 2.27 g/L (5.9 mmol/L) and a mean follow-up of 4 years, intensive multiple risk factor reduction [combining: appropriate diet, smoking cessation, regular physical exercise, weight loss or even, when necessary, lipid-lowering drug treatment to achieve serum LDL-C < 1.10 g/L (2.8 mmol/L) and triglycerides < 1.0 g/L (1.1 mmol/L)], vs the control group receiving usual care, significantly reduced progression of lesions, as reflected by a 47% reduction of the annual stenosis rate of diseased coronary artery segments (the minimum lumen diameter decreased by 0.024 mm vs 0.045 mm in the control group, $p < 0.02$) and by a 4.7% reduction of the incidence of new lesions (observed in 6.1% of coronary segments studied vs 7.6% in the control group, $p = 0.05$).

Surgical ileal bypass

- In the **POSCH** study (*N Engl J Med* 1990;323:946-955), conducted in 838 survivors of a first myocardial infarction, with serum cholesterol ≥ 2.20 g/L (5.7 mmol/L) or serum LDL-C ≥ 1.40 g/L (3.6 mmol/L), with a mean follow-up of 9.7 years, ileal bypass vs the control group assigned to low cholesterol diet only, significantly slowed ($p < 0.001$) coronary atherosclerosis progression, evaluated by a score based on comparison of angiographic data.

Calcium channel blockers and atherosclerosis regression

Calcium channel blockers improve the course of atherosclerosis. Although significant, their effect nevertheless remains much more limited than that of lipid-lowering drugs, especially statins. They reduce the incidence of new coronary lesions or slow the progression of minor lesions (stenoses < 20%), but have no effect on advanced lesions.

● In the **INTACT** study (*Lancet* 1990;335:1109-1113), conducted in 348 patients with a mean age of 53 years, presenting mild coronary atherosclerosis, with a 3-year follow-up, nifedipine (20 mg qid), vs placebo, did not modify the severity of existing coronary lesions, but significantly decreased the number of new stenoses by 28% (p = 0.034) and delayed atherosclerosis progression in patients with mild coronary stenoses (< 20%). The 6-year follow-up (*J Cardiovasc Pharmacol* 1996;28 suppl. 3:10-21) confirmed these results.

● In the **MHIS** study (*Circulation* 1990;82:1940-1953), conducted in 383 patients with a mean age of 51.5 years, presenting 5 to 75% stenoses in at least 4 coronary artery segments, with a 2-year follow-up, nicardipine (30 mg tid), vs placebo, significantly slowed progression of minimal lesions ($\leq$ 20%), which only progressed in 15% of treated patients vs 27% with placebo (p = 0.046), but did not modify the progression or regression of more advanced coronary lesions.

● In the **MIDAS** study (*JAMA* 1996;276:785-791), conducted in 883 hypertensive patients (DBP: 90 to 115 mm Hg), with a mean age of 58.2 ± 8.3 years, isradipine (2.5 to 5 mg bid) was compared to hydrochlorothiazide (12.5 to 25 mg bid). With a follow-up of 3 years, the two drugs did not modify the rate of atherosclerosis progression assessed by B-mode ultrasound imaging of the intimal-medial thickness in carotid arteries.

● ● ●

• • •

● In the **PREVENT** study (*Am J Cardiol* 1998;80:1087-1090 and 71st session of the American Heart Association, 1998), conducted in 825 patients with a mean age of 57 years, with coronary heart disease documented by coronary angiography, amlodipine (5 mg daily for 4 weeks, then 10 mg daily for the rest of the study) vs placebo, with a mean follow-up of 3 years, had no effect on coronary atherosclerosis, as it did not modify either the mean lumen diameter of coronary stenoses < 30% (main endpoint) or that of other stenoses between 30 and 50% or > 50%. In contrast, although no precise explanation can be provided, it stabilized intimal-medial thickness assessed by B-mode ultrasound imaging of the carotid arteries [this thickness was not modified with amlodipine, but increased by an average of 0.04 mm with placebo (p = 0.009)]. Lastly, amlodipine decreased the relative risk of cardiovascular events by 31% (p = 0.01) and the need for coronary reperfusion by coronary angioplasty or bypass graft by 46% (p = 0.001). The role of amlodipine (vs enalapril) on regression of atherosclerosis and cardiovascular events will be evaluated in the CAMELOT study to be conducted in 3,000 patients followed for 2 years.

● In the ongoing **ENCORE** study (*J Cardiovasc Pharmacol* 1997;30 suppl. III:S48-S52), the effect of nifedipine (30 to 60 mg daily), cerivastatin (400 µg daily) or a combination of the two, vs placebo, on endothelial function and coronary atherosclerosis is being evaluated with a follow-up of 2 years in coronary patients treated by coronary angioplasty.

Clinical consequences

Coronary artery atherosclerosis regression has sometimes been accompanied by a favorable effect on cardiovascular events. However, there is not necessarily any correlation between the observed clinical benefit and atherosclerosis regression and studies which have demonstrated delayed progression of coronary lesions were not designed to evaluate the clinical consequences of this effect.

Studies based on lipid-lowering drugs

 In the meta-analysis by **Byington** (*Circulation* 1995;92:2019-2025), based on 4 trials (**PLAC I, PLAC II, REGRESS,** and **KAPS** trials), including a total of 1,891 subjects presenting signs of atherosclerosis and slightly to moderately raised plasma lipids, with a follow-up of 2 to 3 years, pravastatin (40 mg daily) prescribed as monotherapy, vs placebo, significantly decreased the incidence of fatal and nonfatal myocardial infarction by 62% ($p = 0.001$) (observed in 2.4% of cases vs 6.4% with placebo), tended to reduce all cause mortality by 46% ($p = 0.17$) (1.8% of cases vs 3.3% with placebo) and the incidence of fatal or nonfatal cerebrovascular accidents by 62% ($p = 0.054$) (0.7% of cases vs 1.8% with placebo). These favorable results were accompanied by a mean 28% reduction of serum LDL-C; they were observed in male and female patients, regardless of age (> or < 65 years) and even for only slightly elevated serum LDL-C levels, about 1.30 g/L (3.3 mmol/L).

The **National Heart, Lung and Blood Institute** study (*Circulation* 1984;69:313-324), conducted in 116 patients with coronary heart disease, mean serum cholesterol of 3.2 g/L (8.2 mmol/L), and mean serum HDL-cholesterol of 0.39 g/L (1.0 mmol/L), designed to evaluate the effect of cholestyramine (6 g qid) vs placebo on progression of coronary lesions analysed by coronary angiography, did not assess the clinical consequences.

● In the **FATS** study (*N Engl J Med* 1990;323:1289-1298), 146 men over
the age of 62 years presenting with coronary atherosclerosis and
serum apolipoprotein B ≥ 1.25 g/L, received, in addition to diet,
colestipol (10 g tid) associated with niacin (4 g daily) or lovastatin (20
mg bid); with a follow-up of 30 months, the most intensive treatment
(colestipol and lovastatin), vs placebo, significantly reduced the frequency of progression of coronary lesions, significantly increased the
number of cases of regression, and decreased by 73% the incidence of
cardiovascular events (death, myocardial infarction, or myocardial
revascularization), observed in 2 out of 48 patients receiving niacin and
colestipol and 3 out of 46 patients receiving lovastatin and colestipol
vs 10 out of 52 patients with placebo, respectively.

● In the **CLAS II** study (*JAMA* 1990;264:3013-3017) (an extension of the
CLAS study, assessing the results at 4 years), conducted in 162 male
normotensive, non-smoking patients (mean age: 54.5 years) with coronary heart disease, who had undergone coronary artery bypass graft at
least 3 months before inclusion, with serum cholesterol between 1.85
and 3.50 g/L (4.7 to 9.0 mmol/L), colestipol (30 g daily) combined
with niacin (3 to 12 g daily), vs placebo, with a 4-year follow-up, significantly decreased the mean number of coronary atheromatous
lesions which progressed (*p* < 0.03) and the percentage of subjects
who developed new lesions (*p* < 0.04) or who developed an abnormality of their coronary artery bypass graft, but did not decrease the
incidence of major medical events. The 7-year follow-up (*Circulation*
1996;93:34-41) showed that patients with the most marked progression of coronary lesions had a higher risk of a myocardial revascularization procedure, nonfatal acute myocardial infarction, and coronary
death (*p* < 0.05).

● In the **STARS** study (*Lancet* 1992;339:563-569), conducted on 90 male
patients with coronary heart disease, with a mean age of 51 years, a
history of angina or myocardial infarction and serum cholesterol >
2.32 g/L (6.0 mmol/L), and a mean follow-up of 39 months, cholestyramine (8 g bid) combined with low-fat diet and possibly low-calorie
diet (dietary intervention) vs dietary intervention alone and vs usual
care, significantly decreased the incidence of cardiovascular events
(death, myocardial infarction, myocardial revascularization by coronary artery bypass graft or coronary angioplasty, cerebrovascular accident), observed in 1% of cases in the treated group vs 10% in the usual
care group (*p* < 0.01).

● In the **MARS** study (*Ann Intern Med* 1993;119:969-976), conducted in 270 patients with coronary heart disease (mean age: 58 years), presenting stenosis of at least 2 coronary segments, at least one of which was ≥ 50% and serum cholesterol between 1.90 and 2.95 g/L (4.9 to 7.6 mmol/L), with a mean follow-up of 2.2 years, lovastatin (40 mg bid), vs placebo, significantly decreased the mean global change score of progression of coronary lesions and decreased the number of patients presenting at least one new coronary occlusion by one-half to one-third, but did not significantly modify the incidence of coronary events (22 vs 31 with placebo), deaths (2 vs 1), and cancers (6 vs 5).

● In the **HARP** study (*Lancet* 1994;344:1182-1186), conducted in 79 male and female patients with a mean age of 58 years, presenting with coronary heart disease and normal serum cholesterol (mean: 2.12 g/L, i.e. 5.5 mmol/L), active lipid-lowering drug treatment [successive administration of pravastatin (40 mg daily), then niacin (1.5 to 3 g daily), cholestyramine (8 to 16 g daily), and gemfibrozil (600 to 1200 mg daily) in order to obtain serum cholesterol ≤ 1.58 g/L (4.1 mmol/L) and an serum LDL-C/serum HDL-C ratio ≤ 2.0], did not modify the number of coronary events with a 2.5-year follow-up: 8 events observed in 6 patients in the treated group vs 12 events in 10 patients in the control group.

● In the **CCAIT** study (*Circulation* 1994;89:959-968), conducted in 331 patients (mean age: 52 years) with diffuse but not necessarily severe coronary atherosclerosis, fasting serum cholesterol between 2.20 and 3 g/L (5.6 to 7.7 mmol/L) and a 2-year follow-up, lovastatin (20-80 mg daily), vs placebo, significantly slowed the progression of coronary lesions and prevented the appearance of new lesions, especially in patients with more numerous and milder coronary stenoses (< 50%), but did not significantly reduce the incidence of coronary events.

● In the **MAAS** study (*Lancet* 1994;344:633-638), conducted in 381 patients with coronary heart disease, with a mean age of 55 years, presenting stenosis ≥ 20% of at least 2 coronary segments and moderate hypercholesterolemia between 2.10 and 3.10 g/L (5.5 to 8 mmol/L), triglycerides < 3.5 g/L (4.0 mmol/L) and a 4-year follow-up, simvastatin (20 mg daily), vs placebo, significantly slowed progression of the lesions, promoted their regression, and prevented the development of new lesions and new total occlusions, did not modify the number of deaths or myocardial infarctions, but tended to reduce the incidence of coronary angioplasty or coronary artery bypass graft revascularization (NS).

● In the **ACAPS** study (*Circulation* 1994;90:1679-1687), conducted in 910 elderly subjects with a mean age of 62 years, free of any symptomatic cardiovascular disease, who, after 8 weeks of intensive diet, still had a serum LDL-C level between 1.60 and 1.89 g/L (4.1 to 4.9 mmol/L), if they presented no or only one other risk factor, or between 1.30 and 1.59 g/L (3.3 to 4.1 mmol/L) if they presented several risk factors, with a 3-year follow-up, lovastatin (20 to 40 mg daily), vs placebo, only tended to decrease progression of maximal intimal-medial thickness, significantly reduced the number of major cardiovascular events (coronary death, nonfatal myocardial infarction or cerebrovascular accident), observed in 5 cases vs 14 with placebo (p = 0.04) and the number of deaths (1 case vs 8 with placebo; p= 0.02).

● In the **PLAC II** study (*Am J Cardiol* 1995;75:455-459), conducted in 151 patients with coronary heart disease with a mean age of 62.7 years, presenting at least one extracranial carotid lesion defined by an intimal-medial thickness > 1.3 mm on B-mode ultrasound, triglycerides < 3.50 g/L (4.0 mmol/L) and serum LDL-C between the 60th and 90th percentiles, with a follow-up of 3 years, pravastatin (10 to 40 mg daily), vs placebo, significantly decreased the common carotid artery atherosclerosis progression rate by 35%, and significantly decreased, by 61% (p = 0.04), the combined incidence of all coronary events and death from any cause, observed in 7% of cases vs 17% with placebo.

● In the **PLAC I** study (*J Am Coll Cardiol* 1995;26:1133-1139), conducted in 408 patients with coronary heart disease, with a mean age of 57 years, presenting at least one coronary stenosis > 50% or a recent history of myocardial infarction, or coronary angioplasty, serum LDL-C between 1.3 and 1.9 g/L (3.3 to 4.9 mmol/L), and triglycerides ≤ 3 g/L (3.9 mmol/L), with a 3-year follow-up, pravastatin (40 mg daily), vs placebo, significantly decreased, by 40%, atherosclerosis progression, especially for lesions < 50%, and the incidence of new lesions, and also significantly reduced the incidence of fatal or nonfatal myocardial infarction by 60% (p ≤ 0.05) and this beneficial effect was demonstrated by the end of the first year.

● In the **KAPS** study (*Circulation* 1995;92:1758-1764), conducted in 447 men with a mean age of 57 years, mostly free of advanced atherosclerosis (less than 10% had had a myocardial infarction) and presenting serum LDL-C > 1.54 g/L (4.0 mmol/L) and serum cholesterol < 2.90 g/L (7.5 mmol/L) after 2.5 months of lipid-lowering diet, pravastatin (40 mg daily), vs placebo, with a 3-year follow-up, significantly decreased the annual atherosclerosis progression rate in the entire carotid artery by 45% (p = 0.05), but also in the carotid bulb and common carotid artery, but only tended to reduce the number of cardiovascular events (nonfatal and fatal myocardial infarction, myocardial revascularization by bypass graft or coronary angioplasty, cerebrovascular accident, other cardiac death) (11 cases vs 17, NS), and especially fatal and nonfatal myocardial infarction (3 cases vs 8, NS).

● In the **REGRESS** study (*Circulation* 1995;91:2528-2540), conducted in 885 patients with coronary heart disease with a mean age of 56.5 years, presenting at least one coronary stenosis > 50% and serum cholesterol between 1.55 and 3.10 g/L (4.0 to 8.0 mmol/L), with a 2-year follow-up, pravastatin (40 mg daily), vs placebo, significantly slowed coronary atherosclerosis progression, assessed by the variations of mean and minimum lumen diameter, significantly reduced the incidence of new cardiovascular events (fatal or nonfatal myocardial infarction, coronary death, myocardial revascularization by coronary angioplasty or coronary artery bypass graft, permanent or transient cerebrovascular accident) by 38% (p = 0.02), increased the number of patients who remained free of such events (89% vs 81% with placebo, p = 0.002) and significantly decreased the number of Holter-documented ischemic episodes in patients with stable angina (p = 0.026).

● The **BECAIT** study (*Lancet* 1996;347:849-853), conducted in 92 male patients under the age of 45 years following a first myocardial infarction (the number of patients included is less than that of other studies of atherosclerosis regression because this population is relatively small), to evaluate the effect of bezafibrate (200 mg tid), vs placebo, on progression of atherosclerotic lesions, did not assess the clinical consequences.

● The **LCAS** study (*Am J Cardiol* 1997;80:278-286), conducted in 340 men and women aged 35 to 75 years, to evaluate the effect of fluvastatin on coronary atherosclerosis, was not designed to assess its clinical consequences; nevertheless, fluvastatin tended to decrease the number of clinical events (i.e. myocardial infarction, unstable angina requiring hospitalization, and myocardial revascularization by coronary artery bypass graft or coronary angioplasty) or deaths (from any cause, which were reduced by 24.1%, NS).

● In the **Post-CABGT** study (*N Engl J Med* 1997;336:153-162), conducted in 1,351 male and female patients who had undergone coronary artery bypass surgery (1 to 11 years previously), and who had a serum LDL-C between 1.31 and 1.75 g/L (3.4 to 4.5 mmol/L), strict lowering of serum LDL-C below 1.0 g/L (2.6 mmol/L) with lovastatin (40 to 80 mg daily), possibly associated with cholestyramine (8 g daily), significantly decreased, by 29%, the myocardial revascularization rate during follow-up: 6.5% vs 9.2% with moderate treatment achieving a serum LDL-C level between 1.32 and 1.36 g/L (3.4 to 3.5 mmol/L) (*p* = 0.03).

● The **CIS** study (*Eur Heart J* 1997;18:226-234), conducted with simvastatin in 254 males with coronary heart disease, and the **CARS** study (*Am J Cardiol* 1997;79:893-896), conducted with pravastatin in 90 patients with coronary heart disease, were not designed to evaluate the clinical consequences of atherosclerosis regression.

Multifactorial management

● In the **Lifestyle Heart Trial** (*Lancet* 1990;336:129-133), conducted in 48 patients (95% males) with coronary heart disease, with a mean age of 56 years, mean serum cholesterol of 2.24 g/L (5.8 mmol/L), mean serum LDL-C of 1.51 g/L (3.9 mmol/L) and one-, two- or three-vessel disease, with a one-year follow-up, radical modification of lifestyle [combining: dietary intervention (low-fat vegetarian diet), moderate but regular physical exercise, stopping smoking, and stress management training], vs a control group left free not to modify its lifestyle, significantly decreased the average percentage diameter stenosis, even for coronary stenoses > 50%, and also reduced the frequency of angina attacks by 91%, their duration by 42% and their severity by 28%; in contrast, in the control group, these parameters increased by 165%, 95%, and 39%, respectively.

● The **German** study by **Schuler** (*Circulation* 1992;86:1-11), conducted in 113 patients with coronary heart disease, with a one-year follow-up, showed that, vs a control group, regular physical exercise combined with low-fat diet slowed progression of coronary lesions, but it was not designed to assess the clinical consequences of this delayed progression.

● In the **SCRIP** study (*Circulation* 1994;89:975-990), conducted in 300 patients with coronary heart disease (mean age: 56 years) with mean serum cholesterol of 2.27 g/L (5.8 mmol/L) and a mean follow-up of 4 years, intensive multiple risk factor reduction (combining: appropriate diet, smoking cessation, regular physical exercise, weight loss or even, when necessary, lipid-lowering drug treatment), vs the control group receiving usual care, significantly reduced progression of lesions, as reflected by a 47% reduction of the annual stenosis rate of diseased coronary artery segments and by a 4.7% reduction of the incidence of new lesions, also decreased the number of hospitalizations secondary to a clinical event by 39% [25 vs 44 in the control group ($p = 0.05$)], but did not modify the mortality (3 deaths in each group).

Surgical ileal bypass

● In the **POSCH** study (*N Engl J Med* 1990;323:946-955), conducted in 838 survivors of a first myocardial infarction, with serum cholesterol ≥ 2.20 g/L (5.7 mmol/L) or serum LDL-C ≥ 1.40 g/L (3.6 mmol/L), with a mean follow-up of 9.7 years, ileal bypass, vs the control group assigned to low cholesterol diet only, significantly slowed coronary atherosclerosis progression, significantly decreased, by 35%, the combined incidence of nonfatal myocardial infarction and coronary deaths (observed in 82 cases vs 125 in the control group, $p < 0.001$), the frequency of coronary artery bypass grafts (52 cases vs 137 in the control group, $p < 0.0001$) and coronary angioplasty (15 cases vs 33 in the control group; $p = 0.005$), and tended to decrease all cause mortality by 21.7% ($p = 0.16$) and coronary mortality by 28% ($p = 0.11$).

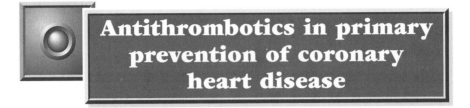

Antithrombotics in primary prevention of coronary heart disease

Although the value of prescription of platelet aggregation inhibitors, especially aspirin, in secondary prevention of ischemic heart disease has now been demonstrated (BMJ 1994;308:81-106), its administration for primary prevention remains controversial because a possible reduction of the myocardial infarction rate can be partially counterbalanced by an increased risk of cerebrovascular accidents.

Aspirin

About ten years ago, two primary prevention studies already reported contradictory results.

● In the **English Physicians' Health** study (*BMJ* 1988;296:313-316), conducted on 5,139 male physicians in apparent good health, 50% of whom were older than 60 on inclusion, aspirin (500 mg daily) vs placebo, with a follow-up of 6 years, did not reduce the incidence of fatal and nonfatal myocardial infarction, had no effect on the incidence of fatal and nonfatal strokes, and significantly decreased the frequency of transient ischemic attacks by about 50% ($2p < 0.05$); it also tended to decrease all cause mortality by 10% (NS).

● In the **American Physicians' Health** study (*N Engl J Med* 1989;321: 129-135), conducted in 22,071 male physicians aged 40 to 84 years, with an average follow-up of 60.2 months, aspirin (325 mg every 2 days) significantly decreased the risk of fatal or nonfatal myocardial infarction by 44% and this reduction was more marked in patients older than 50; it tended to slightly increase the risk of stroke (especially hemorrhagic) and did not modify overall cardiovascular mortality.

The meta-analysis of these two studies by **Hennekens** (*N Engl J Med* 1988;318:923-924), which must be interpreted cautiously because of several major differences between the two protocols, nevertheless showed that prophylactic administration of aspirin in primary prevention reduced the rate of nonfatal myocardial infarction by 33 ± 9%

(p < 0.0001), did not modify the risk of stroke, or could even increase the number of disabling forms and did not reduce the overall cardiovascular mortality.

Two more recent trials have made an interesting contribution to this debate.

● In the **HOT** study (see p. 51), conducted in 18,790 hypertensive patients, 3,080 (16.4%) of whom suffered from angina or presented a history of myocardial infarction, intensive antihypertensive therapy, essentially consisting of felodipine (5 to 10 mg daily), possibly combined with a beta-blocker and/or ACE-inhibitor (low dose or high dose) or even hydrochlorothiazide, with a mean follow-up of 3.8 years, significantly decreased the incidence of major cardiovascular events (myocardial infarction and fatal or nonfatal cerebrovascular accidents, other cardiovascular deaths). In particular, in these patients, aspirin (75 mg daily) vs placebo reduced major cardiovascular events by 15% (p = 0.03) and the total number of myocardial infarctions by 36% (p = 0.002), without modifying the incidence of stroke. It significantly increased nonfatal serious hemorrhages, without increasing the number of fatal hemorrhages.

This study therefore proves, for the first time, that prescription of aspirin to hypertensive patients with well controlled blood pressure significantly reduces major cardiovascular events and especially the number of fatal and nonfatal myocardial infarctions, without increasing the number of fatal hemorrhages or cerebrovascular accidents, but at the cost of a higher incidence of nonfatal hemorrhage.

● In the **Thrombosis Prevention Trial** (*Lancet* 1998;351:233-241), conducted in 5,085 male patients between the ages of 45 and 69 years (mean: 57.5 years) and considered to be at high-risk of developing coronary heart disease because they were situated in the top 20% of the distribution of the risk score, aspirin SR (75 mg daily), alone or coprescribed with warfarin (0.5 to 12.5 mg daily; mean: 4.1 mg daily ensuring a mean INR of 1.47) vs warfarin and placebo decreased ischemic events by 20% (95% CI: 1% to 35%, p = 0.04) almost essentially by a 32% reduction (95% CI: 12% to 48%, p = 0.004) of nonfatal events (this result on nonfatal coronary events was similar to that reported in the **American Physicians'** study). Aspirin also had no effect on the prevention of fatal events and cerebrovascular accidents or on all cause mortality. Aspirin did not decrease fatal coronary events, but reduced the incidence of fatal myocardial infarctions by 65% in the **American Physicians'** study.

The **Thrombosis Prevention Trial** and the **American Physicians'** study therefore agree on two points: aspirin reduces nonfatal ischemic events without increasing the risk of cerebral hemorrhage. It should be stressed, however, that these results, obtained on a selected and very thoroughly followed male population, cannot yet be generalized to the overall population.

In practice, the treatment of 1,000 high-risk subjects by aspirin for one year would prevent about 3 coronary ischemic accidents.

Anticoagulants

Low-dose anticoagulants could have a beneficial role in primary prevention, as there is increasing evidence to show that simultaneous modification of platelet activity and fibrin formation can be more effective than modification of only one of these two processes.

In the **Thrombosis Prevention Trial**, conducted in 5,085 subjects between the ages of 45 and 69 years, at high risk of developing coronary heart disease, administration of warfarin (0.5 to 12.5 mg daily; mean: 4.1 mg daily to obtain an INR of 1.47), either alone or combined with aspirin SR (75 mg daily), vs aspirin and placebo, decreased ischemic events (defined by the sum of coronary deaths and fatal and nonfatal myocardial infarctions) by 21% (95% CI: 4% to 35%, $p = 0.02$) by a 39% reduction (95% CI: 15% to 57%, $p = 0.003$) of fatal accidents, thereby decreasing all cause mortality by 17% (95% CI: 1% to 30%, $p = 0.04$) (this result was obtained despite a significantly higher incidence of ruptured aortic aneurysm or dissection after or during anticoagulant therapy); it had no effect on the prevention of cerebrovascular accidents.

In practice, the treatment of 1,000 high-risk subjects by warfarin for one year would prevent 3 coronary ischemic accidents.

Aspirin and anticoagulants

In the **Thrombosis Prevention Trial** (see p. 108), the warfarin-aspirin combination vs placebo significantly reduced coronary ischemic events by 34% (95% CI: 11% to 51%, $p = 0.006$) at the cost of an increased number of hemorrhagic and fatal cerebrovascular accidents (however, the combination of these two medications prevented 12 times more coronary events than the cerebrovascular accidents it induced). In practice, the treatment of 1,000 high-risk subjects by the warfarin-aspirin combination for one year would prevent about 5 coronary ischemic events.

These results must not mask the fact that primary prevention of coronary heart disease is essentially based on a series of measures designed to modify lifestyle (smoking cessation, regular physical exercise, balanced diet with a reduction of saturated fats, correction of excess weight, etc.). However, it is important to note that these preventive measures can be reinforced in high-risk subjects by using statins, but probably also, in some very selected cases, by using antithrombotic medications (essentially aspirin) prescribed at low doses.

Stable angina and silent myocardial ischemia

Stable angina is the clinical expression of myocardial ischemia, related to the presence of a fixed atherosclerotic coronary stenosis, which prevents adaptation of coronary perfusion to an increased oxygen requirement.

Ischemia can be aggravated by an inappropriate vasomotor response secondary to endothelial dysfunction induced by atherosclerosis: decreased production or increased inactivation of EDRF (endothelium-derived relaxing factor, which appears to be nitric oxide NO) induces paradoxical coronary vasoconstriction during a normally vasodilator stimulus, such as physical effort, mental exercise, or cold. This explains why stable angina is usually observed on effort, but can also occur at rest in 30% of patients.

Although the prognosis of stable angina is relatively good (the annual mortality varies from 1 to 2% according to various published series), the development of a serious event (unstable angina, myocardial infarction, more rarely sudden death) remains difficult to predict. It is now known that these acute accidents are not related to the severity of a pre-existing stenosis, but to usually sudden rupture of a generally slightly raised atheromatous plaque. Certain parameters (multivessel disease, left ventricular dysfunction, low-level positive stress test) have an ominous prognosis because they generally reflect more severe and diffuse coronary disease, and consequently a higher incidence of minor (non-significant) plaques, which are prone to rupture. For the same reasons, silent ischemia could very well represent a prognostic marker only in these high-risk patients.

Drug treatment

The pathophysiology of stable angina provides a clearer understanding of the impact of treatment on prognosis (*JAMA* 1997;277:343-344).

Antianginal drugs eliminate the symptoms (mainly by reducing myocardial oxygen requirements), but their effect on prevention of acute accidents may not be significant. The same applies to myocardial revascularization, which does not prevent the development of myocardial infarction and which reduces mortality only in a limited subgroup of high-risk patients.

Prophylactic treatment by platelet aggregation inhibitors decreases morbidity and mortality because it prevents the thrombotic process accompanying plaque rupture.

One of the essential treatments in stable angina consists of correction of cardiovascular risk factors. Endothelial dysfunction, the first step of the atherosclerotic process, is accelerated by hyperlipidemia, hypertension, smoking, diabetes, and estrogen deficiency. Some serum cholesterol-lowering drugs could also prevent acute coronary accidents by "stabilizing" constituted atheromatous plaques and by improving endothelial function. Similarly, estrogens in postmenopausal women lower the serum cholesterol level, improve endothelial function and could decrease the risk of thrombosis.

Antianginal drugs

The three main classes of antianginal drugs (nitrates, beta-blockers, and calcium channel blockers), have different and synergistic mechanisms of action (see p. 128), justifying a number of drug combinations. The treatment options have been recently completed by potassium channel activators (represented by a single molecule, nicorandil) and trimetazidine.

Current state of knowledge

 Only sublingual nitroglycerin (or its derivatives) allows rapid relief of angina.

2 In prophylactic monotherapy, the various classes of antianginal drugs have been shown to be essentially equivalent for the control of angina and silent ischemia.

Many placebo-controlled studies have shown that nitrates, beta-blockers, calcium channel blockers, potassium channel activators, and trimetazidine reduce the frequency of angina attacks, improve effort capacity (increased total duration and delayed appearance of the ischemic threshold), and decrease ambulatory ischemia recorded by Holter monitoring.

Comparative trials have failed to demonstrate any superiority of one class over another, when the drugs were used at appropriate dosages.

3 **Beta-blockers should be prescribed as first-line treatment, in the absence of contraindications (see p. 131).**

The efficacy of beta-blockers and their recognized cardioprotective effect in unstable angina, acute myocardial infarction, and post-myocardial infarction justify this recent recommendation of the European Society of Cardiology (*Eur Heart J* 1997;18:394-413) and ACC/AHA (*Circulation* 1999; 99:2829-2848).

In patients with stable angina, the **ASIST** study (*Circulation* 1994; 90:762-768), although lacking sufficient statistical power, suggested a beneficial effect of atenolol on the prevention of serious cardiac events. Beta-blockers could prevent plaque rupture and thrombosis responsible for acute coronary accidents, by decreasing the constraint applied to the atheromatous plaque and adrenergic platelet aggregation.

However, as no mortality study has been performed in stable angina, improvement of the prognosis with beta-blocker treatment has yet to be demonstrated in this indication.

4 **Nitrates and calcium channel blockers can be proposed as second-line treatment, along with trimetazidine and potassium channel activators, when beta-blockers are contraindicated or poorly tolerated.**

● The efficacy of nitroglycerin has been known for more than a century (**Murrell**; *Lancet* 1879;1:225-227). Nitrates are generally well tolerated, but their long-term use is limited by the development of tolerance, requiring compliance with a daily treatment-free interval (see p. 128).
Congestive heart failure and left ventricular dysfunction represent the preferential indications of nitrates.

● Among the sustained-release (SR) calcium channel blockers, verapamil SR, and nifedipine SR have been shown to be as effective and as safe as beta-blockers.

In the **APSIS** study (*Eur Heart J* 1996;17:76-81), which included 809 patients, verapamil SR (240 mg bid), compared to metoprolol (200 mg daily), did not modify the combined incidence of death, myocardial infarction, unstable or disabling angina, or peripheral vascular accident (29.3% vs 30.8%), with a median follow-up of 3.4 years.

Similarly, the **TIBET** study (*Eur Heart J* 1996;17:104-112), conducted in 682 patients, did not demonstrate any difference between nifedipine SR (20 to 40 mg bid), atenolol (50 mg bid), or a combination of the two drugs, for the two-year incidence of a serious event, i.e. death, myocardial infarction or unstable angina.

Because of the probable harmful effects of first generation dihydropyridines (see p. 129), it is recommended to only use sustained-release dihydropyridines, in combination with a beta-blocker.

In the absence of sufficient data concerning the most recent dihydropyridines, most authors tend to prefer heart-rate-lowering calcium channel blockers (verapamil or diltiazem), provided there are no signs of left ventricular dysfunction. In the presence of heart failure with alteration of left ventricular systolic function, amlodipine or felodipine can be used, as no harmful effects were demonstrated in the **PRAISE** and **VHeFT III** studies (see p. 254).

5 **Antianginal combinations must be reserved to failures of monotherapy.**

The synergistic mechanisms of action of the various classes of antianginal drugs (see p. 128) are the basis for the evaluation of various combinations. The beta-blocker-dihydropyridine combination has been the most extensively studied, especially in the **TIBET** and **IMAGE** trials (*J Am Coll Cardiol* 1996;27:311-316). The great majority of studies failed to demonstrate any superior efficacy of combinations in terms of improvement of angina and myocar-dial ischemia, except in patients who remained symptomatic with monotherapy.

The most widely recommended combinations are beta-blocker-nitrate and beta-blocker-calcium channel blocker with, in this last case, a preference for sustained-release dihydropyridines in order to avoid the potentially serious adverse effects of heart-rate-lowering calcium channel blockers (excessive bradycardia, heart failure).

Unresolved questions

- **Is antianginal treatment able to improve the prognosis of stable angina?**

  Surprisingly, there is no answer to this fundamental question at the present time. Apart from the fact that a placebo-controlled trial is difficult to perform, it has been estimated that a mortality study would require the inclusion of more than 50,000 patients in order to demonstrate the superiority of one antianginal agent over another, in view of the relatively low incidence of fatal events.

- **Can antianginal medications improve endothelial function, prevent coronary atherosclerosis, and consequently decrease cardiovascular morbidity and mortality?**

  In the **PREVENT** study (see p. 98), which included 825 patients with coronary heart disease, amlodipine did not modify progression of coronary atherosclerosis evaluated by angiography, but decreased overall cardiovascular morbidity and mortality by 31%. The **CAMELOT** study, which should include 3,000 patients, will compare the effects of amlodipine and enalapril on progression of atherosclerosis and reduction of cardiovascular events.

  The **ENCORE I** and **II** studies (*J Cardiovasc Pharmacol* 1997;30 suppl. 3:548-552) are designed to verify whether a calcium channel blocker (nifedipine GITS) and a statin (cerivastatin), alone or in combination, can improve endothelial function of patients with coronary heart disease and whether this effect is associated with atherosclerosis regression.

  The **ACTION** morbidity-mortality study (*Eur Heart J* 1998;19 suppl. I:I20-I32), designed to include 6,000 patients, will evaluate nifedipine GITS (Gastro-Intestinal Therapeutic System) at the dose of 30 or 60 mg daily in addition to freely prescribed antianginal therapy.

  The English **IONA** morbidity-mortality trial is evaluating nicorandil, a potassium channel agonist, in 5,000 patients with stable angina.

Prevention of acute ischemic events

In addition to prevention of atherogenesis by elimination of risk factors, some drugs are also able to improve the prognosis of patients with stable angina. The positive effect of statins is probably not exclusively related to prevention (or regression) of atherosclerosis by a reduction of serum cholesterol (see p. 86), but also involves a stabilizing effect, preventing plaque rupture. The platelet aggregation inhibitor action of aspirin, taken prophylactically, would be useful when the atheromatous plaque becomes unstable.

Current state of knowledge

 Statins used in secondary prevention decrease coronary morbidity and mortality and all cause mortality (see pp. 73 and 74).

This was demonstrated with simvastatin in the **4S** study (*Lancet* 1994;344:1383-1389) (see p. 81) and pravastatin in the **LIPID** study (*N Engl J Med* 1998;339:1349-1357) (see p. 83). In the **CARE** study (*N Engl J Med* 1996;335:1001-1009) (see p. 82), pravastatin only decreased coronary morbidity and mortality. An important finding was that the clinical benefit of statins appeared to be independent of the baseline serum cholesterol level.

In reality, these various studies were performed in patients with a history of myocardial infarction or unstable angina. Only the **4S** study included patients with stable angina, but they represented only 21% of the 4,444 randomized patients. These results can therefore not be strictly extrapolated to the context of stable angina.

The **AVERT** study (see p. 120), performed in patients with stable angina, showed that intensive treatment by statin (atorvastatin 80 mg daily) decreased serum LDL-cholesterol to a much lower level than that obtained with conventional lipid-lowering treatment (0.77 g/L vs 1.19 g/L). Although atorvastatin appeared to reduce the incidence of cardiovascular events, it is unclear whether this is a beneficial effect of the high-dose statin or an effect of coronary angioplasty, systematically performed in the group receiving conventional lipid-lowering treatment.

Low-dose aspirin reduces the combined risk of morbidity and mortality.

Although the efficacy of aspirin in unstable angina, acute myocardial infarction, and post-myocardial infarction has been largely demonstrated, the prescription of aspirin in patients with stable angina was only recommended following the results of the **SAPAT** trial (*Lancet* 1992;340:1421-1425). In this trial, which included 2,035 patients with no history of myocardial infarction and treated with beta-blocker for stable angina, aspirin (75 mg daily), vs placebo, significantly decreased the incidence of a first myocardial infarction or sudden death by 34% over a period of 50 months. Although a marked reduction of all vascular events was observed, the reduction of all cause mortality or cardiovascular mortality was not significant.

 Unresolved questions

● **Should a statin be systematically prescribed regardless of the serum cholesterol level?**

Experimental trials conducted by **Libby** *et al.* (*Circulation* 1998; 97:2433-2444) suggest that lipid-lowering treatment can stabilize vulnerable atheromatous plaques by reducing the activity of certain enzymes (metalloproteinases) which destroy the arterial extracellular matrix, and by promoting accumulation of collagen in the fibrous sheath, thereby limiting the risk of plaque rupture and thrombosis.

● **Can fibrates compete with statins?**

Fibrates have little effect on serum LDL-cholesterol, but increase serum HDL-cholesterol and lower triglycerides. Two studies, **BIP** and **VA-HIT**, have reported discordant results (20th session of the European Society of Cardiology, 1998).

In the **BIP** study, which included 3,122 patients with coronary heart disease (documented coronary insufficiency or myocardial infarction during the previous 6 months), with total serum cholesterol between 1.80 and 2.50 g/L, serum LDL-C < 1.80 g/L, serum HDL-C < 0.45 g/L, and triglycerides < 3 g/L, bezafibrate 400 mg daily, vs placebo, did not delay the appearance of a first event including cardiac death and nonfatal myocardial infarction, although it significantly increased serum HDL-cholesterol and decreased triglycerides.

However, in the **VA-HIT** study, which included 2,531 men with documented ischemic heart disease and serum HDL-cholesterol ≤ 0.40 g/L associated with slightly raised serum LDL cholesterol (≤ 1.40 g/L) and triglycerides < 3 g/L, gemfibrozil (1200 mg daily), vs placebo, decreased the combined risk of cardiac death or myocardial infarction by 22% ($p = 0.006$) with a mean follow-up of 5 years.

The discordance between the results of these two studies could be explained by a higher proportion of high-risk subjects (especially diabetics) in the **VA-HIT** study and by a greater efficacy of fibrates in patients with an initially low serum LDL-cholesterol.

● **What is the place of other platelet aggregation inhibitors?**

Like aspirin, ticlopidine and clopidogrel have demonstrated a beneficial effect in secondary prevention, but their evaluation has not included any studies specifically devoted to stable angina. New antiplatelet drugs, such as GP IIb/IIIa receptor inhibitors have not been used in this indication.

● **Does the probable anti-ischemic effect of angiotensin-converting enzyme inhibitors justify their prescription in stable angina?**

In the **TREND** study (*Circulation* 1996;94:258-265), quinapril (40 mg daily) improved the endothelial dysfunction of normotensive coronary patients without left ventricular dysfunction. In contrast, in the **QUIET** study (*Cardiovasc Drugs Ther* 1993;7:273-282 and 18th session of the European Society of Cardiology, 1996), conducted in 1,750 patients with ischemic heart disease, quinapril (20 mg daily) vs placebo, did not show any beneficial effect in terms of prevention of recurrent ischemic event and death or progression of coronary atherosclerosis with a mean follow-up of 3 years. The results of ongoing studies with perindopril (**EUROPA**), trandolapril (**PEACE**), and ramipril (**HOPE**) are eagerly awaited. These placebo-controlled trials should each include 8,000 to 11,000 patients.

Myocardial revascularization

Medical treatment, coronary angioplasty, and surgery should be considered to be complementary strategies, whose respective place depends on the clinical stage of coronary heart disease.

Current state of knowledge

 Myocardial revascularization is justified in the case of disabling angina despite well conducted drug treatment.

 Surgery and coronary angioplasty are more effective than antianginal drug treatment to reduce the frequency of angina and drug consumption.

 Compared to medical treatment, coronary angioplasty does not improve the prognosis and does not decrease the risk of myocardial infarction. It could even be harmful in low-risk patients.

Few studies have been devoted to comparison of the effects of coronary angioplasty and medical treatment in stable angina and the populations studied had a relatively low spontaneous risk.

In the **ACME** study (*N Engl J Med* 1992;326:10-16), which included 212 patients with stable angina, a positive stress test, and single-vessel disease, coronary angioplasty did not modify the incidence of death and myocardial infarction at 6 months, but improved the clinical symptoms at the expense of a higher repeated revascularization rate.

The **RITA 2** study (*Lancet* 1997;350:461-468) was conducted in 1,018 patients with stable coronary heart disease, most of whom had moderate symptoms, single-vessel or two-vessel disease, with preserved left ventricular function. With a mean follow-up of 2.7 years, coronary angioplasty increased the risk of death or myocardial infarction (6.3% vs, 3.3%, $p = 0.02$), and this difference essentially affected the incidence of myocardial infarction, because of complications related to the interventional procedure. Coronary angioplasty decreased angina symptoms and approximately one in five patients of the medical group underwent myocardial revascularization.

The **MASS** study (*J Am Coll Cardiol* 1995;26:1600-1605) compared coronary angioplasty, surgery, and medical treatment in 214 patients with isolated proximal stenosis of the left anterior descending artery, with no left ventricular dysfunction. With a mean follow-up of 3.5 years, the three strategies gave equivalent results in terms of the incidence of myocardial infarction and mortality (which was zero in the medical treatment group).

The **AVERT** study (71st session of the American Heart Association, 1998) compared coronary angioplasty and intensive statin therapy (atorvastatin 80 mg daily) in 341 patients with stable angina, at low risk because of single-vessel or two-vessel disease (without proximal stenosis of the left anterior descending artery) and left ventricular ejection fraction > 0.40. All patients had to have a serum LDL-cholesterol level > 1.15 g/L and the coronary angioplasty group received conventional lipid-lowering treatment. With a follow-up of 18 months, atorvastatin, compared to coronary angioplasty, decreased the combined incidence of death, myocardial infarction, repeated revascularizations, and hospitalizations for angina (13% vs 21%, p = 0.048). Serious events were equally uncommon in the two groups and the difference essentially concerned rehospitalizations for angina, which could be explained by the frequency of post-coronary angioplasty restenosis.

4 **Compared to medical treatment, coronary bypass surgery using saphenous vein improves the prognosis only in certain high-risk patient groups defined by clinical and angiographic criteria.**

The three major trials comparing surgery and medical treatment were conducted in the 1970s and published in the 1980s: the **CASS** study (*Circulation* 1983;68:939-950; *Circulation* 1990;82: 1629-1646), the **European ECSG** study (*Lancet* 1982;2:1173-1180; *N Engl J Med* 1988;319:332-337), and the **Veterans Administration** study (*N Engl J Med* 1984;311:1333-1339; *Circulation* 1992;86:121-130), including 780, 768, and 686 patients, respectively.

The meta-analysis by **Yusuf** (*Lancet* 1994;344:563-570), based on 7 studies (including the 3 major trials mentioned above), deals with a total of 2,649 patients whose main characteristics were relatively young mean age (51 years), a majority of men (97%), variable angina symptoms (class I or II: 54%), a history of myocardial infarction in 60% of cases, generally preserved left ventricular function (ejection fraction < 50% in 20% of patients), and predominance of three-vessel disease (51% of cases), involving the proximal segment of the left anterior descending artery (LAD) (59% of cases).

This meta-analysis indicated the following elements:

● overall, surgery improved the prognosis: mortality was reduced by 39% at 5 years, 32% at 7 years, and 17% at 10 years. This benefit tended to fade with time because of alteration of the bypass graft (40% occlusion rate at the 10th year), but remained significant at 10 years;

● in the absence of proximal stenosis of the LAD, surgery was beneficial at 5 and 10 years only in the case of stenosis of the left main coronary artery and three-vessel disease;

● the absolute benefit of surgery was more marked in the case of left ventricular dysfunction, history of myocardial infarction, and low-level positive stress test;

● at 10 years, medical treatment tended to be superior to surgery in the group of low-risk patients (who represented 1/3 of the population) defined by a score taking into account age, severity of angina, left ventricular ejection fraction, degree of coronary disease, history of myocardial infarction, diabetes, or hypertension.

The very long-term results (> 10 years), assessed in the **Veterans Administration** study (*Circulation* 1992;86:121-130 and *Am J Cardiol* 1998;81:1393-1399), showed that surgery:

● did not decrease the incidence of myocardial infarction, but improved its prognosis;

● was no longer superior to medical treatment from the 11th year onwards, in terms of clinical symptoms and mortality (including at the 18th year in patients with three-vessel disease and left ventricular dysfunction);

● worsened the prognosis in low-risk patients with single-vessel and two-vessel disease, but also three-vessel disease with normal left ventricular function.

These studies present a number of limitations. Their conclusions cannot be applied to women and to patients over the age of 65, who represented only a very small minority of the study populations. "Intent to treat" statistical analysis also masked the fact that, at 10 years, about 40% of patients initially assigned to medical treatment had undergone surgical intervention. Finally, the results of these trials, initiated more than 20 years ago, do not take into account the subsequent progress in both surgical and medical treatment.

 Compared to surgery, coronary angioplasty does not modify the prognosis and is associated with a high incidence of repeated myocardial revascularizations.

Apart from the **BARI** study (see p. 123), 4 main trials compared surgery and balloon coronary angioplasty: the **RITA** (*Lancet* 1993;343:573-580), **GABI** (*N Engl J Med* 1994;331:1037-1043), **EAST** (*N Engl J Med* 1994;331:1044-1059), and **CABRI** (*Lancet* 1995;346:1179-1184) studies, which randomized 1011, 359, 392, and 1054 patients, respectively. Apart from the **RITA** study, which could include patients with single-vessel disease, the other three studies were exclusively conducted in patients with multi-vessel disease and myocardial revascularization had to be as complete as possible, except in the **CABRI** study. The great majority of patients presented with stable angina and preserved left ventricular function.

With a follow-up ranging from 1 to 3 years, depending on the study, coronary angioplasty and coronary artery bypass graft surgery gave comparable results in terms of mortality and the incidence of nonfatal myocardial infarction. Coronary angioplasty was less effective than surgery to eliminate angina because of the often incomplete nature of the initial myocardial revascularization and the frequency of restenoses, requiring repeated revascularization procedures.

Pocock (*Lancet* 1995;346:1184-1189) reported similar findings for the treatment of single-vessel disease, corresponding to only 732 of the 3,371 patients included in his meta-analysis.

The conclusions of these studies are limited by the highly selective nature of the patients (who represented less than 5% of all coronary patients evaluated), the exclusion of patients with the most severe disease (left main coronary artery disease, proximal three-vessel disease, multiple chronic occlusions, left ventricular dysfunction) and by the progress in coronary angioplasty techniques achieved since these trials (especially stents). The ongoing SOS and ARTS studies are designed to compare bypass grafts and stenting in patients with multiple-vessel disease.

Surgery is superior to coronary angioplasty in diabetic patients with multi-vessel disease and severe ischemia.

This was the conclusion of the **BARI** study (*N Engl J Med* 1996; 335:217-225 and *Circulation* 1997;96:2162-2170), which included 1,829 patients with multi-vessel disease and severe angina or ischemia.

In the 1,476 non-diabetic patients, the mortality rate and combined incidence of death or myocardial infarction were identical 5 years after coronary angioplasty or coronary artery bypass graft, regardless of the severity of the symptoms, left ventricular function, number of stenotic vessels, presence or absence of proximal stenosis of the LAD. However, 50% of patients initially treated by coronary angioplasty subsequently underwent at least a 2nd revascularization within 5 years and surgery was more effective to eliminate angina.

The major finding was that surgery was superior to coronary angioplasty in the 353 diabetic patients, by significantly improving their 5-year survival (80.6% vs 65.5%). However, recent progress in coronary angioplasty (stents and the use of GP IIb/IIIa receptor inhibitors) were not tested in this study, although restenosis after balloon coronary angioplasty is known to be particularly frequent in diabetic patients (*J Am Coll Cardiol* 1998;31:10-19).

Although the register by **O'Keefe** (*Eur Heart J* 1998;19:1696-1703), which included 1,938 diabetic patients, appears to confirm the superiority of surgery over coronary angioplasty in the long term (10-year survival: 60% vs 46%, $p < 0.0001$), it should be noted that the benefit of surgery was only observed in patients receiving oral antidiabetic treatment (sulfonylurea). The difference between the two modes of revascularization was not significant in diabetic patients treated with insulin or diet alone.

Unresolved questions

 What are the real implications of the major trials for the current therapeutic strategy?

Despite the above mentioned limitations of these studies, a number of fundamental principles can be recommended on the basis of their conclusions:

● Myocardial revascularization is indicated when angina is no longer controlled by drugs and interferes with everyday life.

● Coronary angiography is required when noninvasive investigations show severe myocardial ischemia or left ventricular dysfunction likely to have a negative influence on prognosis.

● The choice between surgery and coronary angioplasty depends on the clinical context, the extent of coronary lesions and the degree of left ventricular dysfunction. Schematically:
  • surgery is recommended for stenosis of the left main coronary artery and in three-vessel disease, especially in the presence of left ventricular dysfunction or diabetes mellitus,
  • in contrast, most single-vessel lesions can be treated by coronary angioplasty;
  • in all other cases, the choice depends on the clinician's personal preference, although the indications for coronary angioplasty have been considerably enlarged over recent years. The main limitation of this technique remains restenosis, despite the increasingly frequent use of coronary stents [**STRESS** study (*N Engl J Med* 1994;331:496-501) and **BENESTENT 1** study (*N Engl J Med* 1994;331:489-495 and *J Am Coll Cardiol* 1996;27:255-261)] and the patient must be informed about the possibility of repeated myocardial revascularization.

● At the present time, no study justifies systematic coronary angioplasty in patients with minimally symptomatic stable angina, not presenting any criteria of severity.

Treatment of silent myocardial ischemia

Myocardial ischemia, defined by transient episodes of ST depression on ambulatory ECG monitoring during everyday activities, is present in approximately 50% of patients with stable angina. The important point is that more than 2/3 of these ischemic episodes are completely silent.

Analysis of variations of heart rate and blood pressure preceding the episode of myocardial ischemia shows that the essential mechanism is an increased myocardial oxygen requirement. More rarely, ischemia is due to a sudden fall in the oxygen supply secondary to coronary spasm.

There is no truly satisfactory explanation for the silent nature of the myocardial ischemia. Some authors have suggested a decreased sensitivity and cognitive faculties involving endorphins, while others consider that the episode of ischemia is too brief to cause symptoms or occurs in a limited subendocardial zone.

It is now recognized that myocardial ischemia has the same prognostic significance whether it is symptomatic or asymptomatic. However, in the absence of angina, only demonstration of an improvement of morbidity and mortality would justify targeted treatment. Although silent myocardial ischemia has a definite ominous prognostic value in the context of unstable angina and immediate post-myocardial infarction, its real impact on the outcome of patients with stable angina remains a highly controversial subject.

Current state of knowledge

1 **Silent myocardial ischemia can persist despite control of angina by medical treatment.**

2 **Antianginal drugs decrease the degree of silent myocardial ischemia which can be totally eliminated in one out of two patients.**

Many small randomized placebo-controlled trials have shown that the various classes of antianginal drugs reduce silent myocardial ischemia present on Holter monitoring (reduction of the number of episodes and total duration of ischemia) and on stress testing (prolonged latency of ST depression and increased total effort duration). These findings were confirmed in larger trials, such as the **CAPE** study (*J Am Coll Cardiol* 1994;24:1460-1467) with amlodipine, the **ASIST** study (*Circulation* 1994;90:762-768) with atenolol, or the **TIBET** study (*Eur Heart J* 1996;17:96-103) which evaluated atenolol, nifedipine SR, and a combination of the two.

3 **Beta-blockers are probably more effective than calcium channel blockers to eliminate silent ischemia.**

This was demonstrated by three studies: the study by **Quyyumi** (*Br Heart J* 1987;57:505-511) and especially the more recent **ACIP** and **TIBBS** studies.

In the **ACIP** study (*J Am Coll Cardiol* 1994;24:11-20), conducted in 618 patients, atenolol (50 to 100 mg daily) was found to be superior to diltiazem (60 to 90 mg bid) to totally eliminate ischemia on Holter monitoring at the 12th week (47% vs 32%).

In the **TIBBS** study (*J Am Coll Cardiol* 1995;25:231-238), which included 330 patients, bisoprolol (10 to 20 mg daily) vs nifedipine SR (20 to 40 mg bid) more markedly decreased the number of ischemic episodes and the total duration of ischemia on Holter monitoring. The beta-blocker totally prevented ischemia in a larger proportion of patients (41% vs 15%) and was also the only treatment to reduce the morning peak of silent ischemia.

However, the **TIBET** study (*Eur Heart J* 1996;17:96-103), conducted in 608 patients, did not reveal any difference between atenolol (50 mg bid), nifedipine SR (20 to 40 mg bid), or a combination of the two in terms of improvement of stress test parameters and reduction of ischemia on Holter monitoring. In this trial, nifedipine, less well tolerated than the beta-blocker, was responsible for more frequent discontinuation of treatment (40% vs 27% over a two-year period).

4 **Myocardial revascularization is superior to drug treatment to prevent silent ischemia.**

In the **ACIP** study, 618 patients with stable angina and at least one significant coronary stenosis, a positive stress test, and silent ischemia on Holter monitoring, were randomized to receive three different strategies. The first two treatment arms consisted of antianginal drugs and were designed to either control angina, or eliminate any form of ischemia. The third arm consisted of myocardial revascularization by coronary angioplasty or coronary artery bypass graft. Myocardial revascularization more frequently eliminated any form of ischemia on the Holter monitoring performed at the 12th week (55% vs 39% for the antianginal strategy and 41% for the antiischemic strategy). Analysis of revascularization techniques showed that surgery was more effective than coronary angioplasty.

Unresolved questions

 Does elimination of silent myocardial ischemia, particularly by myocardial revascularization, improve the prognosis of stable angina?

The **ASIST** study (*Circulation* 1994;90:762-768), conducted in

306 patients, was the first study to suggest that atenolol not only prevented silent ischemia, but could also reduce the one-year incidence of serious events: death, resuscitated cardiac arrest, myocardial infarction, or unstable angina.

The two-year results of the ACIP study (*Circulation* 1997;95: 2037-2043) recently supported this hypothesis, by showing that myocardial revascularization (the most effective strategy to eliminate silent ischemia) improved the prognosis compared to angina-guided or ischemia-guided drug treatment. A significant benefit was observed for mortality (1.1% vs 6.6% and 4.4%), the rate of death or myocardial infarction (4.7% vs 12.1% and 8.8%), and the combined rate of death, myocardial infarction, or recurrent cardiac hospitalization (23.1% vs 41.8% and 38.5%). The medical strategy designed to prevent any form of ischemia also tended to be superior to the angina-guided strategy.

These results are in contradiction with those of the TIBET study (*Eur Heart J* 1996;17:104-112) which, with a mean follow-up of two years, failed to demonstrate any relationship between the presence, frequency and total duration of ischemic episodes on Holter monitoring (with or without treatment), and the incidence of cardiac events.

In fact, no definitive conclusions can be drawn from the results of the ACIP study, as this pilot study did not have the statistical power of a mortality study and included only a small number of events. In particular, there is no evidence that reduction of silent ischemia represented an independent factor of improvement of the prognosis.

The ACIP II study, which will include 5,000 patients, should provide an answer to this fundamental question.

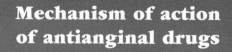

Mechanism of action of antianginal drugs

We will consider the mechanism of action of nitrates, beta-blockers, calcium channel blockers, trimetazidine and nicorandil.

 Nitrates are peripheral and coronary vasodilators, whose antianginal effects are due to an increase of myocardial oxygen supply and a reduction of myocardial oxygen requirements.

Nitrates decrease myocardial oxygen requirements by lowering the preload (venous vasodilatation and decreased venous return) and, to a variable degree, the afterload (reduction of arterial compliance and peripheral resistance). Nitrates also promote the myocardial oxygen supply *via* several mechanisms: dilatation of epicardial coronary vessels and the collateral circulation, coronary dilatation at a site of stenosis, improvement of subendocardial perfusion by reduction of the preload. Nitrates are metabolized in endothelial cells and deliver NO, a powerful vasodilator, directly to smooth muscle cells.

Tolerance observed during continuous treatment must be prevented by observing a treatment-free interval each day, which implies that effective 24-hour protection cannot be achieved. Tolerance is not observed with molsidomine (NO donor similar to nitrates) because spontaneous hydrolysis of its active metabolite, linsidomine, is not enzyme-dependent.

Beta-blockers reduce myocardial oxygen consumption by decreasing heart rate, myocardial contractility, and systolic blood pressure on effort.

The increased blood flow in ischemic myocardium is related to lengthening of diastolic filling and reduction of coronary vasoconstriction on effort (by decreased release of free fatty acids). Although all beta-blockers have been shown to induce an equivalent increase of the duration of effort, the presence of an intrinsic sympathomimetic activity decreases the efficacy on ischemia detected by ambulatory monitoring.

Calcium channel blockers are arterial vasodilators whose antianginal effects are essentially exerted by reduction of myocardial oxygen consumption.

The three main calcium channel blockers are dihydropyridines, diltiazem (belonging to the class of benzothiazepines), and verapamil (belonging to the class of phenylalkylamines). They all reduce the influx of calcium into smooth muscle cells, including myocardial smooth muscle cells, by blocking calcium channels in various ways. The reduction of myocardial oxygen consumption is secondary to arterial vasodilatation, which reduces the afterload, and to the reduction of heart rate on effort, which is observed only with diltiazem and verapamil. Although all calcium channel blockers are negative inotropic agents, the reduction of myocardial contractility is more or less marked *in vivo* because of the reflex sympathetic response. The negative inotropic effect is greater with verapamil and diltiazem.

All calcium channel blockers have a direct coronary vasodilator action, allowing increased perfusion in coronary arteries and collaterals. This action is beneficial in the case of vasoconstriction (antispastic effect), but is more limited in the case of fixed stenosis, in which case it can induce a coronary steal phenomenon due to excess vasodilatation in healthy zones, at the expense of ischemic myocardium.

First generation (immediate-release) dihydropyridines can induce a pro-ischemic effect *via* a coronary steal phenomenon, sudden hypotension, and reflex tachycardia. This harmful effect is no longer observed with second generation sustained-release dihydropyridines.

● **Trimetazidine, devoid of any hemodynamic effects, has a specific metabolic mechanism of action**

At the cellular level, myocardial ischemia results in a reduction of energy production (increased levels of inorganic phosphates, degradation of creatine phosphate, and decreased ATP production), acidosis, calcium overload and formation of free radicals.

Trimetazidine improves the energy yield under conditions of ischemia, by promoting glucose utilization at the expense of fatty acids, which are less profitable in terms of ATP production and which consume more oxygen.

The antianginal effect of trimetazidine was demonstrated in the **TEMS** study (*Br J Clin Pharmacol* 1994;37:279-288).

● **Nicorandil, a potassium channel activator, is a mixed arterial and venous and coronary vasodilator.**

By opening potassium channels and by allowing efflux of K+ ions, nicorandil induces repolarization of vascular smooth muscle cells, closure of voltage-dependent calcium channels and cellular relaxation. The antianginal effect is due to an increased myocardial oxygen supply and a decreased myocardial oxygen consumption. The increased myocardial oxygen supply is due to epicardial coronary vasodilatation. The decreased myocardial oxygen consumption is secondary to a reduction of afterload due to peripheral arterial vasodilatation and a reduction of preload by venous vasodilatation, induced by the complementary nitrate action exerted by the NO_2 radical of the molecule.

Silent myocardial ischemia: Cohn's classification
(*Circulation* 1987;75 suppl. 2:33-37)

● Type 1   *in asymptomatic subjects*
            silent ischemia is discovered during assessment of
            cardiovascular risk factors or on routine tests per-
            formed for particular occupations (airline pilots, etc.)

● Type 2   *after myocardial infarction*

● Type 3   *in angina patients*

Contraindications of antianginal drugs

● Beta-blockers
    Asthma and chronic obstructive airways disease
    NYHA class III-IV heart failure
    Severe arterial disease of the lower limbs
    Raynaud's phenomenon
    Sinus bradycardia < 50 bpm
    > 1st degree atrioventricular block
    Hypotension

● Dihydropyridines
    Hypotension
    Recent transmural myocardial infarction

● Diltiazem and verapamil
    Left ventricular systolic dysfunction
    Sinus bradycardia < 50 bpm
    > 1st degree atrioventricular block
    Hypotension
    Recent transmural myocardial infarction

Angina pectoris: functional classification

		Canadian Cardiovascular Society (CCS) (1)	New York Heart Association (NYHA) (2)
●	Class I	• Angina on violent, rapidly performed or prolonged physical activity or in sportsmen	• No angina for ordinary physical activity
●	Class II	• Angina on rapid walking or on sloping ground or on flat ground after a meal or during cold or windy weather or emotional stress or in the morning after waking • Angina on climbing more than one flight of stairs at normal speed	• Angina on mild exertion
●	Class III	• Angina while walking on flat ground for less than two blocks • Angina on climbing a flight of stairs at normal speed	• Angina for less than ordinary physical activity
●	Class IV	• Angina on walking several steps or during personal hygiene or at rest	• Angina on the slightest exertion or at rest

(1) L. Campeau (*Circulation* 1976;54:522).

(2) The Criteria Committee of the New York Heart Association (*Diseases of the Heart and Blood Vessels. Nomenclature and Criteria for Diagnosis*, 6th ed., Boston, Little, Brown and Co., 1964).

Unstable angina

Unstable angina is at least as frequent as myocardial infarction. In the absence of treatment, it leads to necrosis in the majority of cases and is associated with a risk of sudden death. Modern treatments are able to prevent this unfavorable outcome in more than 90% of patients.

There are several clinical forms of unstable angina, corresponding to angina at rest, accelerated exertional angina, de novo exertional angina (present for less than one month), and post-myocardial infarction angina. As these various clinical presentations do not have the same prognostic significance, it is sometimes difficult to interpret the results of clinical trials conducted in heterogeneous populations. The elaboration of often complex classifications (see p. 155) has not really resolved this problem.

The first mechanism, common to unstable angina and to myocardial infarction, is rupture of an atheromatous plaque, leading to the formation of coronary thrombosis. Lesions likely to rupture generally induce moderate, or even insignificant eccentric stenoses, corresponding to plaques with a lipid-rich histological structure, composed of a soft atheromatous nucleus covered by a fine, fragile, fibrous shell, presenting signs of inflammation. The factors triggering rupture of the plaque are poorly elucidated. The main factors incriminated (but not necessarily validated) are a sudden increase of parietal stress secondary to spasm or a sudden rise in blood pressure, particular vulnerability of the plaque to an extracardiac inflammatory process or intraplaque bleeding from the newly formed vasa vasorum induced by development of the atheroma. Whatever the factors involved, the consequence of plaque rupture is the formation of a fibrin and platelet thrombus, generally nonocclusive, to which is added vasospastic phenomena promoted by activated platelets and thrombin. The marked and often intermittent reduction of coronary perfusion is responsible for myocardial ischemia and the clinical features depend on the intensity of the thrombotic process, the severity of the subendothelial lesions and the presence or absence of a collateral circulation. This last factor explains why complete coronary occlusion is sometimes not accompanied by any myocardial necrosis.

Non-Q-wave myocardial infarction is classically classified with unstable angina, and the clinical syndrome is accompanied by a generally moderate elevation of serum creatine kinase. Elevation of troponin I or T was recently demonstrated to constitute a pejorative prognostic factor in unstable angina.

The initial therapeutic strategy is based on our understanding of the pathophysiological phenomena. The essential objective is to rapidly neutralize activation of platelets and the clotting system by an antithrombotic agent. Anti anginal treatment is designed to relieve symptoms, reduce myocardial oxygen requirements, eliminate vasomotor phenomena, and decrease the stresses applied to the unstable plaque.

Drug treatment

The initial treatment of unstable angina is pharmacological, as, in the very great majority of cases, it is sufficient to prevent early ischemic recurrence and it also prepares for a possible coronary angioplasty, the complications of which are more frequent in a context of unstable angina.

Drug treatment is based on anti-ischemic and antithrombotic agents.

Anti-ischemic drugs

Current state of knowledge

 Nitrates are rightly or wrongly considered to be a major treatment.

However, no morbidity and mortality studies have been conducted with these drugs. Nitrates relieve the symptoms and their anti-ischemic effect is related to coronary vasodilatation and reduction of myocardial oxygen consumption, itself resulting from a reduction of the preload (and afterload at high doses).

Nitrates are usually initially administered by IV infusion, followed by the oral route. IV linsidomine (active metabolite of molsidomine, not inducing any tolerance) is also an effective product (*Eur Heart J* 1997;18:1300-1306).

 Beta-blockers decrease the risk of progression to myocardial infarction.

Beta-blockers relieve symptoms. By inhibiting the effects of catecholamines on the myocardium, they reduce the metabolic activity of the heart and decrease the constraints applied to the unstable atheromatous plaque.

In the **HINT** study (*Br Heart J* 1986;56:400-413), which included 515 patients, oral metoprolol (100 mg bid), vs placebo, decreased the incidence of ischemic recurrence or recurrent myocardial infarction during the first 48 hours by 24%. However, this favorable effect tended to fade after the first week.

In the meta-analysis by **Yusuf** (*JAMA* 1988;260:2253-2263), based on 7 trials including about 5,000 patients, beta-blockers (administered IV then orally in 5 of the 7 trials) significantly decreased the incidence of myocardial infarction by 13%, but did not demonstrate any positive effect on mortality.

❸ **Calcium channel blockers have variable effects depending on the class considered.**

Overall, calcium channel blockers do not decrease either the risk of progression to myocardial infarction or the mortality. This was the conclusion of the meta-analysis by **Held** (*BMJ* 1989;299:1187-1192), based on 6 trials including 1,100 patients, the majority of whom were treated with nifedipine.

Short-acting dihydropyridines should only be used in combination with beta-blockers. In the **HINT** study, oral nifedipine (60 mg daily) increased the risk of early myocardial infarction by 50% vs placebo. Nifedipine did not provide any additional beneficial effect when prescribed in combination with a beta-blocker. On the other hand, addition of nifedipine decreased the risk of ischemic recurrence or myocardial infarction by 32% vs placebo in patients already treated with beta-blockers at the time of onset of unstable angina.

Heart-rate-lowering calcium channel blockers (diltiazem, verapamil) effectively prevent short-term recurrent angina. In a **Dutch** study (*Lancet* 1995;346:1653-1657), IV diltiazem was well tolerated and more effective than IV nitrates to reduce the rate of refractory angina and myocardial infarction during the first 48 hours. In the **DRS** study by **Gibson** (*N Engl J Med* 1986;315:423-429), which included 576 patients with non-Q-wave myocardial infarction, oral diltiazem (90 mg qid), vs placebo, decreased the recurrent myocardial infarction rate and the frequency of refractory angina by one half during the first 14 days, but did not reduce the mortality.

Calcium channel blockers obviously remain the treatment of choice for Prinzmetal angina because of their powerful antispastic action. The dihydropyridines, verapamil, and diltiazem, demonstrated an identical efficacy in this indication. A combination of two different calcium channel blockers was shown to be synergistic in refractory forms of spastic angina.

Unresolved questions

 Should 2 or 3 anti-ischemic drugs be coprescribed?

In practice, calcium channel blockers are usually reserved for contraindications to beta-blockers and failures of beta-blocker-nitrate two-agent therapy. However, the largest study comparing medical treatment and an early invasive strategy (**TIMI IIIB** study, see p. 147) used a triple combination therapy with beta-blocker, diltiazem, and nitrate.

 Is an angiotensin-converting enzyme inhibitor beneficial during the acute phase?

This question is justified in view of a possible anti-ischemic effect of this drug class. However, the answer appears to be no, on the basis of the Argentine **ENAI** study, which included 1,022 patients with unstable angina. Oral enalapril, started during the 24 hours following an episode of rest pain, in addition to conventional treatment, did not modify the incidence of death, myocardial infarction, refractory angina, or emergency revascularization on the 7th day vs placebo (26.9% vs 24.4%). This negative result does not eliminate the possibility of a favorable long-term effect.

 Can early treatment with a statin reduce ischemic events during the acute phase of unstable angina or non-Q-wave myocardial infarction?

This question is being addressed by the ongoing **MIRACL** trial (*Am J Cardiol* 1998;81:578-581), designed to include 2,100 patients randomized to receive placebo or high-dose atorvastatin (80 mg daily) started during the first 4 days of hospitalization. The baseline serum cholesterol level must be < 2.70 g/L, with no lower limit.

Antithrombotic drugs

Current state of knowledge

 IV thrombolysis has not been demonstrated to be effective and may even be harmful.

Angiographic, angioscopic, and histological findings have demonstrated the high frequency of generally nonocclusive intracoronary thromboses in unstable angina and non-Q-wave myocardial infarction. These findings were the basis for trials of IV thrombolysis in this acute coronary syndrome.

Two angiographic studies, **UNASEM** (*Circulation* 1992;86:131-137) and **TIMI IIIA** (*Circulation* 1993;87:38-52) showed that a thrombolytic agent (APSAC in the **UNASEM** study and tPA in the **TIMI IIIA** study), combined with heparin, slightly decreased the degree of coronary stenosis responsible for the clinical syndrome, vs heparin used alone. In fact, a marked angiographic improvement was only obtained in patients initially presenting complete coronary artery occlusion or an image suggestive of intraluminal thrombus and in the non-Q-wave myocardial infarction group.

The **TIMI IIIB** study represents the largest clinical trial devoted to thrombolysis in unstable angina. This study (*Circulation* 1994;89: 1545-1556) included 1,473 patients with unstable angina (2/3 of cases) or non-Q-wave myocardial infarction (1/3 of cases), randomized during the 24 hours following spontaneous pain to receive either IV tPA (0.8 mg/kg over 90 minutes, half as an initial bolus), or placebo, in addition to IV heparin, started immediately, and aspirin (325 mg daily), started on the second day. tPA vs placebo had a harmful effect in the unstable angina group, by significantly increasing the combined rate of death or myocardial infarction at the 6th week (9.1% vs 5.0%). tPA had a neutral effect in the non-Q-wave myocardial infarction group. Thrombolysis also increased the incidence of cerebral hemorrhage, especially in patients over the age of 75.

The failure of thrombolysis in unstable angina has been attributed to the fact that intracoronary thrombi are generally nonocclusive, present at various stages of development and composed of organized fibrin and platelets, in contrast with the erythrocytic nature of recent occlusive thrombus characteristic of Q-wave infarcts.

Aspirin prevents progression to myocardial infarction and decreases cardiac mortality.

Aspirin acts by blocking cyclo-oxygenase. Its action is therefore confined to only one of the more than 80 currently identified pathways of platelet activation.

Aspirin was used at relatively high doses (325 mg to 1300 mg daily) in 3 placebo-controlled studies: the **Veterans Administration** study (*N Engl J Med* 1983;309:396-403), which included 1,266 patients, the **Canadian Multicenter Trial** (*N Engl J Med* 1985; 313:1369-1375), conducted in 555 patients, and the study by **Théroux** (*N Engl J Med* 1988;319:1105-1111), conducted in 479 patients. The concordant results of these 3 trials allowed **Yusuf**, in his meta-analysis (*JAMA* 1988;260:2253-2263), to conclude on a beneficial effect of aspirin, illustrated by a 40% reduction of nonfatal myocardial infarction and a 42% reduction of cardiac mortality.

The dosage of 1300 mg daily used in the **Canadian Multicenter Trial** was responsible for an excess of gastrointestinal disorders. Low-dose aspirin (75 mg daily) was found to be just as effective in the **RISC** study (*Lancet* 1990;336:827-830), which included 796 men during the first 72 hours of an episode of unstable angina or non-Q-wave myocardial infarction. In this study, aspirin, vs placebo, reduced the combined risk of death and myocardial infarction by 57% on the 5th day, 69% on the 30th day and 64% at the 3rd month.

3 **Ticlopidine has been shown to be effective and can be prescribed when aspirin is contraindicated.**

The antiplatelet action of ticlopidine differs from that of aspirin: it does not inhibit cyclo-oxygenase, but inhibits ADP-dependent binding of fibrinogen to GP IIb/IIIa receptors.

In an **Italian** study (*Circulation* 1990;82:17-26), conducted in 652 patients, oral ticlopidine (250 mg bid), started during the first 48 hours of hospitalization, significantly reduced the cumulative rate of vascular deaths and nonfatal myocardial infarction, determined at the 6th month, by 46% vs placebo.

In the absence of a large-scale evaluation and in view of the need for increased laboratory surveillance (risk of thrombocytopenia and neutropenia), it is reasonable to only prescribe ticlopidine to patients presenting contraindications to aspirin.

Unfractionated heparin is effective, especially when it is associated with aspirin.

In the study by **Théroux** (*N Engl J Med* 1988;319:1105-1111), IV heparin without aspirin significantly decreased the incidence of refractory angina and progression to myocardial infarction, vs placebo. However, this positive effect was not observed in the **RISC** study (*Lancet* 1990;336:827-830), in which IV heparin was started later and administered by intermittent injections. Heparin has been held responsible for frequent recurrence of the clinical syndrome after stopping the infusion, but this rebound phenomenon only appears to really exist in the absence of concomitant treatment with aspirin (*N Engl J Med* 1992;327:141-145).

The rationale for the heparin-aspirin combination appears to be demonstrated by the meta-analysis by **Oler** (*JAMA* 1996;276:811-815), who reviewed 6 trials with a total of 1,356 patients, including the study by **Théroux**, the **RISC** study and the **ATACS** study (*Circulation* 1994;89:81-88). Compared to aspirin administered alone, the heparin-aspirin combination decreased the risk of myocardial infarction or death during the randomization period by 33% (7.9% vs 10.4%, $p = 0.06$), at the cost of a major bleeding risk, which, although increased threefold, remained acceptable (1.5%).

5 **Low molecular weight heparins (LMWHs) are going to replace unfractionated heparin.**

● A first trial, the **FRISC** study, showed that dalteparin was superior to placebo in patients receiving aspirin (75 mg daily). In this study (*Lancet* 1996;347:561-568), which included 1,506 patients with unstable angina or non-Q-wave myocardial infarction, dalteparin (120 IU/kg bid SC for 6 days then 7,500 IU daily for 35 to 45 days) significantly decreased the rate of myocardial infarction or death during the first 6 days (1.8% vs 4.8%) and the incidence of myocardial revascularization (0.4% vs 1.2%), with a benefit which persisted on the 40th day.

● Two other studies, **FRIC** and **FRAXIS**, showed that dalteparin and nadroparin gave equivalent results to those of unfractionated heparin.

● In the **FRIC** study (*Circulation* 1997;96:61-68), conducted in 1,482 patients, dalteparin (120 IU/kg bid SC for 6 days) did not modify the incidence of cardiac events (death, myocardial infarction, recurrent angina, myocardial revascularization) on the 6th day compared to unfractionated heparin administered IV for 6 days (initial bolus of 5,000 U followed by infusion of 1000 U/hour adjusted to maintain effective anticoagulation). Continuation of low-dose dalteparin (7,500 IU SC daily) between the 6th and 40th day did not provide any additional benefit compared to aspirin (75 to 165 mg daily) prescribed alone.

● In the **FRAXIS** study (20th session of the European Society of Cardiology, 1998), which included 3,468 patients, the combined rate of deaths, myocardial infarction, and refractory or recurrent angina was the same on the 6th day with unfractionated heparin and nadroparin. As in the **FRIC** study, continuation of nadroparin until the 14th day did not provide any supplementary benefit (evaluated at 14 days and 3 months) compared to a 6-day treatment.

● Enoxaparin appears to be superior to unfractionated heparin on the basis of the **ESSENCE** and **TIMI 11B** studies.

● In the **ESSENCE** study (*N Engl J Med* 1997;337:447-452), which included 3,171 patients with angina at rest or non-Q-wave myocardial infarction and receiving aspirin (100 to 325 mg daily), enoxaparin (1 mg/kg bid SC for a minimum of 48 hours to a maximum of 8 days), compared with unfractionated heparin (initial bolus of 5,000 U followed by an infusion of 1,000 U/hour adjusted to maintain effective anticoagulation, for the same duration), significantly decreased the combined risk of death, myocardial infarction, or recurrent angina at the 14th day (16.6% vs 19.8%) and at one month (19.8% vs 23.3%), and the need for revascularization procedures (27.0% vs 32.2%). The beneficial effect of the LMWH, obvious from the 48th hour, was achieved with an increase of minor but not major bleeding (bruising at injection sites). The results at one year demonstrate persistence of the beneficial effect (47th session of the American College of Cardiology, 1998).

● The **TIMI 11B** study (71st session of the American Heart Association, 1998), conducted in 3,910 patients, confirmed the results of the **ESSENCE** study by demonstrating the superiority of enoxaparin over unfractionated heparin to reduce the combined rate of death, myocardial infarction, or urgent revascularization by the 8th hour and at the 7th and 14th days. The most important endpoint, death or myocardial infarction, was significantly decreased by 20% in the meta-analysis of the 2 studies (**TIMI 11B** and **ESSENCE**). The **TIMI 11B** study did not demonstrate any value of continuing the LMWH after discharge from hospital (until the 43rd day in this study).

Unresolved questions

 Thrombolysis may have a beneficial role in certain cases of extensive subendocardial myocardial infarction which represent a high-risk group.

 Do all LMWHs have the same efficacy?

The discordant results of the **FRIC** and **FRAXIS** studies and the **ESSENCE** and **TIMI 11B** studies tend to suggest that this is not the case. The apparent superiority of enoxaparin could be related to a higher anti–Xa/antithrombin activity ratio.

What is the optimal duration of LMWH treatment?

According to the results of the **FRIC** and **TIMI 11B** studies, continuation of treatment after discharge from hospital does not appear to provide any additional benefit.

What is the cost/efficacy ratio of LMWH treatment?

The preliminary economic analyses performed on data from the **ESSENCE** study are in favor of a lower cost of enoxaparin compared to unfractionated heparin (*Circulation* 1998;97:1702-1707).

Oral anticoagulants prescribed for 3 months, in combination with aspirin, could improve the prognosis.

This was suggested by the results of the **OASIS** pilot study (*Circulation* 1998;98:1064-1070) conducted in 197 patients. Warfarin (at a dosage maintaining the INR between 2 and 2.5), vs no oral anticoagulants, non-significantly reduced the frequency of death, myocardial infarction, or refractory angina (5.1% vs 12.1%), and the rehospitalization rate (7.1% vs 17.2%). Although the risk of bleeding was multiplied by 2.4 (28% vs 12%), there was no significant increase of major bleeding (2% vs 1%).

● Some of the new antithrombotic agents will have an important role to play, but their exact place has yet to be defined according to the strategy adopted (see p. 149).

● **Clopidogrel, a derivative of ticlopidine, does not induce the hematological complications associated with ticlopidine.**

Clopidrogel will be evaluated in unstable angina in the **CURE** study (clopidogrel and aspirin vs aspirin alone), designed to include 9,000 patients. The **CLASSICS** and **CREDO** studies are designed to verify that clopidogrel is as effective as ticlopidine in the prevention of coronary stent thrombosis (71st session of the American Heart Association, 1998).

● **GP IIb/IIIa receptor inhibitors, powerful antiplatelet agents, decrease the morbidity and mortality at one month.**

These molecules block platelet GP IIb/IIIa receptors, which constitute the final step of platelet aggregation, regardless of the pathway of metabolic activation. Two main classes are distinguished: nonspecific inhibitors (c7E3 Fab or abciximab monoclonal antibodies) and specific inhibitors, subdivided into cyclic peptides (eptifibatide) and peptidomimetic agents (lamifiban, tirofiban).

GP IIb/IIIa receptor inhibitors were first evaluated as a treatment to reduce the acute complications of high-risk coronary angioplasty (see pp. 151 and 152). They were then tested as initial treatment of unstable angina by 48-hour IV infusion, in combination with aspirin and, in some studies, with heparin.

Four trials ("the 4 P", see p. 153) have evaluated eptifibatide (**PURSUIT** study), lamifiban (**PARAGON** study), and tirofiban (**PRISM** and **PRISM PLUS** studies) started during the 24 hours following an episode of angina at rest (reflecting unstable angina or non-Q-wave myocardial infarction). All patients also received aspirin. Depending on the study, the GP IIb/IIIa receptor inhibitor was sometimes coprescribed with heparin and compared with heparin. The overall results of these 4 studies, which included a total of approximately 18,000 patients, demonstrated the beneficial effect of GP IIb/IIIa receptor inhibitors, which reduced the mortality and risk of myocardial infarction. The positive result, although more marked during the first week, persisted at the end of the first month with 5 lives saved per 1,000 treated patients and 16 deaths or myocardial infarctions avoided per 1,000 treated patients. Although the overall bleeding risk was slightly increased, no excess of cerebral hemorrhages was observed.

● **Direct thrombin inhibitors have been demonstrated to be effective.**

Unlike heparin, hirudin very specifically inhibits the action of thrombin. It also ensures a more stable degree of anticoagulation.

The **GUSTO IIb** trial (see p. 154) was conducted in more than 12,000 patients, 2/3 of whom presented with unstable angina or non-Q-wave myocardial infarction. All patients received aspirin. Hirudin, vs heparin, provided a modest beneficial effect, which only concerned the reduction of myocardial infarction on the 30th day. Hirudin also increased the bleeding rate.

In the **OASIS** study (*Circulation* 1997;96:769-777), which included 909 patients, hirudin gave more favorable results than heparin, by reducing the combined incidence of death, myocardial infarction, or refractory angina on the 7th day and at 6 months. These data were confirmed by the **OASIS 2** study (*Lancet* 1999;353:429-438), which randomized 10,141 patients: lepirudin (recombinant hirudin), vs heparin, significantly decreased the combined rate of death or myocardial infarction at the 72nd hour and on the 7th day by about 20%. The need for a revascularization procedure and the incidence of heart failure were also decreased by hirudin. These results were obtained with an increase of major bleeding. Persistence of the benefit of hirudin after the acute episode remains to be demonstrated.

In contrast, inogatran did not provide any benefit compared to heparin in the 1,209 patients of the **TRIM** study (*Eur Heart J* 1997;18:1416-1425).

Myocardial revascularization

Although antithrombotic and antianginal medical treatment is usually able to stabilize the clinical symptoms, myocardial revascularization retains two main indications: refractory angina during hospitalization which requires urgent revascularization and, more frequently, persistence of myocardial ischemia on exertion beyond the acute period, related to the fact that rupture of the plaque responsible for the episode of unstable angina induced worsening of the pre-existing stenosis.

Although surgery was the first revascularization procedure to be compared with drug treatment, coronary angioplasty has developed an increasingly important place, despite the fact that unstable angina initially constituted one of its classical contraindications. Progress in this technique (especially the development of stents) has clearly allowed a reduction of the immediate risks related to the procedure and to subsequent restenosis. These improvements have led some authors to advocate systematic coronary angioplasty at an early stage, in the plaque instability phase, with the praiseworthy objective of shortening the hospital stay and preventing recurrence of the clinical syndrome. However, the justification for this so-called aggressive strategy has yet to be demonstrated.

Current state of knowledge

 Urgent myocardial revascularization must be considered in refractory unstable angina.

Refractory angina is defined as persistence of the clinical syndrome for more than 24 to 48 hours after introduction of optimal drug treatment combining aspirin, heparin, IV nitrates, beta-blocker, and possibly calcium channel blocker. Refractory angina has become rare. In 90 to 95% of cases, medical treatment is sufficient to stabilize the clinical syndrome. Except in the emergency situation of refractory angina, it is preferable to wait several days before performing coronary angioplasty, when this strategy has been adopted as the routine procedure.

 Prophylactic use of a thrombolytic agent must be avoided during coronary angioplasty, as it increases the complications related to the procedure.

This was the conclusion reached by the **TAUSA** study (*Circulation* 1994;90:69-77), which included 469 patients receiving aspirin and heparin, and treated with coronary angioplasty during the first 7 days of hospitalization for unstable angina or following early post-myocardial infarction recurrent angina. Compared to placebo, intracoronary thrombolysis (urokinase) combined with coronary angioplasty increased the incidence of acute coronary occlusion (10.2% vs 4.3%), the need for emergency surgery (5.2% vs 2.1%) and early ischemic recurrence (9.9% vs 3.4%).

3 **GP IIb/IIIa receptor inhibitors improve the prognosis of patients treated by coronary angioplasty**

The risk of acute coronary occlusion and subsequent clinical events (death, myocardial infarction, and emergency revascularization) related to coronary angioplasty is higher in unstable angina than in stable angina.

Five large-scale trials have evaluated GP IIb/IIIa receptor inhibitors associated with coronary balloon angioplasty (see pp. 151 and 152).

● Two studies (**EPIC** and **CAPTURE**) tested abciximab and another study (**RESTORE**) tested tirofiban during high-risk coronary angioplasty (especially in the context of unstable angina). In the two studies evaluating abciximab, the beneficial effect of the GP IIb/IIIa receptor inhibitor on a composite criterion (death, myocardial infarction, myocardial revascularization) was significant at 30 days. It remained significant at 3 years in the **EPIC** study, but was no longer apparent at 6 months in the **CAPTURE** study. The main difference between these two protocols concerned the abciximab infusion, which preceded coronary angioplasty by 18 to 24 hours and was stopped rapidly after coronary angioplasty in the **CAPTURE** study, while it was started just before and continued for 12 hours after the procedure in the **EPIC** study. In the **RESTORE** study, tirofiban decreased the combined risk of death, myocardial infarction, or revascularization on the 2nd and 7th day, but the beneficial effect was no longer observed on the 30th day.

● Two other trials, **IMPACT II** and **EPILOG**, evaluated eptifibatide and abciximab, respectively, in elective coronary angioplasty (generally associated with a low risk). The benefit of GP IIb/IIIa receptor inhibitors was very significant on the 30th day in the **EPILOG** study, which also showed that high doses of heparin were unnecessary. In the **IMPACT II** study, the reduction of cardiac events was significant 24 hours after the procedure, but not at 30 days.

What has been established, but is now possibly obsolete

 After the acute phase, surgery (vein bypass graft) improves the prognosis, compared to medical treatment, but only in the case of three-vessel disease or left ventricular dysfunction.

The **Veterans Administration** study (*Circulation* 1989;80:1176-1189), which included 468 men under the age of 70 years, showed that surgery, compared to medical treatment, significantly improved the 5-year survival, but only in patients with three-vessel disease (89% vs 76%) or alteration of left ventricular function (86% vs 73%). Overall, surgery reduced the incidence of symptoms and rehospitalization, at least for the first few years. However, it did not modify the nonfatal myocardial infarction rate (or the 3-year survival, regardless of the subgroup considered), because of a high incidence of perioperative myocardial infarction (11.7%). It should be noted that one-half of patients initially treated medically were subsequently operated over a 10-year period.

The practical implications of the conclusions of this study, conducted during the 1970s, are limited because it does not take into account the progress in revascularization surgery (especially arterial bypass grafts and myocardial protection) and medical treatment.

2 Following the acute phase, coronary angioplasty (balloon dilatation) is equivalent to surgery in terms of mortality and medium-term risk of myocardial infarction.

In fact, no studies have been specifically devoted to comparison of the two revascularization techniques in patients presenting an episode of unstable angina. In the two main trials comparing coronary angioplasty and coronary artery bypass graft, i.e. the **RITA** (*Lancet* 1993;341:573-580) and **CABRI** (*Lancet* 1995;346: 1179-1184) studies, which each included more than 1,000 patients, only 59% of patients in the first study and 15% in the second study presented angina at rest or unstable angina. The Argentine **ERACI** study (*J Am Coll Cardiol* 1993;22:1060-1067) provided more interesting results, as 83% of the study population (unfortunately small: only 127 patients) presented unstable angina.

In any case, the results of these various studies are concordant and are well summarized in two meta-analyses. That published by **Pocock** (*Lancet* 1995;346:1184-1189) concerned 3,371 patients with single- or multi-vessel coronary disease, recruited into 8 trials including the **RITA**, **CABRI**, and **ERACI** studies, but also the **Toulouse trial** (*Circulation* 1992;86 suppl. I:I-372), the **EAST** study (*N Engl J Med* 1994;331:1044-1059), the **Lausanne trial** (*Lancet* 1994;343:1449-1453), the **GABI** study (*N Engl J Med* 1994; 331:1037-1043) and the **MASS** study (*J Am Coll Cardiol* 1995;26: 1600-1605). The meta-analysis by **Sim** (*Am J Cardiol* 1995;76: 1025-1029) was based on 2,943 patients, exclusively with multi-vessel disease, included in 5 trials: **ERACI, RITA, GABI, EAST**, and **CABRI**.

These two meta-analyses concluded on the absence of any difference between coronary angioplasty and coronary artery bypass graft in terms of hospital mortality, mortality during follow-up (ranging from 1 to 5 years, depending on the study) and the combined incidence of death and nonfatal myocardial infarction. During the first year, surgery was more effective to eliminate angina and to decrease the incidence of repeat revascularization, because of the high restenosis rate after coronary angioplasty. The cost of the coronary angioplasty strategy, initially lower, therefore became equivalent to the cost of the surgical strategy after 2 years.

The implication of the conclusions of these studies is limited by the highly selective nature of the patients (exclusion of the most seriously ill patients), insufficient follow-up, and almost complete absence of stents and new antithrombotics during coronary angioplasty.

3 **An early invasive strategy (based on systematic coronary angiography and revascularization whenever possible) does not improve the prognosis compared to a conservative approach.**

This was the conclusion of the **TIMI IIIB** study (*Circulation* 1994;89:1545-1556), which included 1,473 patients within 24 hours of ischemic chest discomfort, considered to represent unstable angina or non-Q-wave myocardial infarction. One of the arms of the trial was a randomization between an early invasive strategy (coronary angiography between the 18th and 48th hour followed by coronary angioplasty or bypass graft depending on coronary anatomy) and a conservative strategy, in which coronary angiography and myocardial revascularization were considered only in the case of failure of medical treatment for the first 6 weeks (spontaneous ischemic recurrence or moderate-to-severe exertional angina or positive stress test performed at the end of hospitalization and at the 6th week).

Compared to the conservative strategy, the invasive strategy did not decrease the combined incidence of death, myocardial infarction, and positive stress test at the 6th week (16.2% vs 18.1%) and did not modify the frequency and severity of angina. However, it reduced the duration of the initial hospitalization as well as the number of rehospitalizations and, in patients over the age of 65, decreased the cumulative rate of death or myocardial infarction (7.9% vs 14.8%).

More recently, the **VANQWISH** study (*N Engl J Med* 1998;338: 1785-1792), which used a similar protocol to that applied in the **TIMI IIIB** study in 920 patients with non-Q-wave myocardial infarction, demonstrated a harmful effect of the early invasive strategy. Compared to the conservative strategy, the early invasive strategy increased the hospital mortality (4.5% vs 1.3%), and the mortality at one month (5% vs 2%) and at one year (12.6% vs 7.9%). It also prolonged the length of hospital stay (9.5 days vs 8.2 days). Approximately 1/3 of patients initially treated medically subsequently required myocardial revascularization during the follow-up period.

At the present time, the two strategies appear to be equivalent based on the results of the **OASIS** study registry (*Lancet* 1998;352: 507-514). This study included almost 8,000 consecutive patients recruited in 6 different countries with coronary angiography rates varying from 15 to 60% and myocardial revascularization rates varying from 6 to 36%. The cumulative rates of cardiovascular mortality or myocardial infarction at 7 days and 6 months were not significantly different between the various countries (9 to 12% at 6 months). The risk of cerebrovascular accident at 6 months was increased in countries in which the invasive strategy was widely adopted, but, on the contrary, the refractory angina rate at 7 days and readmissions for unstable angina at 6 months were decreased.

It would be particularly interesting to conduct a similar study testing recent therapeutic progress, including new antithrombotics and intracoronary stents. The ongoing **RITA III** and **FRISC II** studies

(20th session of the European Society of Cardiology, 1998) may possibly provide more conclusive results in favor of one of these two strategies, invasive or conservative.

Unresolved questions

● **Should a conservative strategy be preferred, which, by using GP IIb/IIIa receptor inhibitors as early as possible, should reduce the indications for coronary angiography and myocardial revascularization?**

The **GUSTO IV** study, which should include 4,500 patients, is evaluating immediate IV infusion of abciximab for 24 or 48 hours with the recommendation to avoid coronary angiography.

● **Or, on the contrary, should an early invasive strategy be systematically adopted, under the protection of powerful antiplatelet treatment to decrease the complications of coronary angioplasty?**

● **What are the respective places of stents and antiplatelet drugs during high-risk coronary angioplasty?**

Stents and antiplatelet drugs both decrease the acute complications of coronary angioplasty. Although stents have reduced the restenosis rate compared to conventional coronary angioplasty, some authors believe that GP IIb/IIIa receptor inhibitors exert similar effects. In the **EPISTENT** study (*Lancet* 1998;352:87-92), which randomized 2,399 patients undergoing coronary angioplasty, abciximab (IV infusion started just before the procedure and continued for 12 hours) decreased stent-related complications. The combined rate of death, myocardial infarction, or emergency revascularization at 30 days was significantly decreased when abciximab was combined with stenting (5.3%) or balloon coronary angioplasty (6.9%) compared to stenting without abciximab (10.8%). The benefit of abciximab was observed regardless of the patient's clinical presentation, especially in patients treated for unstable angina present for less than 48 hours, which represented 35% of all inclusions in this study.

● **What is the cost-efficacy ratio of GP IIb/IIIa receptor inhibitors?**

Although the initial cost of a single treatment is high (approximately 8,000 French Francs for abciximab), the first economic analyses tend to be in favor of a reduction of the total cost when the improvement of the clinical result and reduction of rehospitalizations and myocardial revascularizations are taken into account.

● **How can the group of high-risk patients likely to obtain a real benefit from GP IIb/IIIa receptor inhibitors be precisely defined?**

In the **CAPTURE** study, abciximab was only shown to be effective in the case of elevated troponin T during the first 36 hours of unstable angina (71st session of the American Heart Association, 1998).

● **What are the optimal dose and duration of intravenous GP IIb/IIIa receptor inhibitor treatment and to what degree should heparin, which can increase the bleeding rate, be associated with these drugs?**

● **Should GP IIb/IIIa receptor inhibitor treatment be continued orally?**

Plaque instability and hypercoagulability are known to persist for several weeks after starting treatment (*J Am Coll Cardiol* 1996;27: 964-976), which could explain the progressive attenuation of the beneficial effects of GP IIb/IIIa receptor inhibitors administered exclusively *via* the IV route, reported in several studies. Many ongoing trials are evaluating oral GP IIb/IIIa receptor inhibitors administered for several weeks, either following IV treatment or even in the place of IV treatment.

The preliminary results are encouraging. For example, in the **ORBIT** study (*Circulation* 1997;96 suppl. I:I-385), which included 549 patients (60% following an episode of unstable angina), xemilofiban prescribed orally after coronary angioplasty and continued for one month, tended to reduce the incidence of cardiac events at 3 months, vs placebo. However, the clinical benefit of xemilofiban was not confirmed by the **EXCITE** study, which was prematurely stopped. Similarly, orbofiban gave disappointing results in the **OPUS TIMI 16** study, which had to be stopped prematurely because of an excess mortality in one of the treatment groups (71st session of the American Heart Association, 1998).

New antithrombotic agents

Unstable angina is associated with non-negligible morbidity and mortality, despite the use of heparin, aspirin, and anti-ischemic drugs. In the TIMI IIIB study, the 6-week myocardial infarction and mortality rates were 5.4% and 2.4%, respectively. This explains the development of antithrombotic agents more powerful than aspirin and heparin in this disease, which is highly dependent on fibrin and platelet phenomena.

● **GP IIb/IIIa receptor inhibitors associated with coronary angioplasty.**

The American **EPIC** study (*N Engl J Med* 1994;330:956-961 and *JAMA* 1997;278:479-484), conducted in 2,099 patients, evaluated the effects of abciximab (IV bolus only or bolus followed by continuous infusion) started one hour before coronary angioplasty at high-risk of ischemic complications because the patients were treated for acute myocardial infarction or unstable angina (893 patients) or because the coronary anatomy predisposed to such complications (1,206 patients). Abciximab (bolus followed by continuous infusion), vs placebo, significantly reduced the incidence of nonfatal myocardial infarction and emergency myocardial revascularization at one month. The clinical benefit persisted at 6 months and 3 years. However, the GP IIb/IIIa receptor inhibitor was the most effective in the subgroup of 489 patients treated for unstable angina (*J Am Coll Cardiol* 1997;30:149-156), inducing a significant reduction of mortality (1.8% vs 6.6%) and myocardial infarction rate (2.4% vs 11.1%) at the 6th month. In this study, a marked excess of major bleeding (14% vs 7%) was attributed to the use of high doses of heparin, which led to the design of the **EPILOG** trial.

The **EPILOG** trial (*N Engl J Med* 1997;336:1689-1696) included 2,792 patients undergoing urgent or elective coronary angioplasty. Vs placebo, abciximab (bolus followed by infusion, started one hour before coronary angioplasty and continued for 12 hours after the procedure) significantly decreased the combined rate of death, myocardial infarction, or emergency myocardial revascularization on the 30th day (5.3% vs 11.7%) and this result persisted, without attenuation, at one year. The major finding was that low-dose heparin, adjusted to the patient's body weight, was just as effective as high-dose heparin and did not increase the bleeding risk compared to the control group not receiving abciximab. Early withdrawal of the arterial introducer, during the 6 hours following coronary angioplasty, also contributed to a reduction of the bleeding risk.

In the European **CAPTURE** study (*Lancet* 1997;349:1429-1435), which included 1,265 patients with refractory unstable angina, abciximab infusion for 18 to 24 hours before coronary angioplasty, vs placebo, significantly decreased the combined rate of death, myocardial infarction, or emergency revascularization on the 30th day (11.3% vs 15.9%). The reduction of the number of myocardial infarctions was already marked prior to the coronary angioplasty procedure. However, the benefit did not persist at the 6th month. This result, contrasting with that of the EPIC study, could be explained by the rapid discontinuation of abciximab infusion after coronary angioplasty, which was continued for 12 hours after the procedure in the **EPIC** study.

In the **IMPACT II** study (*Lancet* 1997;349:1422-1428), eptifibatide (24-hour infusion), administered in addition to aspirin and heparin, was tested in 4,010 patients undergoing urgent or elective coronary angioplasty. Vs placebo, eptifibatide decreased the incidence of cardiac events at the 24th hour (6.9% vs 9.3%), but the difference was no longer significant on the 30th day (9.5% vs 11.4%). Eptifibatide did not increase the bleeding rate.

In the American **RESTORE** study (*Circulation* 1997;96:1445-1453), conducted in 2,139 patients undergoing coronary angioplasty within 72 hours after unstable angina or acute myocardial infarction, IV administration of tirofiban (bolus of 10 μg/kg over 3 minutes, followed by infusion for 36 hours at a rate of 0.15 μg/kg/minute), vs placebo, in addition to heparin and aspirin, protected against early adverse cardiac events related to occlusive thrombosis [on the 2nd day, the relative reduction of the combined risk of death, myocardial infarction, another revascularization procedure, was 38% ($p \leq 0.005$) with tirofiban; on the 7th day, the relative reduction of the risk was 27% ($p = 0.022$), essentially because of the reduction of the number of myocardial infarctions and repeat angioplasties]. However, the reduction of cardiac events was no longer significant on the 30th day and tirofiban did not reduce the 6-month restenosis rate (*J Am Coll Cardiol* 1998;32:28-34).

 GP IIb/IIIa receptor inhibitors as the first-line treatment of unstable angina.

Pilot studies such as the Canadian study by **Théroux** (*Circulation* 1996;94:899-905) have shown a favorable tendency of GP IIb/IIIa receptor inhibitors on the course of patients treated for unstable angina. These positive results led to the elaboration of several major clinical trials: **PURSUIT, PARAGON, PRISM,** and **PRISM PLUS** trials (the "4P").

The **PURSUIT** study (*N Engl J Med* 1998;339:436-443), which included 10,948 patients with no age limit, treated with heparin and aspirin, showed that IV eptifibatide, administered within 24 hours of the onset of chest pain (initial bolus of 180 µg/kg followed by infusion of 1.3 or 2.0 µg/kg/minute for at least 72 hours), vs placebo, significantly decreased the incidence of death or myocardial infarction on the 30th day (14.2% vs 15.7%). This absolute reduction of 1.5% was observed by the 96th hour and persisted on the 7th day. Although an excess bleeding rate was observed with eptifibatide, cerebral hemorrhages were not more frequent.

In the **PARAGON** study (*Circulation* 1998;97:2386-2395), conducted in 2,282 patients with unstable angina and receiving aspirin, IV lamifiban (1 or 5 µg/minute) did not provide any significant beneficial effect on the 30th day vs heparin. However, a 33% reduction of the death or myocardial infarction rate was observed at the 6th month in patients treated with low-dose lamifiban, particularly in combination with heparin, and in diabetics (*Circulation* 1997;96 suppl. I:I-474).

In the **PRISM** study (*N Engl J Med* 1998;338:1498-1505), which included 3,232 patients with unstable angina or non-Q-wave myocardial infarction, tirofiban (by continuous infusion for 48 hours), vs heparin, significantly decreased the combined rate of refractory angina, myocardial infarction, or death at the 48th hour (3.8% vs 5.6%) and the mortality rate at 30 days (2.3 vs 3.6%), without no apparent increase of the bleeding rate.

In the **PRISM PLUS** study (*N Engl J Med* 1998;38:1488-1497), which included 1,915 patients, tirofiban, combined with heparin, was more effective than heparin used alone, by significantly reducing the rate of death, myocardial infarction, or refractory angina on the 7th day (12.9% vs 17.9%). The benefit persisted on the 30th day and at the 6th month and the major bleeding rate was only slightly increased. This study was stopped prematurely for the group treated with tirofiban alone (345 patients) due to an excess mortality on the 7th day compared to the group treated with heparin alone (4.6% vs 1.1%).

On the basis of these 4 studies, which recruited almost 18,000 patients, it can be concluded on the beneficial effect of GP IIb/IIIa receptor inhibitors, marked by a significant 1.6% reduction in the absolute risk of death and myocardial infarction at 30 days (or 1 death prevented per 200 treated patients), at the cost of a slightly increased bleeding rate, but with no excess cerebral hemorrhages.

●   **Direct thrombin inhibitors.**

The **GUSTO IIb** trial (*N Engl J Med* 1996;335:775-782) included 12,142 patients treated with aspirin for an acute coronary syndrome, either myocardial infarction (ST elevation in 4,131 patients) or unstable angina or non-Q-wave myocardial infarction (absence of ST elevation in 8,011 patients). Compared to heparin (IV bolus of 5,000 U followed by infusion of 1000 U/hour for 3 to 5 days), hirudin (0.1 mg/kg bolus, followed by infusion of 0.1 mg/kg/hour for 3 to 5 days) significantly decreased the rate of death or myocardial infarction at the 24th hour (1.3% vs 2.1%), but the benefit was no longer significant at the 30th day (8.9% vs 9.8). Hirudin did not modify the mortality (4.5% vs 4.7%), but reduced the incidence of myocardial infarction at 30 days (5.4% vs 6.3%). This modest benefit was observed in the unstable angina group and in the Q-wave myocardial infarction group. Although hirudin did not worsen the major bleeding rate, it nevertheless increased the moderate bleeding rate.

Hirulog, a synthetic peptide, has only been extensively evaluated in unstable angina in combination with coronary angioplasty in the **HASI** study (*N Engl J Med* 1995;333:764-769), which included 4,098 patients. Hirulog, vs high-dose heparin, did not modify the incidence of the main events at 6 months, but decreased the major bleeding rate.

Unstable angina: Braunwald's classification
(*Circulation* 1989;80:410-414)

● Severity of the clinical features

  Class I   • *Severe de novo or crescendo exertional angina*

  Class II   • *Subacute angina at rest:* pain during the previous month, but absent during the last 48 hours

  Class III • *Acute angina at rest:* pain during the previous 48 hours

● Clinical context

  Class A   • *Unstable angina secondary* to extracoronary disease (fever, anemia, hypotension, tachyarrhythmia, hyperthyroidism, respiratory insufficiency.)

  Class B   • *Primary unstable angina:* absence of predisposing extracoronary disease

  Class C   • *Post-myocardial infarction angina:* appearing within the first 2 weeks of the acute phase of myocardial infarction

● Electrocardiographic changes

  ST-T abnormalities present or absent during the painful episode

● Intensity of treatment

  Degree 1   • *Absent or minimal* treatment at the time of onset of unstable angina

  Degree 2   • *Satisfactory* treatment (triple combination antianginal therapy) at the time of onset of unstable angina

  Degree 3   • *Maximal* treatment (triple combination antianginal therapy including IV nitrates) not preventing persistence of unstable angina

Acute myocardial infarction

Myocardial infarction remains a serious disease. It is estimated to be responsible for 5,000 prehospital deaths and 7,000 hospital deaths per year in France. The factors of poor prognosis on the initial assessment have barely changed over the last 30 years; they include mainly advanced age, hypotension, congestive heart failure, tachycardia, anterior myocardial infarction and a history of previous myocardial infarction.

Myocardial infarction is due to occlusive coronary thrombosis in more than 90% of cases. Already suspected by **Herrick** *(JAMA 1912;59:2015-2019), the presence of coronary thrombosis was really only confirmed by the studies by* **Falk** *(Br Heart J 1983;50;127-132),* **Davies** *(Br Heart J 1985; 53:363-369) and* **Dewood** *(N Engl J Med 1986;315:417-421), which showed that this thrombosis was secondary to rupture of an atherosclerotic plaque, generally protruding only slightly into the coronary lumen, but which suddenly becomes unstable; fissuring of the plaque triggers the thrombogenic response of the subendothelial matrix exposed to blood cells.*

Early restoration of coronary perfusion limits the extent of myocardial necrosis, preserves left ventricular function, and improves the prognosis. It has decreased the hospital mortality from 25-30% (regardless of age), before the age of thrombolysis, to approximately 15%, at the present time.

During the first 12 hours, treatment must therefore focus on reopening of the occluded artery by means of IV thrombolysis or coronary angioplasty. Early introduction of treatment is the best guarantee of improvement of the prognosis.

Intravenous thrombolysis

Thrombolysis improves the prognosis, compared to placebo or conventional treatment.

This has been extensively demonstrated with various fibrinolytic agents in several major clinical trials (see pp. 191 to 194): the **GISSI 1** (*Lancet* 1986;1:397-402) and **ISIS 2** (*Lancet* 1988;2:349-360) trials for streptokinase, **ASSET** (*Lancet* 1988;2:525-530) trial for tPA (tissue plasminogen activator), **AIMS** study (*Lancet* 1990;335:427-431) for APSAC (anisoylated plasminogen streptokinase activator complex). Their respective efficacy on coronary reperfusion and improvement of the prognosis has been the subject of a large number of comparative trials (see pp. 195 to 197).

Current state of knowledge

The degree of efficacy of thrombolysis, which varies according to the patient group considered, was evaluated in the meta-analysis by the FTT collaborative group (*Lancet* 1994;343:311-322), based on 9 studies including a total of 58,600 patients.

1 **IV thrombolysis decreases the mortality of patients treated during the first 12 hours of myocardial infarction when the initial ECG shows ST elevation or bundle branch block.**

The absolute benefit at the 5th week is 30 lives saved per 1,000 patients treated before the 6th hour and 20 lives saved per 1,000 patients treated between the 6th hour and the 12th hour (see p. 202). Several studies (**GISSI 1, ISIS 2, AIMS**) have demonstrated persistence of the beneficial effect at one year and beyond.

2 **The beneficial effect is proportionally greater when thrombolysis is started rapidly after onset of the symptoms.**

The absolute gain is 35 lives saved per 1,000 patients treated within the 1st hour, 30% between the 2nd and 3rd hour, 27% between the 4th and 6th hour, and 21% between the 7th and 12th hour. In the meta-analysis by **Boersma** (*Lancet* 1996;348: 771-775), the declining relationship between benefit and the delay before thrombolysis was not linear, but exponential with 65, 37, and 26 lives saved per 1,000 patients treated at the 1st, 2nd, and 3rd hour of myocardial infarction, respectively. The maximal reduction of mortality therefore represented 50% in the **GISSI 1** study in patients treated during the 1st hour of myocardial infarction. These figures argue in favor of the development of prehospital thrombolysis (see p. 201).

3 **The benefit of thrombolysis is significant regardless of age (see p. 199), gender, blood pressure, heart rate, presence or absence of a history of myocardial infarction or diabetes mellitus.**

Thrombolysis is all the more effective in high-risk patients.

Although the relative reduction of mortality, approximately 20%, varies only slightly in the various subgroups analysed, the same does not apply to the absolute benefit, expressed in number of lives saved, which has been shown to be greater in patients with a spontaneously high risk. The number of lives saved per 1,000 treated patients is 49 in the presence of bundle branch block, 37 in the case of anterior myocardial infarction (vs 8 in the case of inferior myocardial infarction), 27 in patients aged 65 to 74 years (vs 11 in patients younger than 55), 62 when SBP was < 100 mm Hg, 33 when heart rate was ≥ 100 b.p.m. (vs 13 when heart rate was < 80 b.p.m.), and 37 in the presence of diabetes (vs 15 in the absence of diabetes).

5 **Thrombolysis is responsible for a slightly increased risk of major bleeding.**

The excess incidence of bleeding is 0.7% for noncerebral hemorrhages and 0.4% for hemorrhagic cerebrovascular accidents. The excess of 4 cerebral hemorrhages is observed on the day of thrombolysis or the following day. It is responsible for: two deaths, one cerebrovascular accident with moderate or severe sequelae and one cerebrovascular accident with no sequelae. These early hemorrhages partly explain the excess mortality observed on the 1st day of thrombolysis, but this is largely counterbalanced by the very marked benefit obtained with treatment between the 2nd and 35th day.

Simoons identified 4 factors predictive of cerebral hemorrhage after thrombolysis: age > 65 years, weight < 70 kg, presence of hypertension on admission and the use of tPA. The presence of these 4 factors increases the risk from 0.75% to 3.5%.

6 **tPA is currently the best thrombolytic agent because it restores coronary perfusion more rapidly and more completely (see pp. 190 and 195).**

(see pp. 190 and 195).

Unresolved questions

 Which patients could benefit from thrombolysis after the 12th hour?

Very late thrombolysis, performed between the 12th and 18th hour of myocardial infarction, provides an absolute benefit of approximately 10 lives saved per 1,000 treated patients. However, this result was not significant in the 9,000 patients included in the meta-analysis by the **FTT collaborative group**. Systematic thrombolysis can therefore not be recommended after the 12th hour, especially as the early treatment-related excess mortality appears to be higher in the case of late treatment.

 Can the indications of thrombolysis be extended to subendocardial myocardial infarction?

Thrombolysis has not been shown to be effective in the absence of ST elevation or bundle branch block. In view of the small number of patients, a large-scale trial needs to be conducted, especially in cases of myocardial infarction with ST depression, which represent a high-risk patient group.

 Is thrombolysis ineffective in cardiogenic shock?

It is usually accepted that cardiogenic shock requires treatment by primary coronary angioplasty, although no large-scale randomized study has compared coronary angioplasty and thrombolysis in this indication. In the meta-analysis by the **FTT collaborative group**, the spontaneous mortality in patients with SBP < 100 mm Hg and heart rate > 100 b.p.m. was greater than 60% and consequently fairly similar to that of cardiogenic shock. In this very high-risk group, thrombolysis prevented 73 deaths per 1,000 treated patients, but the benefit was not significant because of the small number of patients concerned. The ongoing **TACTICS** and **SHOCK** studies are designed to evaluate thrombolysis (alone or combined with counterpulsation), coronary angioplasty and emergency bypass grafts in this indication.

 What is the mechanism for the early excess mortality related to thrombolysis?

The excess mortality (approximately 5 additional deaths per 1,000 treated patients) observed during the first 2 days of thrombolysis, cannot be explained by cerebral hemorrhages alone. The **GISSI I** and **ISIS 2** studies suggested an excess of cardiac rupture, with a higher incidence when treatment was started late (**Honan,** *J Am Coll Cardiol* 1990;16:359-367). The mechanism of cardiac rupture, involving reperfusion lesions, is probably multifactorial: arrhythmia, stunned myocardium, microvascular lesions, and intramyocardial bleeding.

● **How can the results of thrombolysis be improved?**

By the development of prehospital thrombolysis.

The major advantage of thrombolysis resides in the simplicity of its administration, which allows it to be started at the patient's home. Studies of prehospital thrombolysis have shown that this strategy improves the prognosis by shortening the time to introduction of treatment by approximately one hour (see p. 201). It should be noted that prehospital thrombolysis was not assessed in the comparative trials concluding on the superiority of primary coronary angioplasty. Ongoing studies, such as the French **CAP-TIM** study (*Arch Mal Cœur Vaiss* 1998;91(II):33-38) and the American **AIR-PAMI** study, are designed to compare prehospital thrombolysis and primary coronary angioplasty.

By more effective pharmacological treatment to restore coronary perfusion.

The most efficient thrombolytic agent regimen (accelerated-dose tPA) ensures optimal early reperfusion in only one half of patients. New thrombolytic agents and combinations of thrombolytic agents, thrombin inhibitors, and antiplatelet agents are currently being evaluated in a large number of clinical trials. Although it appears relatively easy to increase the coronary reperfusion rate, drug combinations are limited by the increased risk of hemorrhagic complications. We will successively consider the new thrombolytic agents, direct thrombin inhibitors, and GP IIb/IIIa receptor inhibitors.

● *New thrombolytic agents*

Pro-urokinase (saruplase) was equivalent to streptokinase in the **COMPASS** mortality equivalence trial (*J Am Coll Cardiol* 1998; 31:487-493), which included 3,089 patients. In the **BIRD** study (20th session of the European Society of Cardiology, 1998), which randomized 2,400 patients, a single bolus of saruplase was just as safe and effective as the usual administration protocol of a bolus injection followed by IV infusion.

The **TIMI 10B** (*Circulation* 1997;96 suppl. I:I-330) and **ASSENT 1**

(19th session of the European Society of Cardiology, 1997) studies showed TNK-tPA to be very similar to accelerated-dose tPA in terms of coronary reperfusion and safety profile. The **ASSENT 2** mortality study, which should include 16,500 patients, is designed to demonstrate that a single bolus of TNK-tPA gives equivalent results to those of accelerated-dose tPA.

nPA (lanoteplase), compared to tPA, increased the coronary reperfusion rate in the **In-TIME I** trial (*Eur Heart J* 1997;18 suppl.:454). Mortality studies are currently underway, such as the **In-TIME II** equivalence trial, comparing nPA and tPA in 15,000 patients.

Lastly, staphylokinase, evaluated in the **STAR** study, could be superior to tPA in terms of coronary reperfusion.

● *Overall, direct thrombin inhibitors combined with thrombolysis have proved to be disappointing.*

Hirudin was compared to heparin in three preliminary trials, **TIMI 9A** (*Circulation* 1994;90:1624-1630), **GUSTO IIa** (*Circulation* 1994;90:1631-1637), and **HIT III** (*Circulation* 1994;90:1638-1642), which had to be discontinued because of the excess bleeding, especially cerebral hemorrhages, attributed to an excessive dosage of the active drugs.

Lower dosages were used in 3,002 patients in the **TIMI 9B** trial (*Circulation* 1996;94:911-921), in 12,142 patients in the **GUSTO IIb** trial (*N Engl J Med* 1996;335:775-782), and in 1,211 patients in the **HIT IV** trial (*Circulation* 1997;96 suppl. I:I-205). None of these trials demonstrated a clinical benefit of hirudin vs heparin after one month and the bleeding complications were comparable in the two groups.

Similarly, argatroban, evaluated in phase II trials (**AMI** and **ARGA-MI** studies), did not modify the incidence of clinical events, although it increased the tPA-induced coronary reperfusion rate in the **MINT** study (*Circulation* 1997;96 suppl. I:I-331).

Hirulog, a synthetic peptide, gave more favorable results in the **HERO** study (*Circulation* 1997;96:2155-2161), which included 412 patients thrombolysed by streptokinase. Hirulog, compared to heparin, improved early coronary reperfusion and tended to reduce the combined rate of death, cardiogenic shock or recurrent myocardial infarction at one month.

● *GP IIb/IIIa receptor inhibitors are more promising.*

Although their efficacy has been demonstrated in unstable angina and particularly during high-risk coronary angioplasty (see p. 151), these powerful antiplatelet drugs are still under evaluation in acute myocardial infarction.

Small-scale trials, such as **TAMI 8** with abciximab (*J Am Coll Cardiol* 1993;22:381-389), **PARADIGM** with lamifiban (*J Thrombosis Thrombolysis* 1995;2:165-169), and **IMPACT-AMI** with eptifibatide (*Circulation* 1997;95:846-854), showed that GP IIb/IIIa receptor inhibitors improved the early coronary reperfusion obtained with tPA, without increasing the bleeding rate. The clinical benefit of these products has yet to be confirmed by a large-scale trial, such as **TIMI 14B** and **GUSTO IV**, which will evaluate abciximab combined with low-dose thrombolytic agent. The **SPEED** study, the pilot phase of **GUSTO IV**, conducted in 305 patients, demonstrated that a double bolus of reteplase (2 x 5 mg), combined with abciximab, ensured the best coronary reperfusion rate (63% of TIMI grade 3 flow at 60 to 90 minutes) with a good safety profile.

Primary coronary angioplasty vs thrombolysis

Primary coronary angioplasty is performed as the first-line procedure and replaces thrombolysis to rapidly restore coronary perfusion.

The theoretical advantages of primary coronary angioplasty over thrombolysis are widely acknowledged and should improve the prognosis of acute myocardial infarction. By ensuring a higher coronary reperfusion rate, coronary angioplasty reduces the extent of necrosis and the degree of left ventricular dysfunction. By simultaneously treating the thrombotic occlusion and the underlying atheromatous stenosis, it prevents recurrent ischemia. Coronary angioplasty also decreases the bleeding rate.

Current state of knowledge

 The superiority of primary coronary angioplasty was confirmed by a meta-analysis of 7 trials.

In the meta-analysis by **Michels** (*Circulation* 1995;91:4676-4685), based on 7 trials including a total of 1,145 patients, primary coronary angioplasty, compared to IV thrombolysis, significantly reduced the mortality by 54% (i.e. approximately 40 lives saved per 1,000 treated patients) and the combined rate of death or recurrent myocardial infarction at the 6th week by 57%. These results have raised a number of criticisms:

● the limited sample size in each study (compared to those of thrombolysis studies) emphasizes the difficulty of extending this strategy to a large population.

● the studies were conducted by teams selected on the basis of their coronary angioplasty performance, as reflected by a primary success rate greater than 90% and the absence of delay in performing the procedure, which does not reflect clinical reality.

● none of the studies demonstrated a significant improvement of the prognosis, apart from the **PAMI** study (*N Engl J Med* 1993; 328:673-679) and exclusively in a high-risk patient group, defined by anterior myocardial infarction, age > 70 years or tachycardia > 100 b.p.m. on admission.

● coronary angioplasty was not compared to the optimal thrombolytic agent regimen, i.e. accelerated-dose tPA, as used in the **GUSTO I** trial.

2 **The superiority of coronary angioplasty is less marked when it is performed outside of highly experienced centers.**

This was demonstrated by the publication of two large American registers, the **MITI** register (*N Engl J Med* 1996;335:1253-1260) and the **NRMI 2** register (*J Am Coll Cardiol* 1998;31:1240-1245), in which the rather disappointing results of primary coronary angioplasty were attributed to the delayed introduction of treatment and to the numerous unsuccessful attempts of coronary reperfusion. Recently, the French **USIK** register (*J Am Coll Cardiol* 1997;30:1598-1605) did not reveal any difference in mortality on the 5th day after coronary angioplasty or thrombolysis.

The **GUSTO IIb** trial (*N Engl J Med* 1997;336:1621-1628) provided a clearer definition of the limitations of primary coronary angioplasty in the context of a radical strategy. In this trial, 57 hospitals in 9 countries recruited 1,138 patients, who were randomized between primary coronary angioplasty and accelerated-dose tPA IV thrombolysis. The degree of experience of the participating centers was satisfactory (more than 400 angioplasties per year for 85% of teams and more than 75 angioplasties per year for 85% of practitioners). This study showed a slight benefit of primary coronary angioplasty over thrombolysis since the only significant reduction at 30 days concerned a composite endpoint associating death, recurrent myocardial infarction, and disabling cerebrovascular accident (9.6% vs 13.7%, p = 0.033). Mortality (5.7% vs 7.0%), recurrent myocardial infarctions (4.5% vs 6.5%), and cerebrovascular accidents with sequelae (0.2% vs 0.9%) were not significantly different in the 2 treatment arms. A similar result was obtained when the composite endpoint was evaluated at 6 months (14.1% vs 16.1%; NS). The greater benefit of coronary angioplasty in high-risk patients (according to the definition of the PAMI study) was also not confirmed. The discordance between the results of the GUSTO IIb trial and the more favorable results of earlier studies could be explained by a longer intervention delay (1.9 hour vs 1 hour in the PAMI study) and a lower reperfusion rate (TIMI grade 3 perfusion: 73% vs 95% in the PAMI study).

The meta-analysis by Weaver (*JAMA* 1997;278:2093-2098), based on 10 randomized trials, including the GUSTO IIb study and a total of 2,606 patients, concluded on the superiority of primary coronary angioplasty, which reduced mortality by 33% (absolute reduction of 2.1%) and the risk of nonfatal recurrent myocardial infarction by 47% (absolute reduction of 2.4%). However, a population 5 times greater would be necessary to draw any definitive conclusions.

❸ The choice between thrombolysis and coronary angioplasty must therefore be determined case by case, taking into account the available medical structures and evaluation of the risk-benefit ratio.

Primary coronary angioplasty is superior to IV thrombolysis when the occluded coronary artery can be opened by an experienced team, available 24 hours a day, within one hour after medicalized management of the patient.

At the present time, primary coronary angioplasty therefore cannot be recommended as a routine procedure, because the important point is to restore blood flow in the infarct-related artery as rapidly as possible.

The risk-benefit ratio tends to be in favor of coronary angioplasty in the case of anterior or extensive myocardial infarction, in unstable hemodynamic states and in the case of an increased hemorrhagic risk with thrombolysis (especially in elderly subjects).

Unresolved questions

● **What would be the real cost of a generalized primary coronary angioplasty policy?**

The logistic constraints of primary coronary angioplasty explain why only a minority of patients are currently treated by this technique. According to published studies, the development of primary coronary angioplasty should be based on the creation of specialized centers in order to confirm its real superiority over thrombolysis. The cost of such a radical reorganization of coronary emergency care needs to be thoroughly evaluated.

The fact that primary coronary angioplasty shortens the hospital stay in low-risk patients must also be taken into account, as demonstrated by the **PAMI II** study (*J Am Coll Cardiol* 1998;31: 967-972), which included 471 patients considered to be at low risk because they were 70 years or younger, with single-vessel or two-vessel disease, left ventricular ejection fraction > 0.45, successful coronary angioplasty and without persistent arrhythmia. After randomization, accelerated care (brief stay without monitoring in the intensive care unit and no stress test), compared to conventional care shortened the hospital stay (4.2 ± 2.3 days vs 7.1 ± 4.7 days, $p = 0.0001$) and the cost of hospitalization ($p = 0.002$), without affecting the early and 6-month morbidity and mortality.

● **Can the performance of primary coronary angioplasty be improved?**

Balloon coronary angioplasty at the acute phase of myocardial infarction carries a risk of early reocclusion of about 10 to 15% and a restenosis rate of about 30 to 50%. Successful coronary angioplasty also does not prevent the development of a no-reflow phenomenon, i.e. absent or slowed coronary perfusion despite relief of the obstruction, in 10 to 20% of cases. The mechanism of this phenomenon is probably multifactorial: distal embolization, acute endothelial reperfusion lesion, accumulation of neutrophils.

● **Coronary stents**

Coronary stenting reduces the risk of acute occlusion to less than 3%. This was demonstrated by the French **STENTIM I** register (*J Am Coll Cardiol* 1996;27 suppl. A:68A), in which a stent was successfully implanted in 95% of patients. The procedure was followed by IV heparin therapy for 72 hours, in combination with ticlopidine 500 mg daily for one month and long-term aspirin at a dosage of 100 to 250 mg daily. The justification for the ticlopidine-aspirin combination to prevent occlusive stent thromboses was clearly established by publication of the French register (*Circulation* 1996,94:1519-1527) and the ISAR (*N Engl J Med* 1996;334: 1084-1089), STARS (*Circulation* 1997;96 suppl. I:I-594), and FANTASTIC (*Circulation* 1998;98:I-597-603) studies.

In the meta-analysis by Gibson (*Circulation* 1997;96 suppl. I:I-340), based on 20 non-randomized studies, stenting during primary coronary angioplasty in 1,357 patients was associated with low mortality (2.4%), stent thrombosis (1.5%), and emergency coronary artery bypass grafting (1.3%) rates.

The randomized FRESCO study (*J Am Coll Cardiol* 1998;31:1234-1239), conducted in 150 patients, showed that stenting reduces the combined incidence of ischemic events at 6 months as well as the restenosis or reocclusion rate. The superiority of stenting over balloon coronary angioplasty appears to be confirmed by the Dutch study (*Circulation* 1998;97:2502-2505), which included 227 patients and which revealed a significant reduction of the combined rate of death, recurrent myocardial infarction, or repeat revascularization at the 6th month. In the STENT-PAMI study (47th session of the American College of Cardiology, 1998), which randomized 900 patients, the heparin-coated Palmaz-Schatz stent achieved a larger coronary lumen and a reduction of early ischemic recurrences without modifying the incidence of events on the 30th day. The results of clinical and angiographic follow-up at the 6th month have not yet been published. In addition to these randomized trials, the German ALKK register (*Eur Heart J* 1998;19: 917-921) did not reveal any significant improvement of the prognosis with stenting despite successful implantation in 98% of cases.

Several ongoing trials are evaluating the clinical benefit of stenting in the context of primary coronary angioplasty, including the STENTIM II study in France, the PAMI 3 study in the United States and Europe, and the ESCOBAR study in The Netherlands, whose preliminary results appear to confirm the superiority of stenting over simple balloon coronary angioplasty (*Circulation* 1996;94 suppl. I:I-570).

● **GP IIb/IIIa receptor inhibitors (see p. 151)**

In the **GRAPE** pilot study (*Circulation* 1997;96 suppl. I:I-474), IV administration of abciximab, 45 minutes before planned primary coronary angioplasty, was associated with complete reperfusion in 30% of patients.

In the **RAPPORT** study (*Circulation* 1998;98:734-741), abciximab combined with primary coronary angioplasty decreased the combined rate of death, recurrent myocardial infarction, and emergency revascularization by 70% on the 7th day and 39% at the 6th month, at the cost of an excess of major bleeding (16.6% vs 9.5%), probably facilitated by the high doses of heparin used.

GP IIb/IIIa receptor inhibitors are also being compared to stenting combined with primary coronary angioplasty in the ongoing **CADILLAC** study and French **ADMIRAL** study. The **ERASER** study is more specifically devoted to prevention of stent restenosis by abciximab.

Rescue coronary angioplasty

Rescue coronary angioplasty is designed to palliate the failure of thrombolysis. It must be performed as soon as possible after thrombolysis, within a time limit compatible with limitation of the extent of necrosis.

Current state of knowledge

 Rescue coronary angioplasty probably improves the prognosis of anterior myocardial infarction.

In the **RESCUE** study (*Circulation* 1994;90:2280-2284), which only included 151 patients, coronary angioplasty of the left anterior descending artery, which remained occluded (TIMI grade 0 or 1) after IV thrombolysis, significantly improved left ventricular function compared to a conservative strategy and tended to decrease the mortality on the 30th day (5.1% vs 9.6%, NS). The combined rate of death and severe heart failure on the 30th day was significantly decreased (6.4% vs 16.6%).

Unresolved questions

● The value of rescue coronary angioplasty has yet to be demonstrated in low-risk myocardial infarction and in the case of incomplete coronary perfusion (TIMI grade 2).

● The limitations of rescue coronary angioplasty are the same as those of primary coronary angioplasty.

This strategy is hampered by logistic problems, such as the availability of teams experienced in emergency coronary angioplasty. It implies the need for systematic coronary angiography, in the absence of a reliable early marker of post-thrombolysis coronary reperfusion. Unfortunately, compared to primary coronary angioplasty, it increases the incidence of bleeding at the injection site.

● Is very early rescue coronary angioplasty as effective as primary coronary angioplasty?

This appears to be demonstrated by the **PACT** study (47th session of the American College of Cardiology, 1998), which randomized 606 patients to receive either tPA (IV bolus of 50 mg) or placebo before coronary angiography performed in the context of a primary coronary angioplasty strategy. In the case of complete reperfusion (TIMI 3 flow), patients received a second IV bolus (tPA or placebo), otherwise (TIMI 0, 1 or 2 flow) coronary angioplasty was performed. Compared to placebo, the tPA bolus improved coronary perfusion before coronary angioplasty and the left ventricular ejection fraction verified by angiography on the 5th to 7th day was significantly better in the case of TIMI 3 flow on arrival in the coronary angiography room (62% vs 58% for TIMI grade 3 after coronary angioplasty and 55% in the absence of complete reperfusion). In addition, in patients treated by coronary angioplasty, the clinical outcome on the 30th day was comparable whether they had undergone primary coronary angioplasty (placebo group) or rescue coronary angioplasty (tPA group). These results need to be confirmed by a mortality study.

Adjuvant therapy

Although early reperfusion of the infarct-related artery represents a major advance, other treatments have also contributed to the improvement of the prognosis.

A consensus has been reached in favor of the widest possible use of aspirin, beta-blockers, and angiotensin-converting enzyme inhibitors. The value of heparin, nitrates, and magnesium is much more controversial.

In contrast, there are no valid arguments for the prophylactic use of a calcium channel blocker and lidocaine or for systematic coronary angioplasty of a residual stenosis after successful thrombolysis.

Aspirin

The main mechanism of action of aspirin is cyclo-oxygenase inhibition, which prevents the platelet synthesis of thromboxane A2, thereby reducing platelet aggregation in response to various stimuli. A single dose of at least 160 mg of aspirin is sufficient to induce complete cyclo-oxygenase inhibition in less than one hour when a rapid absorption form (chewing gum) is used. A lower dosage may delay the beneficial effect by several hours. In contrast, maintenance treatment at doses of 75 mg daily has been demonstrated to be pharmacologically and clinically sufficient and, in any case, a daily dosage greater than 300 mg is unnecessary.

Current state of knowledge

 The fundamental value of aspirin, alone or in combination with thrombolysis, has been clearly established since the ISIS 2 study.

The **ISIS 2** study (*Lancet* 1988;2:349-360) was conducted in 17,187 patients with no age limit, recruited within the first 24 hours of acute myocardial infarction, and submitted to successive double randomization: streptokinase vs placebo, then oral aspirin (160 mg daily) vs placebo.

 Aspirin, prescribed for one month, vs placebo, reduced the 5-week cardiovascular mortality by 20%.

This beneficial effect, which represented 25 lives saved per 1,000

treated patients, persisted after several years (*Circulation* 1993;88 suppl. I:I-291). Aspirin also decreased the incidence of recurrent myocardial infarction and nonfatal cerebrovascular accidents by almost 50% (10 recurrent myocardial infarctions and 3 cerebrovascular accidents prevented per 1,000 patients). Continuation of aspirin beyond the first month doubled the initial benefit by preventing an additional 40 deaths, recurrent myocardial infarctions, or cerebrovascular accidents per 1,000 treated patients during the first 4 years (*BMJ* 1994;308:81-106).

3 **The beneficial effects of aspirin and thrombolysis are additive.**

Although the mortality at the 5th week was decreased by 20% with aspirin (9.4% vs 11.8%) and by 23% with streptokinase (9.2% vs 12.0%), the streptokinase-aspirin combination was shown to be the most effective regimen, with a 38% reduction of mortality (8.0% vs 13.2%).

Unresolved questions

 It is still unknown whether the main effect of aspirin is to potentiate thrombolysis, prevent reocclusion or limit the microvascular effects of platelet activation.

In the meta-analysis by **Roux** (*J Am Coll Cardiol* 1992;19:671-677), based on 32 trials including almost 5,000 thrombolysed patients, aspirin significantly reduced the coronary reocclusion rate (11% vs 25%, $p < 0.001$) and decreased the incidence of recurrent ischemia (25% vs 41%, $p < 0.001$). This beneficial action was observed regardless of the thrombolytic agent administered, streptokinase, or tPA.

Heparin

Current state of knowledge

 Before the thrombolysis era, heparin decreased the early morbidity and mortality.

Although no large-scale trial has assessed the value of heparin used alone (i.e. without aspirin or thrombolytic agent), the meta-analysis by Collins (*BMJ* 1996;313:652-659), based on 21 small studies including a total of less than 6,000 patients, showed a beneficial effect of heparin during the hospital period in terms of mortality (11.4% vs 14.9%, p = 0.002), cerebrovascular accidents (1.1% vs 2.1%, p = 0.0 1), recurrent myocardial infarctions (6.7% vs 8.2%; NS), and pulmonary embolisms (2.0% vs 3.8%, p < 0.001), at the expense of an excess of severe bleeding (1.9% vs 0.9%, p = 0.01).

Unresolved questions

 Should heparin be associated with thrombolysis?

As the efficacy of aspirin was clearly demonstrated in the **ISIS 2** study, the current issue is whether or not heparin must be associated with aspirin in addition to thrombolysis.

In the **GISSI 2** and **ISIS 3** trials, which included 62,000 patients treated by thrombolysis, heparin was administered by SC injection (12,500 U bid) and introduced late after starting thrombolysis (12 hours in **GISSI 2** and 4 hours in **ISIS 3**). Combined analysis of the results of these two trials showed that the SC heparin-aspirin combination significantly, but only moderately, decreased the early mortality compared to aspirin used alone (6.8% vs 7.3%, i.e. a gain of 5 lives saved per 1,000 treated patients). However, this benefit was only observed during administration of heparin (approximately one week), as the mortality subsequently became identical in the two groups on the 35th day and thereafter.

In the meta-analysis by **Mahaffey** (*Am J Cardiol* 1996;77:551-556), based on 6 trials including 1,735 patients treated by thrombolysis, IV heparin did not provide any major beneficial clinical effect. IV heparin decreased the relative risk of death during the hospital period by 9%, without modifying the incidence of recurrent myocardial infarction and increased the overall hemorrhagic risk. Although these results appear to be independent of the thrombolytic agent used, a number of points need to be mentioned.

● **In combination with streptokinase, heparin can be used *via* the SC or IV routes, but its value has not been formally demonstrated.**

Although the modalities of heparin administration in the **GISSI 2** and **ISIS 3** trials could be considered to be responsible for an underestimation of its beneficial effect, the **GUSTO I** trial showed that this was not the case. In the 20,000 patients treated with streptokinase and aspirin, IV heparin, started immediately (initial bolus of 5,000 U followed by infusion of 1,000 U/hour for at least 48 hours, adjusting the dosage to maintain effective anticoagulation), did not modify the mortality on the 30th day, or the frequency of hemorrhagic cerebrovascular accidents, or the cumulative rate of death or disabling cerebrovascular accident, compared to SC heparin administration (12,500 U bid, started 4 hours after starting thrombolysis and continued for 7 days). In parallel, in the subgroup of patients assessed by angiography (*N Engl J Med* 1993;22:1615-1622), IV heparin, compared to SC heparin, did not improve the early coronary reperfusion rate obtained with streptokinase or the reocclusion rate.

● **Systematic heparin therapy does not appear to be recommanded after thrombolysis by APSAC combined with aspirin.**

This was the conclusion of the **DUCCS 1** study (*J Am Coll Cardiol* 1994;23:11-18), which included 250 patients. IV heparin, started 4 hours after thrombolysis and continued for 4 days, compared to the absence of heparin, did not modify the combined incidence of death, recurrent myocardial infarction, and coronary occlusion and did not improve the coronary reperfusion rate on the 5th day or the left ventricular ejection fraction. On the other hand, it increased the global incidence of hemorrhagic complications, especially potentially fatal complications (4.7% vs 0.8%).

● **Effective IV heparin therapy for 48 hours must be combined with tPA thrombolysis.**

In the **HART** study (*N Engl J Med* 1990;323:1433-1437), which included 205 patients treated by tPA-thrombolysis (100 mg over 3 hours), IV heparin (initial bolus of 5,000 U followed by infusion of 1,000 U/hour) was compared to oral aspirin (80 mg daily). IV heparin, compared to aspirin, increased the coronary reperfusion rate, assessed between the 7th and 24th hour (82% vs 52%, p < 0.0001), although the coronary reperfusion rate was identical on the 7th day.

The **ECSG 6** study (*Br Heart J* 1992;67:122-128) was conducted in 152 patients treated by tPA-thrombolysis and receiving aspirin. Compared to placebo, IV heparin (immediate bolus of 5,000 U followed by continuous infusion of 1,000 U/hour) improved the coronary reperfusion rate, assessed between the 48th and 120th hour (83.4% vs 74.7%).

These studies suggest that low-dose aspirin is not sufficient to prevent early coronary reocclusion after tPA thrombolysis, but that it is at least as effective as heparin in the prevention of late reocclusion. The main objective of early heparin administration is prevention of coronary reocclusion during the first 24 hours. Reocclusions are observed more frequently with tPA than with other thrombolytic agents because of its short plasma half-life, a low systemic fibrinolytic effect, and the paradoxical tPA-induced platelet activation.

● **Low molecular weight heparins, combined with thrombolysis and aspirin, decrease the risk of left intraventricular thrombosis.**

This was the conclusion reached by the **FRAMI** study (*J Am Coll Cardiol* 1997;30:962-969), which included 776 patients with anterior myocardial infarction. Vs placebo, dalteparin SC (150 IU/kg bid during the hospital period) significantly reduced the incidence of left ventricular thrombi detected by echocardiography on the 9th day (14.2% vs 21.9%). However, this result did not affect the risk of arterial embolism, recurrent myocardial infarction, or mortality, and major hemorrhages were more frequent with dalteparin (2.9% vs 0.3%).

Beta-blockers

Beta-blockers inhibit the activity of the sympathetic system, which is increased during acute myocardial infarction. Their anti-ischemic properties are related to the reduction of heart rate, inotropism, and blood pressure, which decreases myocardial oxygen consumption. They exert an antiarrhythmic effect, especially expressed by elevation of the ventricular fibrillation threshold. Their early IV administration decreases the extent of myocardial necrosis, as demonstrated by the **Göteborg Metoprolol Trial** (*Lancet* 1981;2:823-827). They also possess an analgesic effect.

Current state of knowledge

 Before the age of thrombolysis, beta-blockers decreased the early morbidity and mortality.

Two large-scale trials, the **MIAMI** trial and especially the **ISIS 1** trial, as well as the meta-analysis by **Yusuf** based on 27 trials, led to the recommendation of the early use of IV beta-blockers during the acute phase of myocardial infarction.

In the **MIAMI** trial (*Eur Heart J* 1985;6:199-211), which included 5,778 patients within the first 24 hours following myocardial infarction, IV metoprolol (5 mg x 3 every 2 minutes), followed by oral metoprolol (100 mg bid) did not decrease the mortality on the 15th day compared to placebo. However, the study population globally presented a low risk and, in a retrospective analysis, the beta-blocker decreased the mortality by 29% in the patients at greater risk, defined by the presence of at least 3 of the following 8 criteria: age > 60 years, history of myocardial infarction, hypertension, angina, congestive heart failure, diabetes, and treatment with digitalis or diuretics.

The **ISIS 1** trial (*Lancet* 1986;2:57-66), conducted in 16,027 patients randomized at the 5th hour, on average, following acute myocardial infarction, showed that atenolol (5 to 10 mg IV then 100 mg daily orally) significantly decreased the vascular mortality on the 7th day by 14% compared to the control group, and this benefit persisted at one year. It should be noted that the beta-blocker improved the prognosis especially during the first two days, although it increased the need for positive inotropic drugs during this period. Moreover, retrospective analysis of the **ISIS 1** trial also suggests that the beneficial effect of the beta-blocker was essentially related to the prevention of cardiac rupture and ventricular fibrillation.

The meta-analysis by **Yusuf** (*JAMA* 1988;260:2088-2093), based on 27 trials including 27,000 patients, mostly at low risk, showed that beta-blockers induced a significant 13% reduction of hospital mortality, maximal during the first 2 days, as well as a 19% reduction of nonfatal recurrent myocardial infarction and a 16% reduction of resuscitated cardiac arrests.

Unresolved questions

 In the thrombolysis era, when should beta-blockers be introduced?

Although beta-blockers retain all of their indications in the post-myocardial infarction setting, the exact place of their very early use in patients treated by thrombolysis, especially *via* the IV route, has yet to be defined.

The only trial that tried to answer this question was the **TIMI IIB** study (*Circulation* 1991;83:422-437), in which 1,390 patients treated by tPA-thrombolysis and receiving aspirin, were treated with metoprolol, either immediately *via* the IV route (5 mg x 3 followed by 50 to 100 mg bid orally), or later (6th to 8th day) *via* the oral route (50 to 100 mg bid). In this low-risk population, the modalities of administration did not influence the mortality at the 6th day and at the 6th week, but early IV prescription (especially during the first 2 hours following myocardial infarction) significantly decreased recurrent angina (15.4% vs 21.2%) and nonfatal recurrent myocardial infarction (2.3% vs 4.5%) during the first 6 days.

These results were not confirmed by an ancillary study of **GUSTO I** (*J Am Coll Cardiol* 1998;32:634-640), which emphasized the potential danger of using IV beta-blockers after thrombolysis. 75% of the 41,000 patients of this study were treated by atenolol (IV and/or oral) and 44% received the beta-blocker by early IV injection, without randomization. Although the overall mortality on the 30th day was significantly lower in patients treated with beta-blockers, IV administration worsened the prognosis (odds ratio: 1.3; $p = 0.02$) compared to oral beta-blockers introduced after hemodynamic stabilization.

In particular, IV beta-blockers increased the incidence of heart failure, shock, recurrent ischemia, and the need for ventricular pacing.

Although the recommendations of the American College of Cardiology and the American Heart Association (J Am Coll Cardiol 1990;16: 249-292) are in favor of early IV prescription of a beta-blocker in the absence of the usual contraindications (asthma, pulmonary edema, hypotension, bradycardia, or atrioventricular block), especially in the case of sinus tachycardia, tendency to hypertension, and narcotic-refractory pain, the value of IV beta-blocker treatment in patients treated by thrombolysis and its exact place in relation to the other adjuvant treatments (ACE-inhibitors and nitrates) have yet to be defined. Short half-life beta-blockers could be useful in this setting.

Angiotensin-converting enzyme inhibitors

By decreasing the preload and afterload and by preventing neuroendocrine activation, angiotensin-converting enzyme (ACE) inhibitors reduce the extent of myocardial necrosis and the incidence of arrhythmias and prevent left ventricular remodeling. These beneficial effects of ACE-inhibitors during acute myocardial infarction were demonstrated experimentally, then confirmed by clinical trials.

For example, in the **PRACTICAL** study (*Am J Cardiol* 1994;73:1180-1186), captopril, and enalapril, started orally during the first 24 hours (in patients treated by thrombolysis in 70% of cases), improved the ejection fraction and prevented left ventricular dilatation evaluated at the 3rd month.

In the **CATS** study (*Eur Heart J* 1994;15:898-907), oral captopril administered at the same time as thrombolysis in patients with anterior myocardial infarction, reduced the extent of myocardial necrosis, plasma norepinephrine levels, and the frequency of arrhythmias related to coronary reperfusion.

Current state of knowledge

1 In acute myocardial infarction complicated by heart failure or isolated left ventricular dysfunction (left ventricular ejection fraction ≤ 0.40), oral ACE-inhibitors, started late during hospitalization and continued in the long term, very significantly improve the prognosis, saving 42 to 74 lives per 1,000 patients treated for 15 to 42 months.

These results were reported by the **SAVE** (*N Engl J Med* 1992; 327:669-677), **AIRE** (*Lancet* 1993;342:821-828), and **TRACE** (*N Engl J Med* 1995;333:1670-1676) studies, which tested captopril in 2,231 patients (started on average on the 11th day at the initial dose of 6.25 mg, progressively increased to 50 mg tid), ramipril in 2,006 patients (started between the 3rd and 10th day at the initial dose of 2.5 mg, subsequently increased to 10 mg daily) and trandolapril in 1,749 patients (started between the 3rd and 7th day at the initial dose of 1 mg and subsequently increased to 4 mg daily), respectively.

In the **SAVE** study, captopril decreased the mortality by 19% and progression to severe heart failure by 37%, after a follow-up of 42 months.

In the **AIRE** study, at the 15th month, ramipril reduced the mortality by 27% and the risk of developing a first event (death, severe heart failure, myocardial infarction, or cerebrovascular accident) by 19%.

Finally, in the **TRACE** study, trandolapril decreased all cause mortality by 22%, cardiovascular mortality by 25%, sudden death by 24%, and progression to severe heart failure by 29%, with a mean follow-up of 2.2 years.

It should be noted that the beneficial effect of the ACE-inhibitor was observed independently of the other treatments administered (especially thrombolysis, which was used in 33% to 58% of patients depending on the study).

2 In unselected patients with acute myocardial infarction, oral administration of an ACE-inhibitor during the first 24 hours slightly improve the prognosis, by preventing about 5 deaths per 1,000 patients treated for 4 to 6 weeks and this benefit persist at one year.

In the **GISSI 3** study (*Lancet* 1994;343:1115-1122), which included 19,394 patients, oral lisinopril (5 mg then 10 mg daily for 6 weeks) decreased all cause mortality at the 6th week by 12%, even in elderly patients over the age of 70.

In the **ISIS 4** study (*Lancet* 1995;345:669-685), conducted in 58,050 patients, oral captopril (started at an initial dose of 6.25 mg, progressively increased to 50 mg bid) reduced the mortality at one month by 7% and this benefit persisted after one year.

The Chinese **CCS-1** study (*Lancet* 1995;345:686-687), which tested captopril in 13,634 patients, confirmed these results, although the reduction of the one-year mortality was not significant.

The meta-analysis performed by the **ACE-inhibitor Myocardial Infarction collaborative group** (*Circulation* 1998;97:2202-2212), based on the **GISSI 3**, **ISIS 4**, **CCS-1**, and **CONSENSUS II** studies (*N Engl J Med* 1992;327:678-684) and including a total of almost 100,000 patients, concluded that an ACE-inhibitor, started on the day of myocardial infarction and continued for 4 to 6 weeks, prevented 5 deaths per 1,000 treated patients and reduced the risk of heart failure.

Unresolved questions

● **Should ACE-inhibitors be systematically prescribed early in the course of acute myocardial infarction?**

Prescription of an ACE-inhibitor may induce severe hypotension, which may decrease the benefit of successful coronary reperfusion.

The **CONSENSUS II** study (*N Engl J Med* 1992;327:678-684), which included 2,231 unselected patients, half of whom were treated by thrombolysis, was prematurely suspended because enalapril, started on the first day, did not reduce the all cause mortality at the 6th month. This result can be attributed to a significant increase in the incidence of early severe hypotension. However, this study differed from the previous studies by IV administration of the ACE-inhibitor in the beginning of treatment.

When the ACE-inhibitor was administered orally on the first day of myocardial infarction, with progressively increasing doses, in unselected patients treated by thrombolysis in 70% of cases (**GISSI 3** and **ISIS 4** study populations), the main adverse effect was still hypotension (approximately 10% of cases), although it did not appear to have a negative effect on prognosis. The fact that 80% of the benefit in terms of mortality was obtained during the first 7 days argues in favor of the early use of ACE-inhibitors. However, as the benefit of ACE-inhibitors is low in the overall population of unselected myocardial infarction, it is possible that only patients with high-risk myocardial infarction really benefited from treatment. For example, in the **ISIS 4** study, captopril was more effective in patients with a history of myocardial infarction or heart failure (10 lives saved per 1,000 treated patients). The **SMILE** study (*N Engl J Med* 1995;332:80-85), which included 1,556 patients with anterior myocardial infarction, ineligible for thrombolysis, reported similar results. In this high-risk population, oral zofenopril, started during the first 24 hours and continued for 6 weeks, induced a very marked reduction of the one-year mortality (40 lives saved per 1,000 treated patients).

● **Can ACE-inhibitors be replaced by or coprescribed with an angiotensin II AT1 receptor antagonist (see p. 252)?**

Two large-scale ongoing trials have been designed to address this question during the first 10 days after acute myocardial infarction, complicated by congestive heart failure. The **OPTIMAAL** mortality study, which must include 5,000 patients, is comparing losartan (50 mg daily) vs captopril (50 mg tid). The **VALIANT** mortality study, which must include 16,000 patients, is comparing valsartan, captopril, and a combination of the two.

The controversy concerning nitrates

Nitrates decrease myocardial oxygen consumption by reducing the preload (venous vasodilatation), afterload (arterial vasodilatation exclusively at high doses), and wall stress. Vasodilatation of small epicardial arteries can promote the development of collateral vessels and counteracts coronary spasm. Nitroglycerin also has a platelet aggregation inhibitor effect. The studies by **Jugdutt** (*Circulation* 1988;78:906-919) are in favor of a reduction of the extent of myocardial necrosis and improvement of left ventricular function in response to early IV administration of nitroglycerin during the acute phase of myocardial infarction.

Nitrates before the thrombolysis era

A meta-analysis by **Yusuf** (*Lancet* 1988;1:1088-1092) evaluated the effect of IV nitrates (nitroglycerin and sodium nitroprusside). The infusion was started during the first 24 hours following myocardial infarction, was adjusted to decrease systolic blood pressure by 10 to 15% and was generally continued for 24 to 48 hours. IV nitrates decreased mortality by 35% ($p < 0.001$) compared to the control group, but the benefit was particularly marked during the first week and was not maintained thereafter.

Following the publication of the negative results of the **ISIS 4** and **GISSI 3** studies, **Yusuf's** meta-analysis was criticized for being based on 10 already old trials, conducted according to a dubious methodology and on limited sample sizes (30 to 800 patients, i.e. an average of 200 per study).

● **Nitrates in the thrombolysis era**

Two major studies, **GISSI 3** (*Lancet* 1994;343:1115-1122) and **ISIS 4** (*Lancet* 1995;345:669-685) evaluated the effect of nitrates started during the first 24 hours of acute myocardial infarction and continued for 4 to 6 weeks, in patients who were treated by thrombolysis in more than 70% of cases. In the **GISSI 3** study, the nitrate, administered *via* the IV route for 24 hours, followed by the transdermal route, was tested under open-label conditions in a...ost 19,000 patients. In the **ISIS 4** study, the oral nitrate, administered immediately, was compared to placebo in 58,000 patients.

The concordant results of these two large-scale trials were the absence of any favorable effect of nitrates on the mortality at the 5th week and thereafter.

The only positive elements, revealed in the **GISSI 3** study, were a significant 10% reduction of the combined rate of death and left ventricular dysfunction in patients over the age of 70 and in women, and a more marked effect of lisinopril on mortality when nitrates were coprescribed.

The disappointing conclusions of the **GISSI 3** and **ISIS 4** studies, in contradiction with the positive results of the earlier meta-analysis, led to various interpretations.

● Some authors considered that a favorable effect of nitrates could not be excluded, but would only be of limited amplitude and masked by concomitant treatments such as thrombolysis and aspirin.

● According to other authors, a number of biases could have influenced the results of the **GISSI 3** and **ISIS 4** studies, the most obvious being the non-protocol use of a nitrate in more than 50% of patients in the control group, leading to a reduction of the statistical power of these trials. The final result was also assessed on the effect of nitrates at the 5th week, while a possible favorable impact of treatment during the very acute phase of myocardial infarction was not taken into account. A retrospective analysis of the **ISIS 4** study showed a significant reduction of mortality with nitrates during the first 2 days. Similarly, in the **GISSI 3** study, some early complications appeared to be less frequent with nitrates: 20% reduction of cardiogenic shock and ventricular fibrillation, and 50% reduction of septal rupture.

Molsidomine, which has similar vasodilator properties to those of nitrates, has not been shown to be effective. In the **ESPRIM** study (*Lancet* 1994;344:91-97), which included 4,000 patients during the first 24 hours of myocardial infarction, IV linsidomine, followed by oral molsidomine at the 48th hour, did not modify the mortality and incidence of cardiac events during the hospital phase and at one year. As in the **GISSI 3** and **ISIS 4** studies, nitrates were also very frequently used in the placebo group.

● **In conclusion, there is no formal evidence in favor of the systematic use of nitrates during acute myocardial infarction.**

Early IV administration of nitrates can be proposed for analgesic purposes and in certain high-risk groups, such as myocardial infarction complicated by heart failure, extensive anterior myocardial infarction, recurrent myocardial infarctions, and post-myocardial infarction angina, but there is no justification for long-term systematic prescription of oral or transdermal nitrates.

The controversy concerning IV magnesium

Magnesium has many potential beneficial effects: protective effect on the ischemic cell, especially by limiting intracytoplasmic calcium overload, coronary and systemic vasodilatation, antiarrhythmic effect, and platelet aggregation inhibitor effect. Experimental studies suggest that early administration of magnesium during acute myocardial infarction decreases myocardial reperfusion lesions.

IV administration of magnesium during acute myocardial infarction was justified until publication of the ISIS 4 study.

> The meta-analysis by Horner (*Circulation* 1992;86:774-779), based on 8 small trials including a total of 930 patients treated with magnesium, revealed a 54% reduction of mortality (*p* = 0.0006) and a reduction of all arrhythmias, as well as asystoles and electromechanical dissociations. The LIMIT 2 study (*Lancet* 1992;339:1553-1558), conducted in 2,316 patients followed for 28 days, appeared to confirm these results. Vs placebo, IV magnesium sulphate (bolus of 8 mmol over 5 minutes followed by infusion of 65 mmol over 21 hours) significantly decreased all cause mortality by 24% (7.8% vs 10.3%) and the incidence of left ventricular failure by 25%.

● However, the ISIS 4 mega-trial dashed the hopes raised by magnesium.

> One arm of this study (*Lancet* 1995;345:669-685) consisted of open randomization of 58,000 patients, one half receiving IV magnesium sulphate (bolus of 8 mmol over 15 minutes followed by infusion of 72 mmol over 24 hours). Magnesium did not modify the mortality at 5 weeks and one year, but significantly increased the incidence of heart failure, cardiogenic shock, severe hypotension, and episodes of bradycardia. No positive effect on mortality was observed in any of the subgroups analysed.

● The discordant results of the LIMIT 2 and ISIS 4 studies gave rise to a number of controversial discussions.

> They concerned the differences in the study populations (confirmed myocardial infarction in only 65% of patients of the LIMIT 2 study vs 92% in the ISIS 4 study), the more frequent use of thrombolysis in the ISIS 4 study (which could have masked the benefit of magnesium), the slightly higher dosage of magnesium in the ISIS 4 study and especially the shorter delay before administration in the LIMIT 2 study (median: 3 hours after onset of symptoms vs 8 hours in the ISIS 4 study). As retrospective analyses of the various subgroups were not convincing, we can only accept the conclusions of the study with the greatest statistical power.

 The systematic use of IV magnesium therefore cannot be recommended during the acute phase of myocardial infarction.

The **MAGIC** study is designed to evaluate the effects of IV magnesium, started early (before or during thrombolysis or primary coronary angioplasty) in 10,400 patients with relatively high-risk acute myocardial infarction.

Insulin in diabetic patients

Despite recent therapeutic progress, the mortality of myocardial infarction remains particularly high in diabetic patients.

Current state of knowledge

 Early and intensive insulin therapy reduces the long-term mortality of diabetic patients.

> This was the conclusion reached by the **DIGAMI** study (*J Am Coll Cardiol* 1995;26:57-65), which included 620 patients with known diabetes, within the first 24 hours of acute myocardial infarction. Compared to conventional treatment, maintenance of blood glucose between 7 and 11 mmol/L by means of glucose and insulin infusion, followed by insulin injections several times a day for at least 3 months, reduced the one-year mortality by 29% (18.6% vs 26.1%, *p* = 0.027). This benefit was maintained with a mean follow-up of 3.4 years (*BMJ* 1997;314:1512-1515).

Unresolved questions

 What is the exact mechanism of the beneficial effects of insulin?

> In the **DIGAMI** study, the reduction of mortality induced by insulin was particularly marked (relative reduction of 52% at 1 year) in diabetic patients with a low cardiovascular risk, not previously treated by insulin. The observed benefit could possibly be related to discontinuation of oral antidiabetic agents, which are known to exert potentially harmful effects during the post-myocardial infarction period. The ongoing **DIGAMI 2** study is designed to verify this hypothesis.

Drugs which should not be systematically prescribed

● **Calcium channel blockers**

The meta-analysis by **Held** (*BMJ* 1989;299:1187-1192), based on 22 trials combining approximately 18,000 patients randomized a few hours to several days after the onset of acute myocardial infarction, evaluated the following calcium channel blockers: nifedipine (9,400 patients), diltiazem (3,100 (patients), verapamil (3,500 patients), lidoflazine (1,800 patients). Overall, calcium channel blockers, compared to the control group, did not modify the mortality (9.8% vs 9.3%) or recurrent myocardial infarction rate (4.2% vs 4.6%). These results should be discussed according to the calcium channel blocker used.

An unfavorable tendency was observed with rapid-acting nifedipine in several trials, such as the **TRENT** study (*BMJ* 1986;193: 1204-1208) and the **SPRINT II** study (*Arch Intern Med* 1993;153: 345-353). However, no trial has evaluated the latest generation, sustained-release dihydropyridines in acute myocardial infarction.

Among the heart-rate-lowering calcium channel blockers, diltiazem, started between the 3rd and 15th day of acute myocardial infarction in the **MDPIT** study (*N Engl J Med* 1988;319:385-392), which included 2,466 patients, and verapamil, started between the 7th and 15th day in the **DAVIT II** study (*Am J Cardiol* 1990; 66:779-785), conducted in 1,775 patients, vs placebo, demonstrated a favorable effect, to varying degrees, on mortality and/or long-term recurrent myocardial infarction rates, but only in those patients not presenting heart failure or left ventricular dysfunction. They had no effect or were even harmful in patients presenting these disorders.

The **INTERCEPT** study (71st session of the American Heart Association, 1998), conducted in 874 patients treated by thrombolysis for a first acute myocardial infarction without left ventricular dysfunction, assessed the value of diltiazem (300 mg sustained release), started 36 to 96 hours after thrombolysis, in the prevention of recurrent ischemia facilitated by coronary reperfusion. Compared to placebo, the calcium channel blocker decreased the combined rate of cardiac deaths, nonfatal recurrent myocardial infarction or refractory myocardial ischemia at the 6th month by 23% ($p = 0.07$). No survival benefit was observed in this low-risk population.

● **Lidocaine**

Although lidocaine represents the treatment of choice for ventricular arrhythmias during acute myocardial infarction, it can also induce asystoles and high-degree atrioventricular block. The meta-analysis by **Mac Mahon** (*JAMA* 1988;260:1910-1916), based on 14 trials including 7,165 patients, demonstrated a non-significant 38% increase in early mortality with lidocaine. Its prophylactic use is therefore not justified.

Coronary angioplasty apart from primary and rescue coronary angioplasty

Current state of knowledge

1 In the presence of a patent coronary artery after thrombolysis, systematic coronary angioplasty of the residual stenosis is useless, or even harmful.

In the meta-analysis by **Michels** (*Circulation* 1995;91:476-485), systematic coronary angioplasty, performed either immediately after thrombolysis (2,243 patients in 8 trials), or later during hospitalization (5,516 patients in 9 trials), did not decrease the mortality or recurrent myocardial infarction rate at the 6th week and at one year, compared to a conservative strategy, which only considered revascularization in the case of recurrent myocardial ischemia or positive stress test. An unfavorable tendency was even observed for systematic coronary angioplasty when it was performed immediately after thrombolysis or later, after the 4th day of acute myocardial infarction.

The American College of Cardiology and American Heart Association recommendations (*J Am Coll Cardiol* 1996;28:1238-1428) are rarely respected in this field.

2 Myocardial revascularization is justified after thrombolysis when it is performed for recurrent angina or for exercise-induced myocardial ischemia.

In the **DANAMI** study (*Circulation* 1997;96:748-755), which included 1,008 patients treated by thrombolysis who rapidly developed recurrent angina or positive stress test, a revascularization strategy (coronary angioplasty or coronary artery bypass graft surgery) decreased the incidence of recurrent myocardial infarction (5.6% vs 10.5%) and unstable angina (17.9% vs 29.5%) over a median period of 2.4 years, compared to conservative treatment. However, the reduction of mortality (3.6% vs 4.4%) was not significant.

Unresolved questions

 Can the systematic coronary angioplasty strategy benefit from coronary stenting?

The disappointing results of balloon coronary angioplasty were attributed to early reocclusions (in almost 20% of cases) and late restenoses, the incidence of which should be reduced by stenting, as demonstrated by the French **STENTIM I** register. However, the favorable impact of this strategy on prognosis has not been demonstrated.

 Should revascularization, even delayed, be performed for all persistently occluded arteries?

The degree of ventricular remodeling, which is known to play a very important role in the long-term prognosis after myocardial infarction, is worsened by persistent coronary artery occlusion.

Experimental studies by **Hochman** and **Choo** (*Circulation* 1987; 75:299-306) showed that left ventricular dilatation was less marked when coronary revascularization was performed, even late, i.e. after constitution of myocardial necrosis. An improvement of left ventricular function was observed at the 6th month, in small patient series, when coronary angioplasty, performed several days after myocardial infarction, had ensured complete and persistent coronary reperfusion. The impact of these findings on prognosis needs to be defined by a large-scale clinical trial, especially as spontaneous coronary reperfusion, development of the collateral circulation, and treatment by ACE-inhibitors also limit ventricular remodeling.

The French **DECOPI** study, designed to randomize 720 patients, should provide an answer to this question.

The accepted indications
for primary coronary angioplasty

● Contraindication to thrombolysis

● Cardiogenic shock and unstable hemodynamic state

● Patient admitted to an interventional cardiology unit

● Non-contributive electrocardiogram

● Myocardial infarction with suspected coronary artery bypass graft thrombosis

● Recurrent myocardial infarction

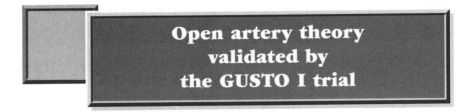

Open artery theory validated by the GUSTO I trial

Although the mechanism of the beneficial effect of thrombolysis has been known for a long time, the GUSTO trial, which included more than 40,000 patients, was the first to establish the link between the degree of coronary reperfusion and improvement of the prognosis.

Current state of knowledge

 The decreased mortality observed after thrombolysis is due to coronary reperfusion, which limits the extent of myocardial infarction and the degree of alteration of left ventricular function.

This was demonstrated with streptokinase in the **ISAM** study (*N Engl J Med* 1986;314:1465-1471), tPA in the **ECSG** study (*BMJ* 1988;297:1374-1379), and APSAC in the **APSIM** study (*J Am Coll Cardiol* 1989;13:988-997).

 The angiographic part of the main **GUSTO I** trial validated the open artery theory: when early reperfusion was optimal and sustained, left ventricular function was more completely preserved and mortality was more markedly decreased.

In this study (*N Engl J Med* 1993;329:1615-1622), 2,431 patients were randomized during the first 6 hours of myocardial infarction to receive either streptokinase, or accelerated-dose tPA, or a tPA-streptokinase combination. After a second randomization, coronary angiography was performed in 94% of patients, either 90 minutes after starting thrombolysis (1,167 patients), or 180 minutes after starting thrombolysis (387 patients), or at the 24th hour (372 patients), or on the 5th-7th day (349 patients).

Independently of the thrombolytic agent strategy, the degree of early coronary reperfusion (at the 90th minute) directly influenced the mortality on the 30th day and the outcome of left ventricular function. The mortality on the 30th day did not exceed 4.4% in the case of optimal coronary reperfusion (TIMI grade 3), but was 7.4% in the case of incomplete coronary reperfusion (TIMI grade 2) and 8.9% in the case of persistent occlusion (TIMI grade 0 or 1). In parallel, left ventricular function was significantly better at the 90th minute and on the 5th-7th day in the case of early complete reperfusion compared to incomplete reperfusion and failure of thrombolysis.

The benefit observed on the 30th day was subsequently amplified: early restoration of TIMI grade 3 flow, compared to absent or incomplete coronary reperfusion, provided an additional gain of 5 lives saved per 100 from 30 days to 2 years (*Circulation* 1998; 97:1549-1556).

③ Accelerated-dose tPA is more effective than the other thrombolytic agent strategies.

Accelerated-dose tPA achieves complete reperfusion at the 90th minute in 54% of cases, a significantly higher proportion than that observed with streptokinase (approximately 30%) or the tPA-streptokinase combination (38%). Although later assessment of coronary reperfusion (180 minutes, 24 hours and 5th-7th day) was identical regardless of the thrombolytic agent strategy, tPA was the most effective strategy to reduce mortality on the 30th day.

In conclusion, this fundamental study therefore demonstrated that the prognosis of myocardial infarction essentially depends on preservation of left ventricular function, which is correlated with early coronary reperfusion, and the quality and maintenance of coronary perfusion. tPA improves survival compared to streptokinase because it restores coronary perfusion earlier and more completely.

Characteristics of thrombolytic agents

Four thrombolytic agents are currently authorized in France for the treatment of acute myocardial infarction: streptokinase, anisoylated plasminogen streptokinase activator complex (APSAC), recombinant tissue plasminogen activator (tPA), and reteplase (rPA).

Streptokinase

Streptokinase is an exogenous protein produced by a strain of streptococcus, which can be responsible for allergic reactions. It induces lysis of fibrinogen and fibrin, with lowering of fibrinogen levels for about twelve hours in view of its long half-life.

Current state of knowledge

 The mode of administration of streptokinase has been standardized: 1.5 MU by IV infusion over 60 minutes.

The formation of antibodies contraindicates subsequent administration of streptokinase more than 5 days after the first dose and for a minimum of 2 years. Combined administration of heparin (SC or IV) does not appear essential according to the results of the **GISSI 2**, **ISIS 3**, and **GUSTO I** studies (see pp. 172 and 173).

Streptokinase improves the prognosis of acute myocardial infarction, as demonstrated by the GISSI 1 and ISIS 2 studies.

The Italian **GISSI 1** study (*Lancet* 1986;1:397-402 and *Lancet* 1987;2:871-874) included almost 12,000 patients with no age limit, during the first 12 hours of acute myocardial infarction. Compared to conventional treatment, streptokinase reduced the hospital mortality by 18% (10.7% vs 13.0%) and this benefit persisted at one year. The improvement of prognosis was more marked when thrombolysis was performed early, with a maximum 47% reduction of death in patients treated during the first hour of acute myocardial infarction. A probable favorable effect was observed in patients treated between the 6th and 9th hour. In this study, the positive effect of streptokinase was only significant for anterior or extensive myocardial infarctions and thrombolysis appeared to be beneficial in patients over the age of 65 years.

The **ISIS 2** study (*Lancet* 1988;2:349-360) is especially recognized as the first major trial that demonstrated the efficacy of aspirin during acute myocardial infarction. Among the 17,000 patients included, with no age limit, during the first 24 hours of myocardial infarction, 8,600 did not receive aspirin, as one half were treated with streptokinase alone and the other half received placebo. Streptokinase, vs placebo, decreased the mortality at the 5th week by 23% (9.2% vs 12.0%) and this result persisted at the 15th month. The beneficial effect was more marked in patients treated before the 4th hour of myocardial infarction, but appeared to persist in those treated after the 12th hour. The improvement of the prognosis was more marked in high-risk subgroups (over the age of 70 years, SBP < 100 mm Hg, history of myocardial infarction, and anterior myocardial infarction).

APSAC (anisoylated plasminogen streptokinase activator complex or anistreplase)

APSAC differs from streptokinase by a simpler mode of administration, a greater affinity for fibrin of the thrombus, a longer plasma half-life (allowing reduction of the early reocclusion rate), but also a much higher cost. Like streptokinase, it can also induce allergic reactions. APSAC was withdrawn from the market in 1998.

Current state of knowledge

 1 The mode of administration of APSAC consists of a single IV bolus of 30 U over 3 to 5 minutes.

Its ease of use made it a thrombolytic agent of choice in several trials of prehospital thrombolysis (**EMIP** and **GREAT** studies: see p. 201). Concomitant heparin therapy increases the bleeding rate and must be avoided, as demonstrated by the **DUCCS 1** study (see p. 173).

Improvement of the prognosis with APSAC was confirmed by the AIMS study.

In this study (*Lancet* 1990;335:427-431), which included 1,258 patients under the age of 70, during the first 6 hours of myocardial infarction, APSAC, vs placebo, significantly decreased the mortality by 47% at one month (6.4% vs 12.1%) and 37% at one year (11.1% vs 17.8%). The beneficial effect was more marked in patients aged 65 to 70 years.

Tissue plasminogen activator (tPA)

tPA is a natural protein manufactured by genetic recombination. It essentially acts on fibrin of the clot and only slightly lowers fibrinogen. Its short half-life, limited fibrinogenolysis and paradoxical platelet activation partly explain the high incidence of early coronary reocclusions, justifying the systematic coprescription of heparin (see p. 173).

Its main disadvantages are a slightly higher bleeding rate than that observed with streptokinase and a 10-fold higher cost of treatment.

Current state of knowledge

 The tPA administration protocol has now been standardized.

So-called accelerated administration (90 minutes) consists of an IV bolus of 15 mg followed by infusion of 0.75 mg/kg over 30 minutes (with a maximum of 50 mg), then 0.5 mg/kg in 60 minutes (without exceeding 35 mg).

The maximal dose must therefore not exceed 100 mg. It must be combined with heparin for at least 48 hours, starting with a bolus of 5,000 U before thrombolysis and continued by an infusion of 1,000 U/hour, adjusting the dosage to maintain the APTT (monitored every 6 hours) between 2 and 2.5 times the initial value.

The combined results of 4 studies, including the **RAAMI** study (*J Am Coll Cardiol* 1992;20:17-23), demonstrated a marked improvement of coronary perfusion with accelerated-dose tPA compared to tPA administered over 3 hours, as in the first major clinical trials. Double-bolus tPA, evaluated in the **COBALT** study (*N Engl J Med* 1997;337:1124-1130), which included 7,169 patients, tended to be harmful, compared to accelerated-dose tPA with, in particular, a non-significant increase of cerebral hemorrhages.

Improvement of the prognosis after tPA thrombolysis was demonstrated by the ASSET trial.

In this trial (*Lancet* 1988;2:525-530), which included 5,011 patients under the age of 75, randomized during the first 5 hours of myocardial infarction, tPA (100 mg over 3 hours), compared to placebo, decreased the mortality at one month by 26% (7.2% vs 9.8%), but with an excess of major bleeding (1.4% vs 0.4%), without modifying the global incidence of cerebrovascular accidents. The effect of tPA was particularly marked in the 66- to 75-year age-group (34% reduction of mortality at one month).

Reteplase (rPA)

Reteplase is a recombinant plasminogen activator with a different structure from that of native tPA by deletion of 3 specific domains of the protein. Its longer plasma half-life allows double-bolus administration. Like tPA, it is produced by genetic engineering, which explains its high cost.

Current state of knowledge

 The mode of administration of reteplase is simple: two IV bolus injections of 10 U (over 1 to 2 minutes) at 30-minute intervals.

 The efficacy of reteplase, the latest thrombolytic agent, has not been studied vs placebo.

It has nevertheless been compared with streptokinase and tPA in mortality studies (see p. 197).

Comparative efficacy of thrombolytic agents

We will successively compare the effects of the various thrombolytic agents on coronary reperfusion and prognosis.

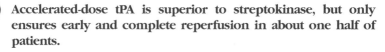

Effects on coronary reperfusion

The **GUSTO** trial demonstrated that only complete (TIMI grade 3), early and persistent coronary reperfusion is able to improve the prognosis of acute myocardial infarction. More than 3 hours after thrombolysis, coronary perfusion is essentially the same, regardless of the thrombolytic agent used.

Current state of knowledge

1 **Accelerated-dose tPA is superior to streptokinase, but only ensures early and complete reperfusion in about one half of patients.**

In the **GUSTO** angiographic trial (*N Engl J Med* 1993;329:1615-1622), complete reperfusion at the 90th minute was obtained in 54% of patients treated with tPA vs only 30% of patients treated with streptokinase ($p < 0.001$). The coronary reocclusion rate (evaluated on the 5th-7th day) was low (about 6%) and did not differ between tPA and streptokinase, which were both combined with aspirin and heparin.

2 **Accelerated-dose tPA is also superior to APSAC.**

In the **TAPS** study (*J Am Coll Cardiol* 1992;19:885-891), complete coronary patency was obtained in 54% of cases at the 60th minute of tPA thrombolysis (vs 40% with APSAC) and in 72% of cases at the 90th minute (vs 54% with APSAC). However, early reocclusions (24th-48th hour) were less frequent with APSAC (2.5% vs 10.3% with tPA).

The **TIMI** 4 study (*J Am Coll Cardiol* 1994;24:1602-1610) reported similar results: complete patency rate of 60% at the 90th minute after accelerated-dose tPA (vs 43% with APSAC) and a lower reocclusion rate with APSAC (2.2% vs 8.8% with tPA between the 18th and 36th hour).

 APSAC appears to be slightly superior to streptokinase.

In the **TEAM 2** study (*Circulation* 1991;83:126-140), the TIMI grade 3 patency rate was 60% after APSAC, vs 53% with streptokinase on the assessment performed between the 90th and 240th minute, but the difference was not significant.

 Reteplase improves early coronary patency compared to accelerated-dose tPA.

In the **RAPID II** study (*Circulation* 1996;94:891-898), complete patency at the 90th minute was obtained in 59.9% of cases with reteplase vs 45.2% with accelerated-dose tPA ($p = 0.01$).

Effects on mortality

Current state of knowledge

 Accelerated-dose tPA improves the prognosis compared to streptokinase.

This finding was confirmed by the **GUSTO I** trial. Two earlier large-scale trials, the **GISSI 2** study (*Lancet* 1990;336:65-71), which included 12,490 patients, and the **ISIS 3** study (*Lancet* 1992;339:753-770), conducted in 41,299 patients, failed to demonstrate any difference of mortality between the 2 thrombolytic agents. However, tPA was administered over 3 or 4 hours, without immediate heparin therapy.

In the **GUSTO I** trial (*N Engl J Med* 1993;329:673-682), 10,396 patients received accelerated-dose tPA combined with immediate IV heparin, while 20,251 patients were treated with streptokinase combined with SC or IV heparin. Compared to streptokinase, tPA significantly decreased the mortality on the 30th day (6.3% vs 7.3%) and the cumulative rate of death or disabling cerebrovascular accident (6.9% vs 7.8%). Although it increased the incidence of hemorrhagic cerebrovascular accidents, the net benefit of tPA therefore represented 9 lives without disabling cerebrovascular accident per 1,000 treated patients. The initial mortality difference persisted throughout follow-up until one year (*Circulation* 1996; 94:1233-1238). The relative benefit was more marked for anterior myocardial infarctions, in patients under the age of 75 and in myocardial infarctions treated by thrombolysis before the 2nd hour.

 APSAC does not improve the prognosis compared to streptokinase.

This was the conclusion of the ISIS 3 study (*Lancet* 1992;339: 753-770), in which 13,773 patients received APSAC and 13,780 patients received streptokinase. Although a positive effect of APSAC could be expected in view of its performance on coronary patency, the mortality, and recurrent myocardial infarction rates at the 35th day and at 6 months were not significantly different with the two thrombolytic agents. These disappointing results could be related to the excess of hemorrhagic cerebrovascular accidents, hypotension, and allergic reactions observed with APSAC compared to streptokinase. It should be noted, however, that one half of patients in this study also received heparin (in addition to aspirin), and this combination could have increased the APSAC-related bleeding rate (see p. 173).

The superiority of reteplase compared to accelerated-dose tPA has not been confirmed.

In the INJECT study (*Lancet* 1995;346:329-336), reteplase did not reduce the mortality at the 35th day and 6th month compared to streptokinase, but this study, which included only 6,000 patients, was an equivalence trial.

The GUSTO III trial (*N Engl J Med* 1997;337:1118-1123), conducted in 15,060 patients, did not show any significant difference between reteplase and accelerated-dose tPA in terms of mortality on the 30th day (7.47% vs 7.24%) and the cumulative rate of deaths and disabling cerebrovascular accidents (7.89% vs 7.91%).

Combinations of thrombolytic agents improve coronary reperfusion compared to streptokinase alone, but considerably increase the bleeding rate.

The theoretical advantages of a combination of thrombolytic agents include a synergistic action, improved coronary patency, prevention of reocclusions, and reduction of the cost of treatment.

The hopes raised by various combinations evaluated in several studies, including the **KAMIT** (*Circulation* 1991;84:540-549) and **TAMI 5** (*Circulation* 1991;83:1543-1556) studies, were not confirmed by the results of the **GUSTO** trial. In this trial, the tPA-streptokinase combination, used at reduced doses in 10,374 patients, ensured early and complete coronary patency in only 38% of patients, with no reduction of the coronary reocclusion rate at the 5th to 7th day. The thrombolytic agent combination vs streptokinase alone also did not decrease the mortality on the 30th day, but increased the risk of cerebral hemorrhage.

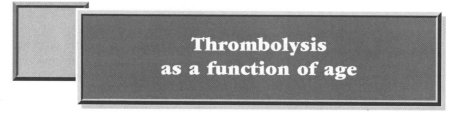

Thrombolysis as a function of age

Age represents an essential prognostic factor in acute myocardial infarction. In the absence of thrombolysis, the mortality on the 35th day, reported in the meta-analysis by the FTT collaborative group (see pp. 134-136), does not exceed 4.6% before the age of 55 years, but represents 8.9% for the 55- to 64-year age-group, 16.1% between 65 and 74 years and 25% in patients over the age of 75 years.

Current state of knowledge

1 **The benefit of thrombolysis, although more marked in younger subjects when expressed in terms of the relative reduction of mortality, is actually greater in elderly subjects in terms of the absolute reduction of mortality.**

The absolute benefit is therefore 27 lives saved per 1,000 treated patients between the ages of 65 and 74 years vs 11 per 1,000 before the age of 55 years and 18 per 1,000 between the ages of 55 and 64 years. After the age of 75 years, i.e. in the group of patients with the highest spontaneous risk, the contribution of thrombolysis (10 lives saved per 1,000 treated patients) is not significant. However, it must be noted that these elderly patients, often excluded from the first thrombolysis studies due to fear of the potential risk of bleeding, represented only 10% of inclusions of the **FTT collaborative group** meta-analysis, while the registers show that this population accounts for 30% of all myocardial infarctions. However, in the current state of our knowledge, there is no evidence that thrombolysis should not be performed exclusively because of advanced age.

2 **Thrombolysis is responsible for a modest excess of cerebrovascular accidents (1.2% vs 0.8%, i.e. 4 additional cerebrovascular accidents per 1,000 treated patients), but this risk increases with age.**

This excess is only observed on the first 2 days and is attributed to cerebral hemorrhage. The bleeding risk certainly increases with age: the excess of early cerebrovascular accidents is 0.6 per 1,000 before the age of 55, but 5.4 per 1,000 between the ages of 55 and 64, 4.1 per 1,000 between the ages of 65 and 74 years and 10.2 per 1,000 in patients over the age of 75 years. Nevertheless, the reduction of mortality between the 2nd and 35th day is in favor of a marked benefit of thrombolysis, regardless of age.

❸ Age has little influence on the choice of thrombolytic agents, except perhaps in patients over the age of 85.

Several comparative trials (ISIS 3, GUSTO I trials) demonstrated an excess of cerebrovascular accidents with tPA and APSAC compared to streptokinase and this excess was accentuated with age. However, in the GUSTO I trial (*Circulation* 1996;94:1826-1833), accelerated-dose tPA appeared to be more effective than streptokinase or a combination of the two in terms of the reduction of the combined rate of death or disabling cerebrovascular accident, regardless of age, except in patients over the age of 85 years. The superiority of tPA (vs streptokinase) was most obvious in the 75-85 year age-group, with 17 deaths or disabling cerebrovascular accidents avoided per 1,000 treated patients vs 5 events avoided in patients younger than 65 years. Over the age of 85 years, streptokinase combined with SC heparin tended to decrease this risk as well as the one-year mortality (40.3% vs 47% with tPA), but the small number of patients concerned (412, i.e. 1% of the total inclusions of the GUSTO trial) did not allow any definitive conclusions.

❹ It is very important to remember that, even despite thrombolysis, aspirin, and beta-blockers, the prognosis of myocardial infarction rapidly deteriorates with age.

In the GUSTO I trial, the mortality at one month was 3.0% before the age of 65, 9.5% between the ages of 65 and 74, 19.6% between the ages of 75 and 85 years and 30.3% over the age of 85 years. These figures emphasize the need to develop more effective treatment in elderly patients.

Prehospital thrombolysis

Prehospital thrombolysis increases the benefit of treatment by shortening the interval between onset of symptoms and reopening of the artery.

● Prehospital thrombolysis trials include the **TEAHAT** (*Am J Cardiol* 1990;65:401-407), **MITI** (*JAMA* 1993;270:1211-1216), **GREAT** (*J Am Coll Cardiol* 1994;23:1-5), and especially the **EMIP** (*N Engl J Med* 1993;329:383-389) trials.

● The **EMIP** trial was conducted in 5,469 patients with no age limit, randomized during the first 6 hours of acute myocardial infarction. Thrombolysis by APSAC (IV bolus of 30 U over 5 minutes) was performed at home (2,750 patients) or on arrival at hospital (2,719 patients). Prehospital thrombolysis gained 55 minutes (median value), as APSAC was injected 130 vs 190 minutes after the onset of symptoms. It non-significantly decreased all cause mortality on the 30th day (9.7% vs 11.1%) and significantly decreased cardiac mortality at the end of the hospital period (8.3% vs 9.8%).

This study demonstrated the feasibility and safety of prehospital thrombolysis when performed by a medical team experienced in intensive care techniques and equipped with the necessary material (especially defibrillator). Despite a time gain of almost one hour, the reduction of all cause mortality was not significant. The benefit could have been masked by the particularly short interval (15 minutes) in the control group, between the patient's admission to hospital and injection of thrombolytic agents, an interval which does not reflect the reality of everyday practice. When the time gain obtained by prehospital thrombolysis was greater than 90 minutes, the reduction of all cause mortality on the 30th day was 42% and statistically significant.

The meta-analysis conducted by the EMIP investigators, based on 5 prehospital thrombolysis trials including a total of about 6,300 patients, showed that this strategy gained approximately one hour and was accompanied by a 17% relative reduction of early all cause mortality ($p = 0.03$).

Late thrombolysis

The indication for thrombolysis can be extended to the first 12 hours.

● The value of late thrombolysis, i.e. performed after the 6th hour of acute myocardial infarction, was specifically evaluated in the TAMI 6 (*Circulation* 1992;85:2090-2099), EMERAS (*Lancet* 1993;342:767-772), and especially in the LATE (*Lancet* 1993;342:759-766) studies.

● The LATE study was conducted in 5,711 patients, randomized during the first 6 to 24 hours of acute myocardial infarction to receive either tPA (100 mg IV over 3 hours) or placebo and concomitant treatment, consisting of oral aspirin, IV heparin, and an oral beta-blocker. tPA reduced the mortality on the 35th day only in patients treated between the 6th and 12th hour: 8.9% vs 12.0%, i.e. a relative reduction of 25% ($p = 0.02$).

Although this study clearly shows that the period of application of thrombolysis can be extended to 12 hours, the mechanism of the benefit related to late coronary revascularization remains controversial: reduction of the extent of necrosis (as it is difficult to reliably estimate the time since onset of complete coronary occlusion), or limitation of left ventricular remodeling.

TIMI classification of coronary perfusion
(*Circulation* 1987;75:817-829)

● Grade 0 (no perfusion): no antegrade flow of contrast agent beyond the occlusion.

● Grade 1 (minimal perfusion): presence of very low antegrade flow beyond the occlusion, unable to entirely opacify the distal bed of the coronary artery.

● Grade 2 (incomplete perfusion): presence of antegrade flow beyond the stenosis, which entirely opacifies the distal bed of the coronary artery, but more slowly (compared to the proximal segment or other normal arteries).

● Grade 3 (complete perfusion): normal, non-slowed antegrade flow beyond the stenosis.

More simply, grades 0 and 1 correspond to occluded coronary arteries and grades 2 and 3 correspond to patent coronary arteries, but only grade 3 reflects optimal perfusion.

Failures of thrombolysis

● Intermittent coronary patency, reflected by often asymptomatic ST segment fluctuation, occurs in almost one third of patients.

● The paradoxical prothrombotic effect is responsible for reocclusions.

● Thrombolysis leaves a residual stenosis which, when it is very tight, predisposes to reocclusion and deterioration of left ventricular function.

● Coronary reocclusion occurs in 8 to 12% of patients during the hospital phase and in 15 to 25% during the 1st year. It eliminates the initial benefit of successful thrombolysis.

● Coronary reperfusion is not synonymous with myocardial reperfusion. Ito (*Circulation* 1992;85:1699-1705), comparing angiography and contrast ultrasonography data, demonstrated absence of tissue flow in 1 case out of 4 despite restoration of complete coronary patency.

Contraindications of thrombolysis
(*Eur Heart J* 1996;17:43-63)

● **Absolute contraindications**

    Cerebrovascular accident

    Trauma or major surgery during the previous 3 weeks

    Gastrointestinal bleeding during the previous month

    Known bleeding diathesis

    Dissecting aneurysm

● **Relative contraindications**

    Transient cerebral ischemic attack during the previous 6 months

    Oral anticoagulant treatment

    Pregnancy

    Recent puncture of a large non-compressible vessel

    Traumatic resuscitation

    Refractory hypertension (SBP > 180 mm Hg)

    Recent Laser treatment to the retina

Post-myocardial infarction

Patients surviving after acute myocardial infarction have a higher risk of morbidity and mortality. In the late 1970s and early 1980s, the annual mortality was estimated to be 8.5-10% during the first two years (the majority of deaths occur during the first three months) and 4-5% during the following three years (Am J Med 1979;67:7-14). More recent studies have shown a marked improvement of the prognosis. The six-month mortality rate of survivors after acute myocardial infarction was 3.5% in GISSI II (Lancet 1990;336:65-71), 4.6% in GISSI I (Lancet 1986;1:397-402 and Lancet 1987;2:871-874), 4.6% in the intervention arm of the ASSET study (Lancet 1988;2:525-530) and generally less than 4% in the thousands of relatively non-selected patients included in the large-scale trials conducted on angiotensin-converting enzyme inhibitors (Circulation 1997;95:1341-1345).

The improvement of prognosis:

● *is parallel to the reduction of the overall number of recurrent myocardial infarctions, with an annual incidence varying between 6 and 10% in the GISSI II and TIMI studies (Am J Cardiol 1988;62:179-185), while the incidence of nonfatal recurrent myocardial infarction was less than 4% at six months, and about 5% at one year (J Am Coll Cardiol 1995;26:900-907);*

● *is due to more effective treatment of the initial phase, based on coronary reperfusion; application of effective secondary prevention measures designed to reduce risk factors (Circulation 1997;95:1341-1345); and finally, the use of 4 treatments whose efficacy has now been clearly demonstrated: beta-blockers, aspirin, angiotensin-converting enzyme inhibitors and statins.*

Beta-blockers

Beta-blockers counteract the harmful action of catecholamines which, by increasing myocardial oxygen consumption (due to increased heart rate and afterload, decreased compliance and left ventricular filling), promote the development of ventricular arrhythmias (see p. 227).

Current state of knowledge

 Beta-blockers significantly reduce post-myocardial infarction morbidity and mortality.

The meta-analysis by **Yusuf** (*JAMA* 1988;260:2088-2093), based on 25 clinical trials including 23,000 patients, showed that beta-blockers, vs a control group, significantly decreased the risk of death by 22% (*p* < 0.001) and the risk of sudden death by 32% (95% CI: -4% to -22%); they also significantly reduced the risk of nonfatal recurrent myocardial infarction by 27% (*p* < 0.001).

It should be stressed that only 25 to 30% of all patients with myocardial infarction were included in the major clinical trials and the patients included were mostly low-risk patients, as the most seriously ill patients were excluded and the mean mortality of the control group was 7.7%, i.e. much lower than that of unselected myocardial infarction. For example, in the **APSI** study (*Am J Cardiol* 1990;65:251-260), the only study to include 66% of patients presenting more severe myocardial infarction than in the other trials, the mortality in the placebo group remained relatively low (12%), much lower than the expected 20%.

It should also be noted that 28% of patients were excluded from the major trials because of contraindications to the use of beta-blockers and that 25-30% of patients discontinued treatment during the trial because of the development of adverse effects.

2 The benefit of beta-blockers in terms of mortality is greater when treatment is instituted early.

This effect was not observed immediately, as the favorable results of the **Göteborg Metoprolol Trial** (*Lancet* 1981;2:823-827), in which metoprolol was administered intravenously (5 mg x 3, at 2-minute intervals) an average of 11 hours after onset of myocardial infarction, were followed by the less favorable results of the **MILIS** trial (*N Engl J Med* 1984;311:218-225) with propranolol and the **MIAMI** trial (*Eur Heart J* 1985;6:199-211) with metoprolol. In practice, it was the **ISIS 1** study (*Lancet* 1986;2:57-66), including 16,027 patients, which demonstrated that atenolol, administered an average of 5 hours after the onset of myocardial infarction, at a dosage of 5 to 10 mg IV, immediately followed by oral treatment (100 mg daily for 7 days), decreased the cardiovascular mortality of the 1st week by 14%.

The absolute benefit of beta-blockers in terms of mortality is greater in high-risk myocardial infarction.

According to the **BBPP** meta-analysis (*Eur Heart J* 1988;9:8-16), mortality was decreased by 32% ($p = 0.006$) in patients with a history of myocardial infarction and by 37% ($p = 0.01$) when previous treatment included digitalis prescribed for heart failure or arrhythmia. In the **BHAT** (*JAMA* 1982;247:1707-1714) and **APSI** studies, mortality was also reduced by almost 50% in the subgroup of patients presenting signs of heart failure.

In contrast, beta-blockers should probably not be administered systematically in patients with a very favorable prognosis: preserved left ventricular function, no residual angina or complex ventricular arrhythmia, and negative stress test.

 The short-term benefit acquired after the acute phase of myocardial infarction persists in the medium-term.

This was demonstrated by the **Norwegian** study and the **APSI** study.

In the **Norwegian** study (*N Engl J Med* 1981;304:801-807), medium-term follow-up showed that the beneficial effect of timolol on all cause mortality observed at the end of the study (2 years) persisted at the 6th year (*N Engl J Med* 1985;313:1055-1058) and survival curves became parallel by the 2nd year after randomization.

In the **APSI** study, medium-term follow-up showed that the significant 48% reduction ($p = 0.019$) of mortality obtained with acebutolol during the first 12 months persisted at 5 years (*Am J Cardiol* 1997;79:587-589) and survival curves became parallel by the 1st year after randomization.

 Myocardial infarction is less serious when it occurs in patients already treated with a beta-blocker.

In the study by **Nidorf** (*BMJ* 1990;300:71-74), on 2,430 consecutive patients hospitalized for myocardial infarction, those who were already treated with a beta-blocker because of hypertension or a history of myocardial infarction had a significantly lower risk of early mortality (28th day) (RR: 0.50, 95% CI: 0.34 to 0.76).

 Apart from those cases in which they are contraindicated, beta-blockers are still insufficiently prescribed.

More specifically, they were prescribed in only 41.5% of cases in the **EPPI I** study (*Arch Mal Cœur Vaiss* 1990;83:1777-1782), 48% of cases in the series reported by **Brand** (*J Am Coll Cardiol* 1995; 25:1432-1436), and 58% of cases in the study by **Viskin** (*J Am Coll Cardiol* 1995;25:1327-1332), in which only 11% of patients received the beta-blocker at a dosage greater than one half of that recommended in the major clinical trials. Finally, they were prescribed in only 30% of cases in the series reported by **Gottlieb** (*N Engl J Med* 1998;339:489-497).

This insufficient prescription of beta-blockers is even more marked in elderly patients > 65 years.

Only 21% of these patients received beta-blockers in the series reported by **Soumerai** (*JAMA* 1997;277:115-121). However, beta-blockers remain useful at this age and their underuse is harmful, as, in this study, based on 5,332 survivors of myocardial infarction, with a mean age of 77.3 years, beta-blockers decreased mortality by 43% with a follow-up of 2 years, for all age-groups (65 to 74 years, 75 to 84 years and ≥ 85 years) compared to those patients not treated with beta-blockers.

In the retrospective study of the **National Cooperative Cardiovascular Project** (*JAMA* 1998;281:623-629), beta-blockers were prescribed after hospitalization for myocardial infarction in only 50% (30.3% to 77.1%) of patients ≤ 65 years not presenting any contraindications to this treatment. This treatment decreased the one-year mortality by 14% in these patients.

Unresolved questions

 Which beta-blocker? At what dosage? For how long? (see p. 230)

 Is beta-blocker treatment still justified after myocardial infarction?

This apparently provocative question deserves to be raised now that coronary reperfusion is performed increasingly frequently during the acute phase of myocardial infarction, and that the open artery concept is at the center of the preoccupations. It must be remembered that most studies demonstrating the efficacy of beta-blockers in post-myocardial infarction were performed before the age of widespread use of thrombolysis and/or primary coronary angioplasty.

Nevertheless, apart from the usual contraindications, beta-blockers are required in the great majority of cases, as they remain the main element of long-term treatment of coronary heart disease.

In practice, it is legitimate to comply with the recommendations of the American Heart Association (*Circulation* 1995;92:2-4) indicating that beta-blockers must be started between the 5th and 28th day of myocardial infarction, especially in high-risk patients, i.e. those presenting a history of myocardial infarction, arrhythmia, residual ischemia, heart failure and/or left ventricular dysfunction, especially in the presence of angina or hypertension. Treatment must be continued for at least six months.

Platelet aggregation inhibitors

Aspirin has replaced the other platelet aggregation inhibitors (sulfinpyrazone, dipyridamole), whose efficacy has not been formally demonstrated.

Aspirin irreversibly inhibits cyclo-oxygenase, which blocks the synthesis of thromboxane A2, a potent platelet aggregant and vasoconstrictor. By preventing platelet aggregation at the site of coronary stenosis, aspirin prevents thrombosis and vasospasm induced by the release of thromboxane A2.

The efficacy of aspirin on platelet activation and endothelial cyclo-oxygenase function can be assessed by assaying the urinary metabolites of thromboxane and prostacyclin.

Current state of knowledge

 In secondary prevention, aspirin reduces all cause mortality and the risk of recurrent myocardial infarction.

The meta-analysis by the **Antiplatelet Trialists' Collaboration** (*BMJ* 1994;308:81-106), based on 11 studies including 14,754 patients, showed that aspirin, prescribed for one year at a dosage of 300 to 1500 mg daily, significantly decreased the risk of nonfatal recurrent myocardial infarction by 31%, the risk of nonfatal cerebrovascular accident by 39%, the risk of death from all causes by 12% and the combined risk of cerebrovascular accident, recurrent myocardial infarction, or vascular death by 25%.

The daily dosage of aspirin is tending to be decreased, as several studies have demonstrated the efficacy of increasingly lower dosages and this is clinically relevant, as gastrointestinal adverse effects are dose-dependent: 75 mg daily in the **SAPAT** study (*Lancet* 1992;340: 1421-1425) conducted in stable angina; 50 mg daily in the **CABADAS** study (*Lancet* 1993;342:257-264) conducted in bypass grafted coronary patients; 30 mg daily in the **Cottbus** study (*Prostaglandins Leukot Essent Fatty Acids* 1991;44:159-169) conducted in post-myocardial infarction.

In practice, aspirin is prescribed more frequently than anticoagulants, as it is systematically indicated in all patients undergoing myocardial revascularization.

 The combination of low-dose aspirin and anticoagulants is not more effective than aspirin prescribed alone at a higher dosage.

The **CARS** study (*Lancet* 1997;350:389-396), conducted in 8,803 patients included 3 to 21 days after acute myocardial infarction, was prematurely suspended after an interim analysis showed no significant difference between the 3 treatment groups. With a median follow-up of 14 months, the estimated incidences of a major event (recurrent myocardial infarction, nonfatal ischemic cerebrovascular accident, or cardiovascular death) at one year were: 8.5% (95% CI: 7.6% to 9.6%) with aspirin 160 mg daily, 8.4% (95% CI: 7.4% to 9.4%) with aspirin 80 mg daily combined with warfarin 3 mg daily and 8.8% (95% CI: 7.6 to 10%) with aspirin 80 mg daily combined with warfarin 1 mg daily. The estimated spontaneous major hemorrhage rates (i.e. not related to an interventional procedure) at one year were 0.74% (95% CI: 0.43% to 1.1%) with aspirin 160 mg daily and 1.4% (95% CI: 0.94% to 1.8%) with aspirin 80 mg daily combined with warfarin 3 mg daily (*p* = 0.014). The combination of low-dose aspirin (80 mg daily) and a fixed low-dose of warfarin (1 or 3 mg daily) after myocardial infarction therefore does not appear to provide any additional clinical benefit compared to that obtained with aspirin alone (160 mg daily).

Unresolved questions

● New antithrombotic agents (clopidogrel, sulodexide) have been compared to aspirin.

In the **CAPRIE** study (*Lancet* 1996;348:1329-1339) conducted in 19,185 patients at high risk of ischemic events, with a history of cerebrovascular accident in 6,431 cases, myocardial infarction in 6,302 cases, and arterial disease of the lower limbs in 6,452 cases, clopidogrel (75 mg daily) (an antithrombotic agent resembling ticlopidine) vs aspirin (325 mg daily), with a follow-up of 1 to 3 years, decreased the risk of new cardiovascular events by 8.7% ($p = 0.043$). However, when risk reduction is analysed as a function of the underlying disease leading to inclusion, the efficacy of clopidogrel vs aspirin was more equivocal: it was markedly superior (25% reduction of the risk) in patients with arterial disease of the lower limbs, modest (8% reduction of the risk) in those with a cerebrovascular accident, and comparable to that of aspirin in patients included because of myocardial infarction.

This apparently heterogeneous efficacy was no longer observed in the study by **Gent** (*Circulation* 1997;96 suppl. I:I-467), which retrospectively analysed the risk of developing a new ischemic event in all patients with a history of myocardial infarction (more or less 35 days before): clopidogrel vs aspirin decreased the relative risk by 7.4%. When all 19,185 patients with thrombotic atherosclerosis were considered, clopidogrel vs aspirin decreased the risk of myocardial infarction by 19.2%.

In the **IPO-V2** study (*J Am Coll Cardiol* 1994;23:27-34), conducted in 4,000 patients with myocardial infarction, sulodexide, another new antithrombotic, was used successfully, but this result needs to be confirmed by further studies.

● No trial of ticlopidine in post-myocardial infarction has been conducted.

● Studies are currently underway with GP IIb/IIIa receptor inhibitors.

Anticoagulants

Anticoagulants are designed to prevent the formation of thrombosis in the stenotic coronary artery and in the left ventricular cavity in contact with the necrotic and/or aneurysmal myocardial zone.

Current state of knowledge

 The combination of fixed low-dose anticoagulant with low-dose aspirin is not more effective than aspirin prescribed alone at a higher dosage (see p. 212).

What is probable

 The efficacy of oral anticoagulants in post-myocardial infarction, controversial for a long time, now appears very probable.

In the Sixty Plus Recurrent Myocardial Infarction Study (*Lancet* 1980;2:990-994), conducted in 878 patients, anticoagulants (acenocoumarin and phenprocoumon; INR: 2.8 to 4.8), vs placebo, with a 2-year follow-up, significantly decreased all cause mortality (p = 0.017) and recurrent myocardial infarction rate (p = 0.0001) at the cost of an increased incidence of major bleeding.

In the WARIS study (*N Engl J Med* 1990;323:147-152), based on 1,214 patients, warfarin, vs placebo, with a follow-up of 37 months, significantly reduced mortality by 24% (p = 0.027), number of recurrent myocardial infarctions by 34% (p = 0.0007), and total number of cerebrovascular accidents by 55% (p = 0.0015), at the cost of an annual severe bleeding rate of 0.60%.

In the ASPECT study (*Lancet* 1994;343:499-503), based on 3,404 patients included during the six weeks after hospitalization, anticoagulant vs placebo, with a follow-up of 37 months, only tended to reduce the number of deaths by 10% (NS), but significantly decreased the incidence of first myocardial recurrent myocardial infarction by 53% and the risk of cerebrovascular accident by 40%, due to a 65% reduction of the incidence of transient cerebral ischemic attacks.

In practice, oral anticoagulants are essentially reserved for contra-indications to aspirin and more severe forms.

The incidence of severe forms has decreased since the increasingly frequent use of early coronary reperfusion. Severe forms consist of extensive anterior myocardial infarction, left ventricular dysfunction, or aneurysm with or without heart failure, left intraventricular thrombosis, atrial fibrillation, history of pulmonary embolism or peripheral arterial embolism.

 Anticoagulants must be prescribed at a dosage ensuring an INR between 2 and 4.

As demonstrated by an ancillary ASPECT study (*J Am Coll Cardiol* 1996;27:1349-1355), this INR value is associated with the lowest number of accidents, of the order of 3 hemorrhages or thromboembolic accidents per 100 patient/years, and ensures the most effective protection.

Unresolved questions

● Is aspirin as effective as oral anticoagulants?

The EPSIM study (*N Engl J Med* 1982;307:701-708), conducted in 1,303 patients included an average of 11.4 days after acute myocardial infarction, did not observe any significant difference between aspirin (0.5 g tid) and acenocoumarol (PT: 25% to 35%) in terms of all cause mortality, incidence of cardiac deaths and recurrent myocardial infarctions. Bleeding complications were 4 times more frequent with anticoagulants.

In the APRICOT study (*Circulation* 1983;87:1524-1530), a very specific study, as it was conducted in 300 patients in whom thrombolysis achieved patency of the infarct-related artery, the reocclusion, recurrent myocardial infarction, and coronary reperfusion rates were not significantly different at the 3rd month with aspirin (325 mg daily) and with warfarin (INR: 2.8 to 4.0).

Angiotensin-converting enzyme inhibitors

The favorable action of angiotensin-converting enzyme (ACE) inhibitors in post-myocardial infarction is multifactorial: they decrease left ventricular remodeling, prevent left ventricular hypertrophy-dilatation and increase the left ventricular ejection fraction. They also lower neuroendocrine activation and prevent the harmful long-term effects of this essential compensatory mechanism. They decrease the prevalence of ventricular tachycardia and sudden death, and, finally, they very probably exert an anti-ischemic action and promote physiological fibrinolysis (see pp. 235 and 236).

Current state of knowledge

1 **Prescribed in addition to conventional treatment, ACE-inhibitors significantly decrease post-myocardial infarction mortality.**

They were prescribed less than 24 hours after the onset of symptoms in unselected patients with myocardial infarction [CONSENSUS II (*N Engl J Med* 1992;327:678-684), GISSI 3 (*Lancet* 1994; 343:1115-1122), ISIS 4 (*Lancet* 1995;345:669-685), and CCS-1 (*Lancet* 1995;345:686-687) studies] or in patients selected according to the presence of isolated left ventricular dysfunction or congestive heart failure, in whom they were used early [CATS (*Eur Heart J* 1994;15:898-907) and SMILE (*N Engl J Med* 1995;332:80-85) studies] or late (SAVE, AIRE, and TRACE studies).

2 **The beneficial effect on mortality is moderate when the ACE-inhibitor is administered very early in the course of unselected myocardial infarction.**

It only becomes statistically significant when studied on a very large number of patients (almost 100,000).

3 **Their beneficial effect on mortality is much more marked in patients with myocardial infarction selected because of the presence of heart failure and/or left ventricular dysfunction (left ventricular ejection fraction ≤ 0.35 to 0.40).**

The risk of death was decreased by 19% (p = 0.019) with a follow-up of 42 months in the SAVE study (*N Engl J Med* 1992;327:669-677) conducted with captopril; by 27% (*p* = 0.002) with a follow-up of 15 months in the AIRE study (*Lancet* 1993;342:821-828) conducted with ramipril and by 22% ($p = 0.001$) with a follow-up of 2 to 4 years in the **TRACE** study (*N Engl J Med* 1995;333:1670-1676) conducted with trandolapril.

The number of lives saved per 1,000 treated patients is a function of the mortality of the control group: 42, 74, and 114, for control group mortalities of 24.6%, 42.3%, and 38.9%, in the **SAVE, TRACE,** and **AIREX** (*Lancet* 1997;349:1493-1497) studies, respectively.

4 **The beta-blocker-ACE-inhibitor combination is synergistic.**

In the trials which demonstrated the efficacy of ACE-inhibitors, beta-blockers could constitute part of standard treatment.

In the **SAVE** study, the beta-blocker-ACE-inhibitor combination, used in 34% of patients, had a cumulative effect on reduction of mortality, which was decreased by only 31% with beta-blockers vs 45% with the beta-blocker-captopril combination.

In the **TRACE** study, the greatest reduction of mortality observed with trandolapril was obtained in the subgroup of patients treated with beta-blockers at the time of randomization: RR: 0.60 vs 0.78 for the overall population [*N Engl J Med* 1996;334:1546 (letter)].

In the **AIRE** study, retrospective analysis of 2,006 patients with a history of myocardial infarction complicated by heart failure, showed that beta-blockers (prescribed in 20% of cases) were an independent predictive factor of a 34% reduction of all cause mortality (95% CI: 10% to 51%, $p = 0.008$) and a 43% reduction of the risk of developing severe heart failure (95% CI: 18% to 60%, $p = 0.002$) (*J Am Coll Cardiol* 1998;31 suppl. A:32A).

Unresolved questions

 What is the maximum dosage?

Probably that recommended in the large-scale trials, bearing in mind that, in practice, ACE-inhibitors are prescribed at much lower dosages. Satisfactory results have also been obtained with the lower doses used in more recent trials [captopril 100 mg daily in the **ISIS** 4 study, or even 75 mg daily in the **PRACTICAL** study (*Am J Cardiol* 1994;73:1180-1186)].

For how long?

The duration of treatment is still controversial. While treatment was continued for almost 4 years in the **SAVE** study, a more recent meta-analysis by the **ACE-inhibitor Myocardial Infarction collaborative group** (*Circulation* 1996;94 suppl. I:90), based on patients included in the **CONSENSUS II, GISSI 3, ISIS 4,** and **CCS-1** studies, showed that the majority (80%) of the beneficial effect of the ACE-inhibitor on mortality was obtained by the first week of treatment. It is now known that this effect is maintained at one year, even when the ACE-inhibitor is stopped at the 6th week, which is why some authors propose treatment with an ACE-inhibitor only during the first 4 to 6 weeks after myocardial infarction, although it can be subsequently reintroduced in the case of congestive heart failure or a more marked deterioration of left ventricular function (*J Am Coll Cardiol* 1996;27:337-344).

Is the vasodilator effect of ACE-inhibitors decreased by aspirin?

Aspirin has been reported to attenuate the vasodilator effects of enalapril in severe heart failure (*J Am Coll Cardiol* 1992;20:1549-1555). A retrospective analysis (*Am J Cardiol* 1997;79:115-119) of the **CONSENSUS II** results confirmed the negative effect of this combination on mortality. These data are awaiting confirmation. It should simply be stressed that ACE-inhibitors stimulate prostaglandin synthesis by preventing degradation of bradykinin, while aspirin and non-steroidal anti-inflammatory drugs inhibit this synthesis.

Anti-ischemic effect of ACE-inhibitors

ACE-inhibitors probably exert an anti-ischemic effect, which is only observed after several months of treatment and therefore cannot be demonstrated during the first 6 weeks of acute myocardial infarction; a recent meta-analysis by **Tajer** (*Circulation* 1996;94 suppl. I:90), analysing the short-term anti-ischemic effects of ACE-inhibitors in 1,022 patients of the **ENAI** study (conducted in unstable angina) evaluated at 7 days, 19,394 patients of **GISSI 3** evaluated at 42 days and 58,050 patients of **ISIS 4** evaluated at 35 days, showed that the recurrent ischemia rate (17.4%) with ACE-inhibitors was identical to that of the control group (17%), as were the myocardial infarction or recurrent myocardial infarction rates: 3.84% with ACE-inhibitor vs 3.65% in the control group.

Statins

Statins reduce the instability of young atheromatous plaques by decreasing the lipid load, as young plaques have a large lipid nucleus and a thin fibrous capsule, and are therefore at greater risk of rupture. Statins also decrease platelet aggregation, the thrombosis risk, and endothelial dysfunction.

Current state of knowledge

1 At the present time, simvastatin and pravastatin are the only lipid-lowering drugs which have been shown to improve the post-myocardial infarction prognosis.

The beneficial effect concerns both a reduction of coronary morbidity and mortality (4S, CARE, LIPID studies), as well as all cause mortality (4S and LIPID studies).

2 It is important to lower serum LDL-cholesterol (LDL-C) as close as possible to 1.0 g/L (2.6 mmol/L), as a beneficial effect is still perceptible even at the lowest percentiles.

In the 4S study (see p. 81), simvastatin markedly and significantly decreased the incidence of major coronary events to the same degree (35%, p = 0.0013 and 36%, p = 0.0004, respectively), whether serum LDL-C was only moderately raised (1.16 to 1.70 g/L, i.e. 3.0 to 4.0 mmol/L) or much higher (2.05 to 2.71 g/L, i.e. 5.3 to 7.0 mmol/L).

In the **CARE** study (see p. 82), pravastatin continued to significantly reduce mortality by 24% (p = 0.002), even for serum LDL-C levels between 1.16 and 1.74 g/L (3.0 and 4.5 mmol/L).

In the **Post-CABGT** study (see p. 94), conducted in patients who had undergone coronary artery bypass graft surgery, a more marked reduction of serum LDL-C below 1.0 g/L (2.6 mmol/L), obtained with lovastatin, significantly decreased the myocardial revascularization rate by 29% vs less intensive treatment, which simply lowered serum LDL-C to between 1.32 and 1.36 g/L (3.4 to 3.5 mmol/L) (p = 0.03).

In the **CARS** study (see p. 95), lowering of serum LDL-C to around 1.0 g/L (2.58 mmol/L) significantly decreased the percentage of patients with progression of coronary stenoses.

 Statins can decrease progression of coronary atherosclerosis, prevent the formation of new lesions, or even induce regression of old lesions (see p. 90).

In terms of health economy, treatment with statins is less expensive than may appear at first sight.

In the **4S** study (see p. 81), simvastatin significantly decreased the cost of treatment of coronary heart disease by reducing the number and duration of hospitalizations and by decreasing the number of myocardial revascularization procedures (*Circulation* 1996; 93:1796-1802).

Nitrates

The potential value of nitrates in post-myocardial infarction is based on their anti-ischemic, vasodilator, and platelet aggregation inhibitor properties, mediated by the action of nitric oxide [NO, identified as being *endothelium-derived relaxing factor* (EDRF)], for which nitrates constitute the prodrug.

Unresolved questions

 The long-term efficacy of nitrates has not been demonstrated in controlled trials (see p. 180).

However, sustained-release nitrates are widely used; they were included in post-hospital prescriptions in almost 50% of cases in the **EPPI II** survey (*Arch Mal Cœur Vaiss* 1995;88:1261-1266).

In practice, it is reasonable to avoid prescribing nitrates in monotherapy, but to coprescribe them with drugs possessing demonstrated beneficial effects: aspirin, beta-blockers, and/or ACE-inhibitors.

Calcium channel blockers

The use of calcium channel blockers in coronary heart disease is theoretically justified, as they decrease arterial and arteriolar smooth muscle tone. They therefore induce marked arterial vasodilatation of normal and stenotic coronary segments and decrease the afterload. They increase coronary blood flow and can also relieve coronary spasm. They consequently decrease myocardial oxygen consumption and protect the myocardium from the harmful effects of ischemia, which are known to be accentuated by an influx of calcium ions. Finally, they can also reduce the extent of experimental myocardial infarction.

In practice, despite their pharmacological and hemodynamic disparities, as indicated in the review by **Guize** (*J Mal Vasc* 1997;22:222-228), calcium channel blockers are very effective in the treatment of spastic angina and acute and chronic coronary insufficiency. However, they can be harmful in acute myocardial infarction and, for a long time, there use in post-myocardial infarction was controversial.

Current state of knowledge

 Systematic prescription of calcium channel blockers, especially first generation dihydropyridines, is not justified in post-myocardial infarction.

Early administration of calcium channel blockers following myocardial infarction did not demonstrate any benefit in terms of mortality and an excess mortality was even observed with rapid-acting dihydropyridines [**SPRINT I and II** studies (*Eur Heart J* 1988;9: 354-364 and *Eur Heart J* 1988;9 suppl. 1:1-350)].

Nevertheless, against all apparent logic, calcium channel blockers are still widely used: they were included in 58% of post-hospital prescriptions in the EPPI I survey (*Arch Mal Cœur Vaiss* 1990;83: 1777-1782); represented 35.1% of post-hospital prescriptions in the EPPI II survey (*Arch Mal Cœur Vaiss* 1995;88:1261-1266); and, finally, in the elderly, they are used three times more frequently than beta-blockers, which are nevertheless more effective (*JAMA* 1997;277:115-121).

2 **In the absence of left ventricular dysfunction, diltiazem and verapamil could represent an alternative to beta-blockers when this therapeutic category is contraindicated or poorly tolerated.**

In the DRS study (*N Engl J Med* 1986;315:423-429), diltiazem appeared to be beneficial in non-Q-wave myocardial infarction, especially by reducing refractory angina and nonfatal myocardial infarction on the 14th day, but without modifying mortality.

In the MDPIT study (*N Engl J Med* 1988;319:385-392), conducted in 2,466 patients, diltiazem (60 mg qid), started 3 to 15 days after acute myocardial infarction, did not modify all cause mortality, but tended to reduce the incidence of the first recurrent cardiac event, i.e. cardiac death or nonfatal recurrent myocardial infarction, by 11% (NS), with a follow-up of 25 months. Diltiazem also reduced the number of cardiac events in the 1,909 patients not presenting any radiological signs of pulmonary congestion.

In the DAVIT II study (*Am J Cardiol* 1990;66:779-785), verapamil started at the dosage of 360 mg daily between the 7th and 15th day after myocardial infarction in unselected patients, vs placebo, significantly reduced the combined incidence of death or recurrent myocardial infarction, with a follow-up of 16 months.

However, in the CRIS study (*Am J Cardiol* 1996;77:365-369), conducted in 1,073 patients with myocardial infarction, but no history of severe heart failure, included an average of 13.8 days (7 to 21) after myocardial infarction, with a mean follow-up of 23.5 months, verapamil SR (360 mg daily) administered in addition to conventional treatment (consisting of nitrates in 80% of cases, while beta-blockers were prohibited during the study), vs placebo, significantly reduced the frequency of residual angina, but only tended to reduce (NS) the number of recurrent myocardial infarctions and had no effect on mortality.

In the **INTERCEPT** study (71st session of the American Heart Association, 1998), conducted in 874 patients with myocardial infarction treated by streptokinase or urokinase, diltiazem SR 300 mg daily vs placebo, administered for 36 to 96 hours after thrombolysis in combination with aspirin (160 mg daily), with a follow-up of 6 months, decreased: nonfatal recurrent myocardial infarctions by 26%, episodes of refractory ischemia by 26%, cardiovascular events (cardiac deaths, nonfatal recurrent myocardial infarctions, and refractory myocardial ischemia) by 23% and the need for coronary angioplasty or coronary artery bypass grafting by 42%.

Antiarrhythmic drugs

Current state of knowledge

 Class I antiarrhythmic drugs must not be systematically prescribed in post-myocardial infarction in the presence of simple ventricular premature depolarizations (see pp. 300, 302, and 303).

Although class I antiarrhythmic drugs can decrease or even eliminate ventricular premature depolarizations, they do not reduce all cause mortality and the incidence of sudden death. In the **CAST I** and **II** studies (*N Engl J Med* 1989;321:406-412 and 1992;327: 227-233), encainide, flecainide, and moricizine, systematically prescribed after myocardial infarction, were even responsible for significant excess mortality.

Although it is not justified to prescribe these drugs in patients with an estimated low risk of sudden death because they do not provide any advantage in terms of survival and may even be harmful, they may nevertheless be beneficial in certain individual patients.

A meta-analysis by **Hine** (*JAMA* 1989;262:3037-3040), based on 10 trials with a total of 4,122 patients included 2 to 60 days after myocardial infarction, with a mean follow-up of 3 to 24 months, showed that empirical long-term prescription of antiarrhythmic drugs after myocardial infarction did not provide any constant prophylactic effect on late mortality.

A meta-analysis by **Teo** (*JAMA* 1993;270:1589-1595), based on 138 trials including more than 98,000 patients, evaluated the effect on mortality of various antiarrhythmic drugs prescribed prophylactically after myocardial infarction. Overall, class I antiarrhythmic drugs significantly increased the mortality [odds ratio (OR) 1.14, 95% CI: 1.01 to 1.28, $p = 0.03$]. Their harmful effects vary according to the group considered: a simple unfavorable tendency for classes Ia and Ib, but significant excess mortality for class Ic antiarrhythmic drugs.

2 **Amiodarone may be useful in post-myocardial infarction.**

This was demonstrated by the **EMIAT** and **CAMIAT** trials (see p. 302).

In the **EMIAT** trial (*Lancet* 1997;349:667-674), conducted in 1,486 patients with a left ventricular ejection fraction ≤ 0.40, in the presence or absence of ventricular arrhythmias, amiodarone did not modify all cause mortality or cardiac mortality, but significantly reduced the risk of arrhythmic death by 35% ($p = 0.05$).

In the **CAMIAT** trial (*Lancet* 1997;349:675-682), conducted in 1,202 patients presenting frequent or repetitive ventricular premature depolarizations (≥ 10/hour or at least one run of ventricular tachycardia), amiodarone significantly decreased the incidence of ventricular fibrillation or arrhythmic death ($p = 0.016$).

In the **ATMA** meta-analysis (see p. 258), based on 13 trials including 6,553 patients, 89% of whom presented a history of myocardial infarction and who had a mean left ventricular ejection fraction of 0.31 and 18 ventricular premature depolarizations/hour, amiodarone significantly reduced all cause mortality by 13% to 15% and arrhythmic deaths by 29%.

Control of risk factors

Current state of knowledge

 Although neglected for a long time in the context of secondary prevention, control of risk factors now appears essential.

The absolute benefit (total reduction of number of events per 1,000 patients treated for one year) is five-fold higher than that observed in primary prevention (*Arch Mal Cœur Vaiss* 1995;88 suppl. III:51-7). It appears that:

● reduction of serum cholesterol remains an important objective when the serum cholesterol level exceeds 2 g/L and/or when serum LDL-C is > 1.25 g/L (3.2 mmol/L);

● smoking cessation must be obtained, as an ex-smoker's risk rapidly decreases by one half, even after myocardial infarction, and becomes similar to that of non-smokers after 2 to 3 years;

● control of hypertension reduces recurrent myocardial infarctions and coronary mortality by 20%. Retrospective analysis showed that ramipril significantly reduced all cause mortality by 32% (95% CI: 1% to 54%, $p = 0.04$) in the subgroup of hypertensive patients [who represented 28% subjects of the **AIRE** study (*J Am Coll Cardiol* 1998;31 suppl. A:211A)], but not in the group of normotensive subjects (NS). A tendency to reduction of morbidity associated with heart failure ($p = 0.07$) was also observed in the group of hypertensive patients, but not in the normotensive patients (NS). According to the **HOT** study (see p. 51), it is unnecessary to lower blood pressure below 140/85 mm Hg because, even if these low figures are well tolerated, they do not provide any additional benefit.

● dietary measures consist of reduction of total caloric intake in the case of obesity, reduction of unsaturated fatty acids, and increased intake of alpha-linoleic acid (olive oil) and omega-3-eicosapentaenoic acid (fatty fish) (**DART** study, see p. 79) significantly reduce the risk of recurrent myocardial infarction and death by as much as 70%. A vitamin A and E supplement also appears to be useful (**CHAOS** study, see p. 77);

● regular physical exercise contributes to better control of risk factors and reduces cardiovascular mortality by 20 to 25% (*Circulation* 1989;80:234-244);

● management of stress reactions and certain psychological factors such as the type A profile gives encouraging results.

 In everyday practice, post-myocardial infarction control of risk factors is far from satisfactory.

The **ASPIRE** study (*Heart* 1996;75:334-342), conducted in Great Britain in 2,583 patients under the age of 70 who had experienced one of the following 4 major coronary events: coronary artery bypass graft, coronary angioplasty, myocardial infarction, acute coronary insufficiency, showed that 10% to 27% of these patients continued to smoke, 75% were still overweight, 25% remained hypertensive and 75% had a serum cholesterol level > 2.0 g/L (5.2 mmol/L). Furthermore, only 33% of them were treated with beta-blockers and 20% of patients with a history of myocardial infarction were not or no longer treated with aspirin at follow-up.

Place of beta-blockers

Although beta-blockers have been used in post-myocardial infarction since 1965, it nevertheless took almost 15 years before they became an integral part of post-hospital prescription.

First attempts

● The first attempts by **Snow** (*Lancet* 1965;2:551-553), **Reynolds** and **Whitlock** (*Br Heart J* 1972;31:252-259), **Lambert** (*Lancet* 1972;1: 793-794) presented a number of methodological biases: small sample size, inclusion of patients in whom the diagnosis of myocardial infarction was uncertain. Their results were inconclusive and the **MIS** study (*BMJ* 1977;2:419-421) did not improve this situation, as, despite the inclusion of 3,038 patients and the demonstration of a significant reduction of cardiac mortality and sudden deaths observed with a follow-up of 1 to 3 years, it used practolol, which was subsequently withdrawn from the market because of its serious adverse effects.

It was only in the 1980s that large-scale randomized multicenter trials clearly demonstrated the value of beta-blockers in post-myocardial infarction.

However, when looked upon more closely, it appears that it was not always very easy to reach a precise opinion based on real-time reading, as they were published, of the often contradictory results of these trials.

Four favorable trials

● The **Norwegian** study (*N Engl J Med* 1981;304:801-807), conducted in 1,884 patients, 945 of whom received timolol (20 mg daily).

The **BHAT** study (*JAMA* 1982;247:1707-1714), conducted in 3,837 patients, 1,916 of whom received propranolol (180 to 240 mg daily).

The **sotalol trial** (*Lancet* 1982;1:1142-1147), conducted in 1456 patients, 873 of whom received sotalol (320 mg daily).

The study by **Hansteen** (*BMJ* 1982;284:155-160), conducted in 560 high-risk patients presenting with left ventricular failure or ventricular arrhythmias, 278 of whom received propranolol (160 mg daily).

In all these trials, the beta-blocker, started orally between the 1st and 3rd week of post-myocardial infarction, decreased mortality, the number of sudden deaths, and the recurrent myocardial infarction rate to varying degrees and more or less significantly depending on the study.

Three neutral trials

● The **ASPS** study (*Eur Heart J* 1983;4:367-375), conducted in 529 patients, 263 of whom received pindolol (15 mg daily).

The **EIS** study (*Eur Heart J* 1982;3:583-586 and 1984;5:189-202), conducted in 1741 patients, 858 of whom received oxprenolol (320 mg daily).

The **LIT** study (*Eur Heart J* 1987;8:1056-1064), conducted in 2,395 patients, 1,195 of whom received metoprolol (200 mg daily).

In these three studies, the beta-blocker, administered orally, vs placebo, did not modify either all cause mortality or the incidence of sudden death or fatal recurrent myocardial infarction.

ISIS 1 and the meta-analyses

● In this climate of persistent doubt, it was the results of **ISIS 1** (*Lancet* 1986;2:57-66), in which atenolol was administered right from the acute phase of myocardial infarction (see p. 175), and those of 2 meta-analyses (by the **Beta-Blocker Pooling Project** and **Yusuf**), which finally and definitively tilted the scales in favor of beta-blockers.

● The **Beta-Blocker Pooling Project** (*Eur Heart J* 1988;9:8-16) analysed 9 secondary prevention trials selected according to rigorous criteria, including a total of 13,679 patients treated with 7 different beta-blockers.

● The meta-analysis by **Yusuf** (*JAMA* 1988;260:2088-2093) analysed 25 randomized trials including more than 23,000 patients. In 8 of these trials, oral or IV beta-blocker treatment was started rapidly during the hospital phase.

In the medium-term (1 to 3 years), beta-blockers were found to significantly decrease the risk of death by 22% to 24% ($p < 0.001$), sudden death by 32%, and nonfatal recurrent myocardial infarction by 27% ($p < 0.001$).

Mechanism of action of beta-blockers

● The cardioprotection provided by beta-blockers is multifactorial and essentially due to:

● their anti-ischemic effect; they reduce myocardial oxygen consumption (by slowing heart rate and reducing myocardial contractility and blood pressure); they improve coronary blood flow (due to bradycardia and lengthening of end-diastole) and subendocardial perfusion, which is particularly sensitive to ischemia; finally, experimentally, they reduce the extent of myocardial infarction;

● their antiarrhythmic effect: they increase the ventricular fibrillation threshold and decrease the number of ventricular premature depolarizations and episodes of ventricular tachycardia on Holter monitoring; they significantly reduce the incidence of sudden death;

● an antithrombotic effect has been less clearly demonstrated.

● Beta-blockers are generally well tolerated. However, they can be responsible for adverse effects: bradycardia and/or hypotension which resolve after stopping treatment, asthenia, vasomotor disorders of the extremities, asthma, lipid abnormalities (raised triglycerides and decreased serum HDL-C levels). They are not recommended in patients with decompensated diabetes mellitus or active arterial disease of the lower limbs and, classically, in the case of heart failure, which they tend to aggravate (however, ideas are dramatically changing on this point, see p. 267).

Unresolved questions

 Which beta-blocker should be prescribed?

At least theoretically, those drugs whose beneficial effect has been demonstrated in a large-scale clinical trial, i.e. acebutolol, metoprolol, propranolol, timolol and for which the Agence française du Médicament (French Drug Agency) has authorized the indication "long-term treatment after myocardial infarction (reduction of mortality)" (*Et Eval Cardiovasc* 1997; 4:49-56).

However, it is reasonable to raise the question of whether the favorable effect of beta-blockers constitutes a class effect, which can be extended to all molecules of this category. According to **Boissel** (*Les bétabloquants*, Vol. 1. ICI-Pharma ed., Paris, 1990; 150-161), there is no unequivocal answer to this question as, although the reduction of mortality appears to be attributable to the beta-adrenergic blocking effect, the accessory properties of these substances may also influence the intensity of this reduction.

Carvedilol may also have an important place in this indication in the future, as many studies have shown that this new beta-blocker, also possessing alpha-blocking, vasodilator, and antioxidant properties, achieves favorable results in heart failure which is known to be very often secondary to ischemic heart disease.

At what dosage?

Theoretically, at the dosage demonstrated to be effective in large-scale clinical trials. **Viskin** (*J Am Coll Cardiol* 1995;25:1327-1332) showed that only 6% of patients treated with a beta-blocker after myocardial infarction received treatment at the dosage recommended in the large-scale trials.

For how long?

The optimal duration of beta-blocker treatment remains uncertain because none of the published trials was designed to determine this duration and, in the majority of studies, the follow-up barely exceeded 1 to 3 years. In practice, it appears legitimate to continue the beta-blocker for two years when it is well tolerated. After this time, the annual risk of a coronary event is much lower and, based on the results of the large-scale trials, it is unclear whether beta-blocker treatment is still effective. The advantages and disadvantages of continuing this treatment, which must not be interrupted suddenly to avoid a possible rebound phenomenon, must therefore be weighed up in each individual case.

● **What about intrinsic sympathomimetic activity of beta-blockers?**

Based on the discordant or poor results of some studies, this property was initially considered to be harmful (especially due to the fact that reduction of mortality had to be correlated with reduction of the resting heart rate, only slightly or not at all decreased by beta-blockers possessing an intrinsic sympathomimetic activity). The **APSI** study subsequently demonstrated the efficacy of acebutolol, which reduced all cause mortality by 48%. At the present time, it is unclear whether the intrinsic sympathomimetic activity is harmful in secondary prevention, but, according to **Boissel** (*op. cit.* p.230), evidence to the contrary is insufficient to provide a clear-cut answer to this controversy.

Post-hospital prescription

No matter how useful, beta-blockers must not be prescribed alone in post-myocardial infarction, as they do not constitute the entire post-hospital prescription. They must be coprescribed with a number of medications whose efficacy has now been demonstrated: aspirin (100 to 320 mg daily, or even lower doses), ACE-inhibitor when there are signs of heart failure and/or when the left ventricular ejection fraction is ≤ 0.35 to 0.40, and finally, in the case of hypercholesterolemia, lipid-lowering drugs, and especially statins, which the **4S, CARE** and **LIPID** studies have clearly shown to decrease coronary morbidity and mortality (**4S, CARE** and **LIPID** studies) and all cause mortality (**4S** and **LIPID** studies), even when baseline serum cholesterol is only moderately raised (**CARE** and **LIPID** studies and lower quartile of **4S** study).

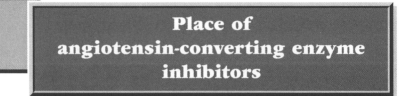

Place of angiotensin-converting enzyme inhibitors

Myocardial infarction is responsible for remodeling of the left ventricular cavity, characterized by three simultaneous processes: expansion of the myocardial infarction, leading to thinning and lengthening of the necrotic zone (this early phenomenon predisposes to the development of ventricular aneurysm and thrombosis); ventricular dilatation (this immediate compensatory process is designed to maintain systolic volume); finally, reactive hypertrophy of non-infarcted myocardial segments. This physiological process is initially compensatory, but finally becomes self-destructive, predisposing to the development of chronic heart failure.

First studies

Since the first studies by **Pfeffer** (*Circ Res* 1985;57:84-95) conducted with captopril in rats, ACE-inhibitors, venous and arterial vasodilators, are known to prevent or delay dilatation of cardiac cavities secondary to myocardial infarction and improve the survival of treated animals.

Three years later, these data were confirmed in man by two randomized, double-blind, placebo-controlled trials.

In the study by **Sharpe** (*Lancet* 1988;1:255-258), conducted in 60 patients with asymptomatic acute Q-wave myocardial infarction, not treated by thrombolysis or beta-blocker, but presenting a left ventricular ejection fraction < 0.45, captopril, administered orally (25 mg tid) vs placebo decreased end-diastolic and end-systolic volumes, increased stroke volume and improved left ventricular ejection fraction; in contrast, these parameters were worsened at 1, 3, 6, 9 and 12 months with placebo and with furosemide.

In the study by **Pfeffer** (*N Engl J Med* 1988;319:80-86), conducted in 59 patients presenting a first anterior myocardial infarction with no signs of congestive heart failure, but whose isotope left ventricular ejection fraction was < 0.45, captopril (25 mg then 50 mg daily), prescribed in addition to usual treatment from the 20th day onwards, decreased the degree of ventricular dilatation and increased exercise duration, after one month.

These two publications opened the way to a whole series of large-scale trials in which ACE-inhibitors were administered in addition to conventional treatment.

Classification of large-scale clinical trials

● Early use (less than 24 hours after onset of symptoms) in unselected myocardial infarction (**CONSENSUS II, PRACTICAL, ISIS 4, GISSI 3**, and **CCS-1** studies).

In the **CONSENSUS II** study (*N Engl J Med* 1992;327:678-684), conducted in 6,090 patients, IV enalapril (1 mg/hour for 2 hours), followed by oral enalapril (20 mg daily) tended to increase mortality at 1 and 6 months (NS). Various reasons for this increased mortality were proposed: inadequate dosage of ACE-inhibitor? Its early use induced or promoted systemic hypotension which increased subendocardial ischemia? The ACE-inhibitor delayed healing of the myocardial infarction? Or, more simply, did this study fail to identify a subgroup of patients who would have benefited from treatment, due to the absence of long-term follow-up?

In the **GISSI 3** study (*Lancet* 1994;343:1115-1122), conducted in 19,000 unselected patients with a follow-up of 6 weeks, oral lisinopril (5 then 10 mg daily) vs placebo significantly reduced mortality by 12% (6.3% in this group vs 7.1% with placebo, $2p = 0.03$), and this benefit was even more marked in women and in patients over the age of 70 ($p < 0.03$).

In the **PRACTICAL** study (*Am J Cardiol* 1994;73:1180-1186), designed to assess the course of isotope left ventricular function in 225 patients randomized to receive oral captopril (18.75 to 75 mg daily), enalapril (3.75 to 15 mg daily) or placebo, with a follow-up of 3 months, the ACE-inhibitor, vs placebo, increased left ventricular ejection fraction ($0.47 \pm 0.01\%$ vs $0.45 \pm 0.01\%$, $p = 0.005$) and decreased left ventricular dilatation, even in patients whose ventricular ejection fraction was > 0.40. The beneficial effect of captopril was similar to that of enalapril.

In the **ISIS 4** study (*Lancet* 1995;345:669-685), conducted in 58,050 patients, oral captopril (6.25 to 100 mg daily) vs placebo, with a follow-up of 5 weeks, decreased mortality by 7% (7.19% in this group vs 7.69% with placebo, $2p = 0.02$).

In the CCS-1 study (*Lancet* 1995;345:686-687), conducted in 13,634 patients, captopril (6.25 mg then 12.5 mg 2 hours later then 12.5 mg tid), administered orally for 4 weeks, vs placebo, tended to decrease mortality (9.05% in this group vs 9.59% with placebo, NS).

● **Use in patients with myocardial infarction selected because of a high risk (SMILE study) or signs of heart failure and/or left ventricular ejection fraction < 0.40 (SAVE, AIRE, TRACE studies).**

● **Early use**

In the **SMILE** study (*N Engl J Med* 1995;332:80-85), conducted in 1,556 patients included less than 24 hours after the first signs of anterior myocardial infarction, ineligible for thrombolysis due to a contraindication or late hospitalization, zofenopril (ACE-inhibitor with a similar structure to that of captopril), administered orally at an increasing dosage of 7.5 to 60 mg daily for 6 weeks, after which the ACE-inhibitor was stopped:

● significantly decreased the combined risk of death and heart failure by 34% ($p = 0.018$) at 6 weeks. This beneficial result was essentially obtained by a significant 46% reduction of the heart failure rate ($p = 0.018$), while the 25% reduction of the risk of death was not statistically significant ($p = 0.19$);

● significantly reduced all cause mortality at one year (10% in this group vs 14.1% with placebo, $p = 0.011$).

● **Late use**

In the **SAVE** study (*N Engl J Med* 1992;327:669-677), conducted in 2,231 patients, one third of whom were thrombolysed, presenting a left ventricular ejection fraction ≤ 0.40 (average of 0.31), in the absence of any clinical signs of congestive heart failure, captopril was administered orally in addition to conventional treatment, an average of 11 days (3 to 16 days) after myocardial infarction, at increasing doses (12.5 to 150 mg daily). With a follow-up of 42 months, captopril vs placebo significantly decreased all cause mortality by 19% ($p = 0.019$, cardiovascular mortality by 21% ($p = 0.014$), and the risk of fatal or nonfatal recurrent myocardial infarction by 25% ($p = 0.015$).

In the **AIRE** study (*Lancet* 1993;342:821-828), conducted in 2,006 patients, two-thirds of whom were thrombolysed and who all presented signs of heart failure, oral ramipril, administered an average of 5 days (3 to 10 days) after the onset of myocardial infarction at a dosage of 5 then 10 mg daily, vs placebo, significantly decreased mortality by 27% ($p = 0.002$) (this result was observed from the 1st week of treatment and became significant from the 30th day) and the development of a first cardiovascular event by 19% ($p = 0.008$), with a follow-up of 15 months.

In the **TRACE** study (*N Engl J Med* 1995;333:1670-1676), conducted in 1,747 patients with or without left heart failure, whose left ventricular ejection fraction was ≤ 0.35, trandolapril, administered orally (4 mg daily) an average of 4 days (3 to 7 days) after myocardial infarction, vs placebo, significantly decreased mortality by 22% (34.7% in this group vs 42.3% with placebo, $p = 0.00065$), with a follow-up of 2 to 4 years.

Practical conclusions of large-scale clinical trials

Two concepts are clearly demonstrated by the results of these clinical trials.

During the first 4 weeks of myocardial infarction, ACE-inhibitors, when systematically prescribed, provide only a slight benefit in terms of mortality.

The meta-analysis by **Latini** (*Circulation* 1995;93:3132-3137) which included the **GISSI 3, ISIS 4, CCS-1, CONSENSUS II** trials and another 2,175 subjects treated in 11 smaller trials, showed that, overall, on more than 100,000 patients, ACE-inhibitors only slightly reduced the mortality at one month: 7.27% in 50,496 treated patients vs 7.73% in 50,467 control patients ($p = 0.006$). This benefit is only clinically important (4.6 lives saved per 1,000 patients treated, $p = 0.006$) because it is expressed in relation to a very large number of patients.

These data were confirmed by the **ACE-inhibitor Myocardial Infarction collaborative group** (*Circulation* 1998;97;2202-2212), which systematically reviewed the individual data of 98,496 patients included in 4 major trials (**CONSENSUS II, GISSI 3, ISIS 4,** and **CCS-1**), in which the ACE-inhibitor was started during the acute phase (0 to 36 hours) of myocardial infarction and continued for only 4 to 6 weeks: at 1 month, ACE-inhibitors, compared to the control group, reduced mortality by 7% [7.1% vs 7.6% (95% CI: 2% to 11%, $2p < 0.004$)], which represents approximately 5 lives saved per 1,000 patients treated. The majority of this beneficial effect was obtained during the first week of treatment. The absolute benefit was greater in the case of high-risk myocardial infarction (anterior myocardial infarction, signs of heart failure, Killip class II or III, heart rate on admission > 100 b.p.m.). ACE-inhibitors also significantly reduced the incidence of nonfatal heart failure (14.6% vs 15.2%, $2p = 0.01$) at the cost of an absolute excess of persistent hypotension (17.6% vs 9.3%, $2p < 0.01$) and renal dysfunction (1.3% vs 0.6%, $2p < 0.01$).

● **In contrast, prescription of an ACE-inhibitor is essentially justified in certain selected cases of high-risk myocardial infarction.**

High-risk myocardial infarction corresponds to anterior or extensive myocardial infarction, or myocardial infarction complicated by left ventricular dysfunction or congestive heart failure. These serious forms have become less frequent since the systematic use of revascularization procedures (thrombolysis and/or coronary angioplasty) during the acute phase of myocardial infarction.

Multifactorial mechanism of action of ACE-inhibitors

● They decrease ventricular remodeling, prevent left ventricular dilatation, and increase the left ventricular ejection fraction, which explains why, in the **SAVE** study, the beneficial result of captopril on mortality was only obtained after the first year of treatment.

 They attenuate neuroendocrine activation, already present at the early stage of isolated ventricular dysfunction; they consequently oppose this essential compensatory mechanism, which can be harmful because: it increases heart rate and afterload by inducing arterial vasoconstriction; it increases myocardial oxygen consumption and coronary vasoconstriction; it induces myocardial deterioration *via* angiotensin II, which is directly cardiotoxic; finally, it can be responsible for ventricular arrhythmias.

Attenuation of the early neuroendocrine response explains the favorable action of ramipril on mortality, observed in the **AIRE** study from the first week of treatment and significant from the 30th day (these patients presented more severe disease than in the **SAVE** study).

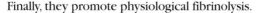 They decrease the prevalence of ventricular tachycardia, as demonstrated for the first time in the **VHeFT II** study (*Circulation* 1993;87 suppl. 6:149-155), conducted with enalapril in patients with chronic congestive heart failure, generally secondary to ischemic heart disease. This was also demonstrated in the **SAVE** study (*J Am Coll Cardiol* 1993;21 suppl. 2:130A), in which captopril tended to decrease ventricular arrhythmias and sudden death by 19% (NS). Finally, this effect was recently proven by the **TRACE** study (*N Engl J Med* 1995;333:1670-1676), which was the first to show that an ACE-inhibitor, trandolapril in this case, significantly reduced the incidence of sudden death by 24% ($p = 0.03$).

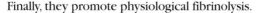 They probably have an anti-ischemic action, already reported in the **SOLVD** curative study (*N Engl J Med* 1992;327:685-691), conducted in patients mostly presenting with ischemic heart failure, in which enalapril induced a nonsignificant ($p < 0.0711$) reduction of the risk of fatal myocardial infarction. The subsequent meta-analysis of the **SOLVD** curative and preventive studies, performed by **Yusuf** (*Lancet* 1992;340:1173-1178), showed that enalapril vs placebo significantly decreased the incidence of myocardial infarction or recurrent myocardial infarction and that of hospitalizations for *de novo* angina or worsening of angina, by 23% ($p < 0.001$). It should be stressed that the anti-ischemic effect is a late effect, which cannot be demonstrated at the 5th week of treatment (*Circulation* 1996;94 suppl. I:90).

The mechanisms of the anti-ischemic effect of ACE-inhibitors are now known. The anti-ischemic effect is not due to an increased oxygen supply, which is only slightly altered by ACE-inhibitors, which exert only a mild coronary vasodilator action and have no effect on coronary blood flow. This effect is essentially due to a marked reduction of myocardial oxygen requirements: reduction of wall stress by reduction of preload and afterload; attenuation of adrenergic stimulation, resulting in slowing of heart rate; improvement of subendocardial perfusion; restoration of a normal coronary lumen by inhibition of the inducer effect of angiotensin II on growth factors responsible for smooth muscle cell hypertrophy, medial thickening, and increased collagen.

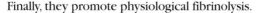 Finally, they promote physiological fibrinolysis.

Practical use of ACE-inhibitors

 Patients treated in large-scale clinical trials are highly selected, as illustrated by the inclusion rates in the **SAVE** (6% of evaluated patients), **AIRE** (6.5%), and **GISSI 3** (45%) studies. These populations therefore do not reflect the patient populations treated in everyday practice in cardiac intensive care units.

• There is no evidence to suggest that ACE-inhibitors should be prescribed systematically to all patients with acute myocardial infarction. According to their current indications, they can be safely administered to patients of either sex, even elderly patients, and to patients already receiving conventional treatment because their beneficial effect is added to that of medications already shown to be effective in this setting: thrombolytic agents, beta-blockers, aspirin, and statins.

• ACE-inhibitors must be prescribed at gradually increasing doses, in order to achieve, as far as possible, the dosages recommended in the major trials (e.g. captopril 150 mg daily in the **SAVE** study, the dosage was well tolerated by 70 to 75% of patients who completed the study). Can similar results be obtained with lower dosages, already used in the more recent trials (captopril 100 mg daily in the **ISIS 4** study, or even 75 mg daily in the **PRACTICAL** study)? This question has still not been clearly elucidated following the contradictory results of the **ATLAS** and **NETWORK** studies (see pp. 251 and 252).

• The duration of ACE-inhibitor treatment is a subject of debate. Although captopril was continued for almost 4 years in the **SAVE** study, a meta-analysis by **Tajer** (*Circulation* 1996;94 suppl. I:90), based on patients included in the **CONSENSUS II**, **GISSI 3**, **ISIS 4**, and **CCS-1** studies, showed that 80% of the beneficial effect of the ACE-inhibitor on mortality was obtained by the first week.

• In the **GISSI 3** study, the beneficial effect on mortality and severe left ventricular dysfunction, persisted at the 6th month, even when the ACE-inhibitor had been stopped at the 6th week, which is why these authors now recommend ACE-inhibitor treatment only during the first 4 to 6 weeks after myocardial infarction, although it can be subsequently reintroduced in the case of congestive heart failure or a more marked deterioration of left ventricular function (*J Am Coll Cardiol* 1996;27:337-344).

ACE-inhibitors represents a substantial reduction of the cost of treatment, as demonstrated by the cost/efficacy analysis performed on the results of the **SOLVD** study (*J Card Fail* 1995;1:371-379).

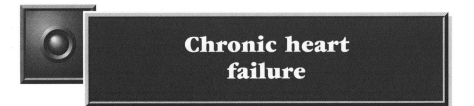

Chronic heart failure

Ventricular failure, the commonest form of heart failure, is defined by a reduction of stroke volume and/or increased filling pressure. It results in intense stimulation of neuroendocrine systems (sympathetic system and renin-angiotensin-aldosterone system), leading to elevation of plasma noradrenaline, angiotensin II and vasopressin levels. Initially beneficial, this compensatory mechanism becomes harmful in the long term, predisposing to the creation of a vicious circle and perpetuation of heart failure. Ventricular failure also disturbs the baroreflex, as prolonged stimulation of aortic, carotid or pulmonary receptors modifies vagal activation and the inhibitory response of sympathetic tone.

*Heart failure has a poor prognosis right from the appearance of clinical signs; before the use of vasodilators and angiotensin-converting enzyme inhibitors (ACE-inhibitors), the one-year mortality was close to 50% in patients with NYHA class IV heart failure. Even with current treatments, the 4-year mortality of patients with mild-to-moderate heart failure was about 50% with hydralazine-isosorbide dinitrate in the **VHeFT I** study (N Engl J Med 1986;314:1547-1552) and 41% with enalapril in the **VHeFT II** study (N Engl J Med 1991;325:303-310).*

Excess secretion of aldosterone increases salt and water retention, blood volume, and consequently preload; experimentally, it has a harmful action on the myocardium of hypertensive rats (Circ Res 1990;67:1355-1364), by predisposing to the development of myocardial fibrosis; it also increases potassium excretion with a risk of hypokalemia, predisposing to arrhythmias.

*The treatment of heart failure has been defined by the **Guidelines** of the American College of Cardiology/American Heart Association (Circulation 1995;92:2764-2784), the recent recommendations of the European Society of Cardiology (Eur Heart J 1997;18:736-753), and general reviews by **Young** (Curr Opin Cardiol 1997;12:407-417) and **Massie** (Lancet 1998;352 suppl.I: 29-33) based on the results of the main clinical trials.*

Diuretics

Diuretics are the basis of the treatment of congestive heart failure. Three classes are distinguished: Henle loop diuretics, essentially furosemide, which act on the ascending limb; thiazides, which also act on the dilution segment; and potassium-sparing diuretics, which act on the distal convoluted tubule and inhibit resorption of sodium in exchange for potassium and proton (H+ ions) excretion, thereby reducing the urinary potassium excretion and alkalinizing the urine.

By decreasing intracellular sodium and therefore intracellular calcium, diuretics induce relaxation of arterial and venous vascular smooth muscle and consequently lower the ventricular preload and afterload.

Current state of knowledge

 Diuretics are an essential element of the treatment of congestive heart failure and acute pulmonary edema.

Long-term treatment with potassium-lowering diuretics is accompanied by an increased risk of death from arrhythmia.

This was demonstrated in the study by **Cooper** (*Circulation* 1997;96 suppl. I:I-711), who retrospectively analysed the 6,797 patients of the **SOLVD** study (left ventricular ejection fraction < 0.35) to determine the relationship between the use of diuretics and the risk of arrhythmic death. Univariate analysis showed that diuretic treatment, compared to the absence of diuretics, was significantly correlated with arrhythmic death (RR: 1.85, 95% CI: 1.52 to 2.24, p = 0.0001). Only potassium-lowering diuretics were significantly associated with arrhythmic death (RR: 1.33, 95% CI: 1.05 to 1.69, p = 0.018) possibly *via* electrolyte disturbances. Treatment with potassium-sparing diuretics, either alone or in combination with a potassium-lowering diuretic, was not associated with an increased risk of arrhythmic death.

Similar results were observed in the retrospective study by **Neuberg** (*Circulation* 1998;98 suppl. I:I-300), conducted in 1,153 patients of the **PRAISE** study (see p. 254) (NYHA class IIIb-IV; left ventricular ejection fraction < 0.30), mostly treated by furosemide (10 to 480 mg daily). High doses of diuretics were found to be an independent predictive factor for sudden death (p = 0.023) and death from all causes (p = 0.012).

3 **The combination of spironolactone (an aldosterone receptor antagonist) with standard treatment for heart failure improves the prognosis by decreasing mortality.**

This was demonstrated by the RALES study (*Am J Cardiol* 1996; 78:902-907) and 71st session of the American Heart Association, 1998), which evaluated the effect of spironolactone (25 to 50 mg daily) vs placebo, prescribed in addition to standard treatment (ACE-inhibitor, furosemide, or even digitalis), on the survival of 1,663 patients with severe heart failure (NYHA class III-IV; left ventricular ejection fraction < 0.35). This study, with a planned follow-up of 2 to 3 years, was discontinued 18 months before its scheduled term because spironolactone vs placebo significantly decreased mortality from congestive heart failure and sudden death by 27% (p < 0.001) [283 deaths (34%) vs 372 deaths (44%)]. According to this study, addition of spironolactone to standard treatment of heart failure in 1,000 patients for 2 years would prevent 77 deaths and avoid 290 hospital admissions not followed by death.

Unresolved questions

● **Does long-term treatment with diuretics, administered continuously between acute episodes of congestive heart failure, decrease the mortality and/or morbidity of the disease?**

Although they are irreplaceable in the short-term to decrease congestion, long-term treatment with diuretics may be responsible for certain harmful effects, as they stimulate neuroendocrine systems (angiotensin II and catecholamines), perpetuating the vicious circle of heart failure. Under these conditions, should the dosage be reduced, or should treatment be administered intermittently? And if so, at what stage of the disease?

Cardiotonic treatment

Cardiotonic treatment, *via* its positive inotropic effect, is designed to reduce the end-systolic volume, increase the stroke volume, and indirectly decrease the end-diastolic volume and signs of congestion.

Digitalis glucosides

Digitalis glucosides act by inhibiting the sodium pump, inducing an elevation of intracellular sodium, which inhibits efflux of calcium by Na^+-Ca^{++} exchange, thereby increasing the quantity of calcium available to contractile sites. They also restore baroreflex sensitivity, altered during heart failure, and consequently decrease peripheral resistance. Digoxin simultaneously exerts positive inotropic effects and a beneficial action on the neuroendocrine reaction. It is still not known which of these two actions is more important. Low doses of digoxin may have little or no effect on hemodynamic parameters, but nevertheless reduce neuroendocrine abnormalities, while, on the contrary, higher doses improve the hemodynamics, but do not have any significant effect on neuroendocrine parameters (*Circulation* 1995;92:1801-1807).

The efficacy of digitalis was controversial for a long time (see p. 263). It was initially thought to be only effective in congestive heart failure secondary to atrial fibrillation, with no effect in chronic heart failure with normal sinus rhythm. The **DIG** study (*N Engl J Med* 1997;336: 525-533) helped to further our knowledge (see p. 264).

Current state of knowledge

1 **Digoxin does not modify all cause mortality, but significantly reduces the combined risk of hospitalization and death from heart failure.**

In the **DIG** study (see p. 264), conducted in 7,788 patients with chronic heart failure and normal sinus rhythm (mostly NYHA class II-III), digoxin (0.125 to 0.50 mg daily) vs placebo, administered in addition to ACE-inhibitor and diuretics, with a follow-up of 4 years, did not modify all cause mortality, but significantly decreased the combined number of hospitalizations and deaths from heart failure, with a trend towards an increased mortality due to arrhythmia or myocardial infarction (NS).

Prescription of digitalis is therefore legitimate in the treatment of chronic systolic heart failure with atrial fibrillation or normal sinus rhythm, especially in the presence of ventricular dilatation, provided blood volume is maintained, and the failing heart still possesses a certain contractile reserve.

New inotropic agents

Great hopes were placed in the new inotropic agents, which were thought to be more powerful and better tolerated that digitalis. These new inotropic agents consist of:

● sympathomimetics, which activate cyclic AMP synthesis by stimulation of myocardial beta-1 receptors (prenalterol, L-dopa, xamoterol, ibopamine) or vascular beta-2 receptors, which are also responsible for arterial vasodilatation (salbutamol, terbutaline, pirbuterol);

● phosphodiesterase inhibitors, which inhibit the breakdown of cyclic AMP by inhibiting phosphodiesterase, the enzyme responsible for this breakdown, and therefore prolong the action of cAMP (amrinone, milrinone, enoximone, pimobendan).

In practice, none of these inotropic agents have been granted a Marketing Authorization for oral use.

Current state of knowledge

 The new inotropic agents are effective on functional parameters in the short-term.

For example, in the **Western Enoximone Study** (*Am Heart J* 1991;121:1471-1479), enoximone (50 mg tid), prescribed in addition to conventional treatment for 12 weeks, in 164 patients with mild-to-moderate heart failure (42% with NYHA class II and 58% with NYHA class III and isotope left ventricular ejection fraction ≤ 0.45), vs placebo, improved the symptoms and signs of heart failure and also significantly increased ($p = 0.012$) exercise time at the 4th week, but this effect was no longer significant after the 12th week.

2　Their long-term prescription cannot be recommended.

The efficacy of the new inotropic agents tapers off with time due to desensitization of beta-adrenergic receptors; they can also be harmful because of their adverse effects (hypotension, gastrointestinal disorders, thrombocytopenia, and especially a proarrhythmic effect with ventricular premature depolarizations or tachycardia) and a particularly marked excess mortality in patients with the most severe heart failure (NYHA class IV).

In the **PROMISE** study (*N Engl J Med* 1991;325:1468-1475), conducted in 1,088 patients with severe heart failure (NYHA class IV), the number of deaths was significantly increased by 53% with milrinone ($p = 0.006$) after 6 months of treatment.

In the **PICO** study (*Heart* 1990;76:223-231), conducted in 317 patients with NYHA class II-III heart failure and left ventricular ejection fraction of 0.20, with a follow-up of 6 months, addition of pimobendan (a phosphodiesterase inhibitor with the positive inotropic and vasodilator properties of this therapeutic category) to conventional treatment, vs placebo, improved exercise duration without significantly modifying oxygen consumption on maximum exercise and increased the risk of death 1.8-fold (95% CI: 0.9 to 3.5).

In the **PRIME II** study (*Lancet* 1997;349:971-977), conducted in 1,906 patients with severe heart failure (NYHA class III-IV) and a follow-up of approximately 1 year, addition of oral ibopamine (devoid of any positive inotropic properties, but able to induce renal and peripheral vasodilatation, which reduces the neuroendocrine reaction) at the dosage of 100 mg tid, to optimal conventional treatment, vs placebo, significantly increased mortality [25% vs 20% with placebo (RR: 1.26; 95% CI: 1.04 to 1.53, $p = 0.017$)].

In the **Vesnarinone Trial** (*N Engl J Med* 1998;339:180-186), conducted in 3,833 patients with severe heart failure (NYHA class III-IV and left ventricular ejection fraction ≤ 0.30) despite optimal treatment, vesnarinone (60 or 30 mg daily) vs placebo, prescribed at the dosage of 60 mg daily in addition to conventional treatment, with a mean follow-up of 286 days, was accompanied by a higher death rate (22.9% vs 18.9%) and a lower survival ($p = 0.02$) attributed to an increased number of sudden deaths, presumably due to arrhythmia. In contrast, the quality of life was improved by vesnarinone 8 ($p < 0.001$) and 16 ($p = 0.003$) weeks after randomization. At the dosage of 30 mg daily, vesnarinone tended to have the same effect as at 60 mg daily, but without any significant difference vs placebo. In conclusion, in this population, treatment with vesnarinone was accompanied by a dose-dependent increase of mortality, probably due to an increase of arrhythmic deaths.

Vasodilator therapy

Since publication of the **VHeFT I** study (*N Engl J Med* 1986;314:1547-1552), vasodilator therapy is an integral part of the treatment of heart failure. It is designed to counteract the harmful effects of the compensatory mechanisms of left ventricular dysfunction, i.e. hyperactivity of the sympathetic and renin-angiotensin-aldosterone systems, which accentuate peripheral vasoconstriction and salt and water retention.

This treatment involves the use of venous vasodilators (nitrates, molsidomine), arterial vasodilators (hydralazine, dihydropyridines), which induce arterial and venous smooth muscle relaxation, decreasing the resistance to left ventricular ejection, and increasing the capacitance of the venous reservoir, and ACE-inhibitors, which act by decreasing the synthesis of angiotensin II, whose vasoconstrictor, anti-natriuretic, and mitogenic effects can accentuate heart failure.

Finally, this approach is also based on angiotensin II AT1 receptor antagonists, a new therapeutic category, which is starting to be used in this indication (**ELITE** and **RESOLVD** studies, see pp. 252 and 253).

Current state of knowledge

1 **Hydralazine and isosorbide dinitrate combination vasodilator therapy improves the prognosis of chronic congestive heart failure.**

In the **VHeFT 1** study, including 642 patients with mild-to-moderate (NYHA class II-III) chronic congestive heart failure and left ventricular ejection fraction < 0.45, addition of the hydralazine (300 mg daily)-isosorbide dinitrate (160 mg daily) combination to conventional treatment (digoxin and diuretics) significantly decreased ($p < 0.028$) mortality by 34% at 2 years and 36% at 3 years.

2 **Prazosin vasodilator therapy does not modify the prognosis of congestive heart failure.**

In the **VHeFT 1** study, including 642 patients with mild-to-moderate (NYHA class II-III) chronic congestive heart failure and left ventricular ejection fraction < 0.45, addition of prazosin (20 mg daily), an alpha-adrenergic receptor antagonist, to conventional treatment (digoxin and diuretics) vs placebo, did not modify the mortality, with a mean follow-up of 2.3 years.

3 **ACE-inhibitors improve the prognosis of congestive heart failure at all stages of the disease.**

● **Severe heart failure**

In the **CONSENSUS** study (*N Engl J Med* 1987;316:1429-1435), based on 253 patients with NYHA class IV heart failure, the addition of enalapril (2.5 to 40 mg daily) to conventional treatment, vs placebo, significantly improved the symptoms and decreased the risk of mortality at 6 and 12 months by 40% ($p = 0.002$) and 31% ($p = 0.001$), respectively.

● **Mild-to-moderate heart failure**

In the curative arm of the **SOLVD** study (*N Engl J Med* 1991;325: 293-302), based on 2,569 patients with NYHA class II-III heart failure and left ventricular ejection fraction ≤ 0.35, addition of enalapril (2.5 to 20 mg daily, with an average of 16.6 mg daily) to conventional treatment significantly decreased the number of deaths (especially death from worsening heart failure) by 16% ($p = 0.0036$) and the combined risk of death and hospitalizations for heart failure by 26% ($p = 0.0001$), with a mean follow-up of 41.4 months.

In the **VHeFT II** study (*N Engl J Med* 1991;325:303-310), based on 804 patients with NYHA class II-III heart failure, enalapril (20 mg daily) was found to be more effective than the hydralazine (300 mg daily)-isosorbide dinitrate (160 mg daily) combination. With a mean follow-up of 2.5 years, enalapril significantly decreased mortality, especially the number of sudden deaths, by 28% (p = 0.016).

● **Isolated left ventricular dysfunction**

In the preventive arm of the **SOLVD** study (*N Engl J Med* 1992;327: 685-691), based on 4,228 patients with NYHA class I-II heart failure and left ventricular ejection fraction ≤ 0.35 and a mean follow-up of 37.4 months, enalapril (2.5 to 20 mg daily) vs placebo significantly reduced the number of deaths or hospitalizations for heart failure by 20% (p < 0.001), but only tended to reduce all cause mortality by 8% (NS) and cardiovascular mortality by 12% (NS) and this beneficial effect vs placebo only started to be observed after the 18th month.

4 **ACE-inhibitors after myocardial infarction reduce morbidity and improve the symptoms and survival, when the left ventricular ejection fraction is less than 0.35 to 0.40 (see p. 233).**

A meta-analysis by **Garg** and **Yusuf** (*JAMA* 1995;273:1450-1456), based on 32 trials including a total of 7,105 patients with congestive heart failure, evaluated the effects of ACE-inhibitors on mortality and morbidity in congestive heart failure. With a minimum follow-up of 10 weeks (> 3 months in 54% of patients), ACE-inhibitors vs placebo significantly decreased all cause mortality, reduced the combined incidence of deaths and hospitalizations for congestive heart failure, and especially decreased mortality from worsening heart failure. They tended to reduce sudden deaths or deaths considered to be due to arrhythmia and deaths from myocardial infarction. Finally, they reduced the incidence of fatal and nonfatal myocardial infarction, and non-significantly decreased the overall incidence of cerebrovascular accident, pulmonary embolism, and other thromboembolic events.

This meta-analysis confirms the major value of ACE-inhibitors, which improve survival, decrease morbidity, relieve symptoms, and increase exercise capacity in patients with symptomatic chronic heart failure or isolated systolic left ventricular dysfunction. They should therefore be very widely prescribed from the first stages of heart failure. Subgroup analysis shows that the reduction of mortality and number of hospitalizations for heart failure is independent of age, gender, NYHA functional class and etiology of heart disease. Only a left ventricular ejection fraction ≤ 0.25 is predictive of an even greater efficacy of ACE-inhibitors.

In practice, although ACE-inhibitors now represent a significant progress in the treatment of heart failure, it must be remembered that only 30% to 40% of eligible patients are treated with these agents. Furthermore, the dosages used in everyday practice are much lower than those used in the major clinical trials and the majority of patients treated with ACE-inhibitors are treated at dosages that may be ineffective to reduce morbidity and mortality.

Unresolved questions

● **Are large-scale clinical trials representative of the population of unselected heart failure patients treated in France?**

The majority of these trials were performed in the United States, in specialized settings, on highly selected patients: under-representation of female patients, age an average of 10 years lower than that of the population of heart failure patients seen in our departments, over-representation of ischemic heart disease, and under-representation of hypertensive heart disease according to the epidemiological data of the **Framingham** study (*N Engl J Med* 1997;336:1350-1355) and the **RECIF** study (*Et Eval Cardiovasc* 1996;3:117-164) conducted in the Ile-de-France region.

● **What is the optimal dose of ACE-inhibitors?**

Are the dosages recommended in the major clinical trials the optimal dosages ensuring maximum benefit from the action of the ACE-inhibitor or, on the contrary, could the same results be obtained with lower dosages?

It must be remembered that the empirical preference given to low-dose ACE-inhibitors in everyday practice is based on the undemonstrated belief that they exert a similar benefit to that of high doses, with a lower incidence of adverse effects. However, most of the major clinical trials have clearly indicated that patients tolerate high dosages of ACE-inhibitors, whose efficacy has now been demonstrated.

Are the effects of ACE-inhibitors on survival dose-dependent?

● Two ongoing studies are trying to determine whether low-dose ACE-inhibitors are as effective as high doses to reduce the morbidity and mortality of heart failure.

The **ATLAS** study (*Arch Mal Cœur Vaiss* 1994;87:45-50 and 47th session of the American College of Cardiology, 1998) included 3,164 patients with NYHA class II-IV heart failure (left ventricular ejection fraction ≤ 0.30, mean: 23%), treated with lisinopril (2.5 to 5.0 mg daily) in addition to diuretics, possibly combined with digitalis; after randomization, some patients also received either high-dose lisinopril (32.5 to 35 mg daily) or placebo. With a mean follow-up of 46 months, during which 1383 deaths occurred, high-dose vs low-dose lisinopril did not significantly modify cardiovascular or all cause mortality, the main endpoint of the study, but decreased the combined risk of all cause mortality and hospitalizations by 12% (*p* = 0.002). High dosages were able to be administered to 90% of the patients randomized to this arm, with a low percentage of adverse events requiring discontinuation of treatment: 1.1% vs 0.6% for hypotension and 1.3% vs 0.8% for impaired renal function. According to **Packer**, the study coordinator, high-dose lisinopril had a significantly greater effect on mortality and morbidity, while remaining well tolerated; more generally, optimal use of ACE-inhibitors could prevent as many as 60,000 deaths and 100,000 hospitalizations in the United States each year.

The **NETWORK** study (this is not an acronym, the study is called Network because it is conducted in a *network* of centers in Great Britain) (*Eur Heart J* 1998;19:481-489), included 1,532 patients (mean age: 70 years) with NYHA class II-IV heart failure, who received enalapril (2.5 mg, 5 mg or 10 mg bid) in addition to conventional treatment. With a follow-up of 6 months, low-dose enalapril (2.5 mg bid) was as effective as the intermediate (5 mg bid) or high (10 mg bid) dosages on reduction of the relative risk of combined events constituting the study endpoint: deaths, hospitalizations for heart failure or deterioration of heart failure, observed in 12.3%, 12.9%, and 14.7% of cases, respectively. The mortality in each group was 4.2%, 3.3%, and 2.9%. Overall, this study failed to demonstrate a relationship between dosage and response to treatment with enalapril.

Should short-acting or long-acting ACE-inhibitors be used?

At least theoretically, short-acting ACE-inhibitors may not provide complete 24-hour protection and may therefore be less effective. Due to their pharmacokinetics, they can also induce, right from the first dose, a brief, but potentially severe fall in blood pressure, particularly harmful in elderly patients, in patients with low SBP and/or with unstable hemodynamics.

However, the duration of action of an ACE-inhibitor depends not only on its affinity for angiotensin-converting enzyme, but also on the dosage used. Consequently, a high dose of a short-acting ACE-inhibitor may have a more prolonged effect than a low dose of a long-acting ACE-inhibitor. It is also often difficult, in clinical practice, to establish dose-equivalencies between the various ACE-inhibitors.

Based on current data, ACE-inhibitors appear to be interchangeable, as their beneficial effect is probably due to an effect specific to this therapeutic category.

Is the beneficial effect of long-term ACE-inhibitors due to their action on afterload or is it related to a specific effect independent of any action on the blood pressure load?

Reviewing the data of the **SOLVD** studies, **Yusuf** (*Lancet* 1992; 340:1173-1178) showed that the patients who obtained the greatest benefit from ACE-inhibitors in terms of prevention of coronary events were those whose blood pressure was reduced in the long-term by at least 6 mm Hg for SBP and 4 mm Hg for DBP, without any reactive tachycardia.

The **PREDICT Coversyl**® (perindopril) study, currently underway in France in 4,000 patients with ischemic heart failure, is evaluating, with a minimum follow-up of 2 years, the effect on cardiovascular morbidity and mortality of a therapeutic strategy based on a reduction of SBP by at least 10 mm Hg obtained with increasing doses of perindopril (2 then 4 then 8 mg daily) vs a therapeutic strategy using low-dose perindopril (2 mg daily).

What will be the place of angiotensin II AT1 receptor antagonists in heart failure (see p. 180)?

In the **ELITE** study (*Lancet* 1997;349:477-452), conducted in 722 patients with a mean age of 74 years, presenting NYHA class II

(65%) or III (34%) heart failure, with a mean left ventricular ejection fraction of 0.31, losartan (50 mg daily), an angiotensin II AT1 receptor antagonist, prescribed in addition to conventional treatment, with a follow-up of 12 months, was significantly better tolerated (main endpoint) than captopril (50 mg tid). Although the percentage of patients (10.5%) with persistent elevation of serum creatinine was the same in the 2 groups, losartan was responsible for fewer drop-outs from the trial because of adverse effects (12.2% vs 20.8% with captopril, $p = 0.002$); it tended to reduce the combined risk of death and/or hospitalizations for heart failure by 32% (9.4% vs 13.2%, $p = 0.075$), especially by reducing all cause mortality (4.8% vs 8.7%, $p = 0.02$) and more particularly sudden death.

The results of this first study, showing that angiotensin II AT1 receptor blockade reduces the mortality of heart failure, need to be confirmed. Publication of the results of the prematurely discontinued **RESOLVD** study will certainly provide more information. This study compared the effects of candesartan, enalapril, and a combination of the two on functional capacity, exercise tolerance, ventricular function, and neuroendocrine status in patients with moderate-to-severe heart failure (NYHA class II-IV; left ventricular ejection fraction ≤ 0.40). Other studies are still underway: **ELITE II** (losartan), **VAL-HeFt** (valsartan), and **CHARM** (candesartan).

Calcium channel blockers

Current state of knowledge

 Despite their vasodilator properties, calcium channel blockers cannot be routinely recommended.

Firstly, because some of them (diltiazem and verapamil), whose negative inotropic action is more marked than the peripheral vasodilator action, can worsen left ventricular failure and, secondly, because the efficacy of new generation dihydropyridines, such as amlodipine (studied in **PRAISE**) and felodipine (evaluated in **VHeFT III**), has not been formally demonstrated.

In the **PRAISE** study (*N Engl J Med* 1996;335:1107-1114), conducted in 1,153 patients with NYHA class III-IV heart failure and left ventricular ejection fraction < 0.30 (average of 0.21), amlodipine (5 mg bid), combined with conventional treatment comprising digoxin, diuretics, and ACE-inhibitor, vs placebo, with a median follow-up of 13.8 months, tended to decrease the combined risk of fatal and nonfatal events and the risk of death by 9% (NS). It did not modify these parameters in patients with ischemic heart disease, but significantly reduced the combined risk of fatal and nonfatal events by 31% ($p = 0.04$) and the risk of death by 46% ($p = 0.001$) in patients with nonischemic heart disease.

This finding led to the design of the ongoing **PRAISE 2** study, evaluating the effect of amlodipine vs placebo on cardiovascular morbidity and mortality and all cause mortality in 1,800 patients with non-ischemic heart failure (NYHA class III-IV; left ventricular ejection fraction < 0.30) treated with ACE-inhibitors, diuretics, and digoxin.

In the **VHeFT III** study (*Circulation* 1997;96:856-863), based on 450 patients with NYHA class II-III heart failure and left ventricular ejection fraction ≤ 0.45 (average of 0.30), felodipine SR (5 mg bid) combined with conventional treatment (enalapril: 97% of cases; diuretics: 89%; digoxin: 75%), vs placebo, with a mean follow-up of 18 months, significantly reduced blood pressure, and also:

● at 3 months, significantly increased left ventricular ejection fraction ($p = 0.001$) and reduced plasma levels of atrial natriuretic factor, but did not improve exercise capacity, quality of life, or number of hospitalizations;

● in the longer term, it did not modify mortality (13.8% vs 12.8%) and hospitalization rate (43% vs 42%). The favorable effects observed on left ventricular ejection fraction and plasma atrial natriuretic factor did not persist, but felodipine SR prevented deterioration of exercise capacity and quality of life.

In this context, the results of the **MACH 1** study (*Clin Cardiol* 1997; 20:320-326) conducted in 2,500 patients with NYHA class II-IV heart failure, were eagerly awaited. This study, with a follow-up of 3 years, was designed to evaluate the effect of mibefradil (50 to 100 mg daily) (a calcium channel blocking agent, potent peripheral and coronary vasodilator devoid of negative inotropic effects, but able to slow heart rate), prescribed in addition to conventional treatment (diuretic and ACE-inhibitors) on symptoms and cardiovascular morbidity and mortality. The study was stopped prematurely (20th Congress of the European Society of Cardiology, 1998) after two years of follow-up because mibefradil tended to increase mortality by 12% (NS). This excess mortality, attributed to a proarrhythmic effect (torsades de pointes), was observed in many subgroups, especially in patients already treated with antiarrhythmic agents, beta-blockers, or statins and led to discontinuation of the development of mibefradil.

Beta-blockers

For a long time, heart failure constituted a formal contraindication to the use of beta-blockers. It may therefore be surprising to consider prescribing them in the treatment of this disease. However, this paradox is only apparent, as heart failure stimulates neuroendocrine systems including the sympathetic system creating, in the long term, a situation which becomes harmful as it worsens heart failure (see p. 274).

According to the **Guidelines** of the American College of Cardiology/ American Heart Association Task Force Report (*Circulation* 1995;92: 2764-2784), the use of beta-blockers in the treatment of chronic heart failure is still under investigation. However, ideas are rapidly changing in the light of the studies conducted with carvedilol, a new generation beta-blocker possessing alpha-blocking, antioxidant, and antiproliferative properties (see pp. 268-270) and especially with the results of the **CIBIS II** (see p. 272) and **MERIT-HF** (see p. 272) studies, which demonstrated, for the first time, a reduction of all cause mortality with bisoprolol and metoprolol, respectively.

It is therefore now legitimate to use beta-blockers in certain selected patients. However, as these agents can depress left ventricular function, it is a wise precaution to institute treatment in hospital and to prescribe them at gradually increasing dosages, starting with a low dose (so-called dose-ranging period).

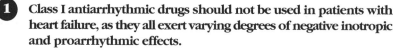

Antiarrhythmic drugs

Current state of knowledge

 Class I antiarrhythmic drugs should not be used in patients with heart failure, as they all exert varying degrees of negative inotropic and proarrhythmic effects.

 Although no individual trial has formally demonstrated that beta-blockers improve the prognosis, the meta-analyses by **Doughty** and **Heidenreich** (see pp. 270 and 271) show that they decrease all cause mortality.

Among the class III antiarrhythmic drugs, amiodarone and dofetilide do not have any harmful effects on the all cause mortality of heart failure.

These were the conclusions reached by the **EMIAT** and **CAMIAT** studies (see p. 302), conducted with amiodarone, and the **DIA-MOND-CHF** study, conducted with dofetilide (see p. 258).

Unresolved questions

● Does amiodarone improve survival?

● Three trials report contradictory results.

In the **GESICA** study (*Lancet* 1994;344:493-498), amiodarone improved survival. In this study, conducted in 516 patients with NYHA class II-IV heart failure and left ventricular ejection fraction ≤ 0.35 and non-sustained ventricular tachycardia with a mean follow-up of 13 months, amiodarone (600 mg daily for 14 days, then 300 mg daily), combined with conventional treatment, vs placebo, significantly reduced mortality by 28% ($p = 0.024$) (this reduction concerned both sudden deaths and deaths due to progressive heart failure) and decreased the combined risk of death or hospitalization by 31% ($p = 0.0024$).

In the **EPAMSA** study (*Am Heart J* 1995;130:494-500), conducted in 127 patients with left ventricular ejection fraction < 0.35 and asymptomatic ventricular arrhythmia (Lown class II and IV) and a follow-up of one year, amiodarone (800 mg daily for 2 weeks then

400 mg daily), vs the control group which did not receive an antiarrhythmic drugs, reduced all cause mortality [10.5% vs 28.6% (odds ratio (OR): 0.29; 95% CI: 0.10 to 0.84; log-rank test 0.02)] and the sudden death rate [7.0% vs 20.4% (OR: 0.29, 95% CI: 0.08 to 1.00; log-rank test 0.04)].

In the **STAT-CHF** study (*N Engl J Med* 1995;333:77-82), amiodarone did not modify all cause mortality, but tended to prolong survival of patients with nonischemic heart disease. In this study, conducted in 674 patients with NYHA class III-IV heart failure, left ventricular ejection fraction ≤ 0.40, and presenting at least 10 asymptomatic ventricular premature depolarizations/hour on continuous Holter ECG monitoring, amiodarone (800 mg daily for 14 days, then 400 mg daily for 50 weeks, and finally 300 mg daily), vs placebo, with a median follow-up of 45 months, did not significantly modify all cause mortality or the sudden death rate, but significantly increased the left ventricular ejection fraction (thereby confirming the absence of a systematic correlation between improvement of this parameter and survival).

The discordant results of the **GESICA** and **STAT-CHF** studies can probably be explained by the much higher proportion of patients with nonischemic heart disease in the **GESICA** study (61%) than in the **STAT-CHF** study (29%).

● The results of a meta-analysis are in favor of amiodarone.

In the **ATMA** meta-analysis (*Lancet* 1997;350:1417-1424), based on 13 trials (including 8 performed in post-myocardial infarction and 5 in heart failure), including a total of 6,553 patients, 89% of whom had a history of myocardial infarction, with a mean left ventricular ejection fraction of 0.31 and an average of 18 ventricular premature depolarizations/hour, amiodarone (400 mg daily to 1,000 mg/week, prescribed after a loading dose varying between 400 mg daily for 28 days and 800 mg daily for 14 days), with a follow-up of 6 months to 4.5 years, reduced all cause mortality by 13% (*p* = 0.030) to 15% (*p* = 0.081), depending on the statistical method adopted, and arrhythmic deaths by 29% (*p* = 0.0003) at the price of a 1% excess annual risk of pulmonary adverse effects.

 What about dofetilide?

In the **DIAMOND-CHF** study (*J Am Coll Cardiol* 1998;31 suppl. A:33A), conducted in 1,518 patients with significant alteration of left ventricular function (left ventricular ejection fraction < 0.35), with a follow-up of 3 years, dofetilide (0.25 to 1 mg daily) vs placebo did not modify either the all cause mortality or the number of arrhythmic deaths; in contrast it significantly reduced the incidence of hospitalizations for heart failure by 25% (RR: 0.75%; 95% CI: 0.63 to 0.89, $p < 0.001$), both in patients in sinus rhythm or with atrial fibrillation.

Anticoagulants

Is the systematic prescription of anticoagulants justified in heart failure? In the absence of controlled studies, no definitive conclusions can be drawn and many uncertainties still persist (*Am J Cardiol* 1998;31:745-748).

Current state of knowledge

 The thromboembolic risk actually appears to be lower than that based on the findings of old anatomical studies.

This risk was 2.5 per 100 patient-years in the **VHeFT I** study, 1.6 in the **SOLVD** study and 2.2 in the **VHeFT II** study.

 The thromboembolic risk increases in a certain number of circumstances.

The thromboembolic risk is increased in the case of advanced heart failure (marked reduction of left ventricular ejection fraction and cardiac dilatation), rheumatic heart disease, especially involving the mitral valve, atrial fibrillation, mobile left intraventricular thrombus, a history of thromboembolic disease and, finally, decreased maximum oxygen consumption on effort, as demonstrated by the **VHeFT I** study.

 The annual hemorrhage rate with anticoagulants is of the order of 5 to 6%, while the fatal hemorrhage rate is about 0.8%.

Unresolved questions

● **Does long-term anticoagulant treatment improve the prognosis of heart failure?**

Although it did not answer all aspects of this fundamental question, retrospective analysis (*J Am Coll Cardiol* 1998;31:749-753) of the 6,797 patients included in the SOLVD studies provided an important element: warfarin improves survival and decreases morbidity.

Multivariate analysis of these patients with left ventricular dysfunction (left ventricular ejection fraction ≤ 0.35) showed that warfarin, with a follow-up of 3 to 4 years, significantly decreased all cause mortality by 24% [hazard ratio (HR): 0.76; 95% CI: 0.65% to 0.89%, $p = 0.0006$] and the combined risk of death or hospitalization for heart failure by 18% (HR: 0.82; 95% CI: 0.72% to 0.93%, $p = 0.0002$). This beneficial effect was not significantly influenced by age, left ventricular ejection fraction, NYHA functional class, etiology of heart disease, or the presence of atrial fibrillation.

● **Does long-term platelet aggregation inhibitor treatment improve the prognosis of heart failure?**

A retrospective analysis (*J Am Coll Cardiol* 1998;31:419-425) of the 6,797 patients included in the SOLVD studies provided a partial answer: platelet aggregation inhibitors improve survival and reduce morbidity.

In these patients with left ventricular dysfunction (left ventricular ejection fraction ≤ 0.35) followed for 3 to 4 years, platelet aggregation inhibitors significantly reduced all cause mortality by 18% [adjusted hazard ratio (HR): 0.82; 95% CI: 0.7% to 0.92%, $p = 0.0005$] and the risk of death or hospitalization for heart failure by 19% (adjusted HR: 0.81; 95% CI: 0.74% to 0.89%, $p < 0.0001$).

● **Other information will be probably be provided by the ongoing HELAS study (8th European meeting of the Société Française de Cardiologie, 1997), designed to compare:**

    ● warfarin (INR: 2.0 to 3.0) vs aspirin (325 mg daily) in 3,000 patients with heart failure (NYHA class II, left ventricular ejection fraction < 0.30) secondary to myocardial infarction:

    ● and warfarin vs placebo in another 3,000 patients with the same degree of heart failure, but secondary to dilated cardiomyopathy.

Functional signs of heart failure
New York Heart Association (NYHA) classification

Class I   No limitation of ordinary physical exercise, which does not cause fatigue, dyspnea, or palpitations

Class II   Slight limitation of ordinary physical exercise, which induces fatigue, dyspnea, palpitations, or angina

Class III   Marked limitation of ordinary physical exercise with no symptoms at rest

Class IV   Any physical exercise is impossible without discomfort; symptoms of heart failure are present even at rest and are increased on effort.

The Criteria Committee of the New York Heart Association (*Diseases of the Heart and Blood Vessels. Nomenclature and Criteria for Diagnosis*, 6th ed., Boston, Little, Brown and Co., 1964, p. 114).

ACE-inhibitors: pharmacological data

● All ACE-inhibitors, except captopril and lisinopril, are inactive prodrugs that only become active after hydrolysis.

● All ACE-inhibitors are eliminated without biotransformation except for:

  • trandolapril and fosinopril, which have a mixed hepatorenal elimination;

  • ramipril, which forms inactive metabolites eliminated in the urine and bile.

Contraindications to the use of ACE-inhibitors

Serum creatinine > 200 µmol/L
History of bilateral renal artery stenosis
Serum potassium > 5.5 mEq/L
Severe valvular stenosis
SBP ≤ 100 mm Hg; when SBP is between 100 and 110 mm Hg, strict blood pressure control is necessary.
Although, in the ISIS 4 study, symptomatic hypotension (approximately 10% of cases) or cardiogenic shock (5% of cases) was more frequent with ACE-inhibitors than with placebo, the mortality was similar in the 2 groups, very probably because of the particularly attentive surveillance of these patients.

The controversy concerning digitalis glucosides

Are digitalis glucosides effective in the treatment of chronic heart failure? Withering already asked these questions in 1785: how can we identify patients? How can we measure the clinical response? How can we avoid the risks of this treatment?

Digitalis glucosides are classically considered to have a weak inotropic action, a narrow therapeutic margin compared to their toxic effects, and to be possibly harmful in ischemic heart disease by increasing myocardial oxygen consumption, by promoting contraction of healthy zones and consequently the appearance of dyskinesias and by facilitating the development of ventricular arrhythmias.

However, we now know that, although their inotropic effect increases myocardial oxygen consumption, they have a favorable influence on the overall energy balance by decreasing ventricular volumes and wall tension and by slowing heart rate. Furthermore, retrospective analysis of the studies used to reach the conclusion that digitalis treatment could reduce the survival of patients with myocardial infarction, showed that the patients treated with digitalis actually presented the least favorable prognosis due to the presence of heart failure.

Studies before DIG

The studies devoted to the assessment of the efficacy of digitalis glucosides in the 1980s evaluated the consequences of the introduction or temporary discontinuation of digoxin treatment. Some studies were in favor of digoxin by demonstrating its efficacy on objective criteria, while others were unfavorable, as they failed to demonstrate any significant improvement of these parameters. Finally, other studies reached mixed conclusions due to the inconstant beneficial effects of digoxin. Critical analysis of these studies reveals the presence of many methodological biases and shows that they did not provide information concerning the effects of digoxin on major cardiovascular events.

● Subsequent randomized controlled clinical trials [**Captopril Digoxin Study** (*JAMA* 1988;259:539-544), **Xamoterol Digoxin Study** (*Lancet* 1988;1:489-493), **PROVED** (*J Am Coll Cardiol* 1993;22:955-962), **RADIANCE** (*N Engl J Med* 1993;329:1-7)] showed the beneficial effect of digoxin in chronic heart failure with normal sinus rhythm. It should be noted that, in the major clinical trials that demonstrated the efficacy of angiotensin-converting enzyme (ACE) inhibitors on the survival of patients with chronic heart failure, these medications were associated with diuretics and digitalis glucosides [digitalis glucosides were used in 92% of patients of the **CONSENSUS** study (*N Engl J Med* 1987;316:1429-1435) and 65.7% of patients of the curative arm of the **SOLVD** study (*N Engl J Med* 1991;325:293-302)].

● The meta-analysis by **Jaeschke** (*Am J Med* 1990;88:279-286) showed that only 12% (3 to 20%) of patients with chronic heart failure and normal sinus rhythm obtained a marked clinical benefit from digoxin. The essential problem concerns the identification of patients likely to respond to digoxin, due to the marked interindividual variations and the fact that the findings on physical examination are poorly correlated with symptoms, exercise capacity, and degree of left ventricular dysfunction.

In this climate of uncertainty, the results of the **DIG** study, designed to evaluate the effect of digoxin on mortality and frequency of hospitalizations, were eagerly awaited.

DIG study

● In the **DIG** study (*N Engl J Med* 1997;336:525-533), conducted in 7,788 patients with chronic heart failure (secondary to ischemic heart disease in 69.1% of cases) and normal sinus rhythm, 84% of whom were classified as NYHA class II-III, presenting a mean left ventricular ejection fraction of 0.32, digoxin (0.125 to 0.50 mg daily, i.e. 0.25 mg in 70% of cases) administered in addition to diuretics and ACE-inhibitor, vs placebo, with a follow-up of 37 months, had no significant influence on all cause mortality, regardless of the left ventricular ejection fraction and the etiology of the heart disease [it actually tended to reduce mortality from heart failure by 12% ($p = 0.06$), but also tended to increase the number of deaths from arrhythmia or myocardial infarction (NS)]. In contrast, digoxin significantly decreased the number of hospitalizations for worsening of heart failure by 28% (*p*

< 0.001) and the combined risk of deaths and hospitalizations for heart failure by 25% ($p < 0.001$). The beneficial effect of digoxin was more marked in patients at greater risk, i.e. NYHA class III-IV, left ventricular ejection fraction < 0.25, cardiothoracic ratio > 0.55. In this study, the mean plasma digoxin level at 12 months was 0.80 ng/mL (1.02 nmol/L), much lower than that classically recommended, which is situated between 1.2 and 2 ng/mL.

● According to **Packer** (*N Engl J Med* 1997;336:575-576), the results of the **DIG** study provide evidence in favor of both the supporters and the opponents of digoxin.

　● For the supporters of digitalis, this study shows that digoxin is effective in the treatment of heart failure and can be prescribed with complete safety. It decreased the risk of hospitalization for heart failure and this benefit, observed rapidly after starting treatment, persisted for more than 4 years, suggesting that the short-term improvement reported in earlier studies may be maintained in the long-term. This study also shows that beneficial effects are also observed in patients not previously treated with digoxin, consequently refuting the assertion that sudden withdrawal of digoxin was responsible for worsening of heart failure. Finally, this study shows that the beneficial effect of digoxin is not accompanied by any adverse effect on mortality.

　● The opponents of digitalis glucosides emphasized the fact that the **DIG** study raises major questions about the efficacy and safety of use of digoxin, as, although it may have slightly decreased the risk of death related to worsening of heart failure (and who can say with certainty whether the patients died from heart failure or with heart failure?), it was responsible for an excess of arrhythmic deaths, which represented most of the cardiovascular deaths. Furthermore, although digoxin reduced the risk of hospitalization for heart failure, it significantly increased the risk of hospitalization for other cardiovascular events. From this point of view, this study confirms, without attenuating, the fears concerning the ease of use of digoxin, as harmful effects were observed for plasma digoxin levels situated at the lower limit of the therapeutic range.

　● In practice, therefore, digoxin is probably neither as effective as was hoped, nor as dangerous as was feared. It is therefore legitimate to continue to use digoxin in the treatment of chronic heart failure when symptoms persist despite prescription of diuretics and especially ACE-inhibitors.

Beta-blocker treatment in heart failure

Waagstein (Br Heart J *1975;37:1022-1036) was the first author to use metoprolol in the treatment of chronic heart failure; this success was confirmed by the BHAT study* (JAMA *1982;247:1707-1714) conducted with propranolol after myocardial infarction.*

MDC and CIBIS studies

● Two large-scale randomized studies, MDC and CIBIS, were conducted in the early 1990s.

   ● In the MDC study (*Lancet* 1993;342:1441-1446), based on 383 patients with NYHA class II-III heart failure (secondary to idiopathic dilated cardiomyopathy) with left ventricular ejection fraction < 0.40, metoprolol (administered at gradually increasing doses to reach 100-150 mg daily over 6 weeks) combined with conventional treatment, vs placebo, with a follow-up of 12 to 18 months, did not modify all cause mortality, but tended to reduce the combined risk of death or deterioration of heart failure to the point of needing transplantation by 34% ($p = 0.058$).

   ● In the CIBIS study (*Circulation* 1994;90:1765-1773), based on 641 patients with NYHA class III-IV chronic heart failure (secondary to ischemic heart disease or dilated cardiomyopathy), with left ventricular ejection fraction < 0.40, addition of bisoprolol (5 mg daily) to conventional treatment, vs placebo, with a follow-up of 1.9 year, did not reduce mortality, but decreased the incidence of hospitalizations for acute episodes of cardiac decompensation.

Studies with carvedilol

● More recent studies were conducted with carvedilol, a new generation beta-blocker possessing alpha-blocking (and therefore vasodilator), antioxidant, and antiproliferative properties, in the context of the **US Carvedilol Heart Failure Study**, including studies conducted in mild (366 patients), moderate [**MOCHA** (345 patients) and **PRECISE** (278 patients) studies], and severe heart failure (105 patients). All patients suffered from ischemic or nonischemic heart disease, they presented signs of heart failure for at least 3 months with a left ventricular ejection fraction ≤ 0.35 and had been treated for at least 2 months with diuretics, ACE-inhibitor and, when necessary, digoxin. The 6-minute walk distance was between 426 and 550 m in the mild heart failure study, between 150 and 425 m in the moderate heart failure studies (**MOCHA** and **PRECISE** studies) and < 150 m in the severe heart failure study.

● In the **US Carvedilol Heart Failure Study** (*N Engl J Med* 1996;334: 1349-1355), based on 1,094 patients with chronic heart failure, mostly NYHA class II-III, carvedilol (starting with a dose of 6.25 mg daily, increased to 25 or 50 mg bid, when well tolerated), combined with conventional treatment, vs placebo, with a median follow-up of 6.5 months, significantly decreased mortality by 65% ($p < 0.001$), reduced the risk of hospitalization for cardiovascular disease by 27% ($p = 0.036$) and the combined risk of death or hospitalization by 38% ($p < 0.001$). Deterioration of heart failure related to an adverse effect of treatment was more frequent with placebo than with carvedilol.

These very favorable results were slightly tempered by **Pfeffer** (*N Engl J Med* 1996;334:1396-1397), based on a certain number of arguments: the deaths occurring during the period evaluating the safety of carvedilol were not taken into account in the statistical analysis of the mortality of this group (however, they represented 24% of the total number of deaths occurring with carvedilol), a number of patients (1.4%) in whom heart failure deteriorated during this same period were not randomized in the study; the spectacular reduction of mortality observed with carvedilol was actually based on only 53 deaths occurring over a period of slightly less than 7 months, a small number compared to the fact that the beneficial effect of ACE-inhibitors vs placebo on survival was demonstrated on more than 1,300 deaths (**CONSENSUS**, **SOLVD**, and **VHeFT II** studies).

● In the **mild heart failure study** (*Circulation* 1996;94:2800-2806), the addition of carvedilol 6.25 mg to 25 mg bid, or even 50 mg bid for patients weighing more than 85 kg, in 366 patients with NYHA class II-III heart failure, vs placebo, with a follow-up of 12 months, significantly decreased the risk of worsening of heart failure by 48% (p = 0.008), which occurred in 11% of cases with carvedilol vs 21% with placebo. This effect of carvedilol was not influenced by gender, age, ethnic origin, etiology of heart failure, or initial value of left ventricular ejection fraction. Carvedilol also significantly improved left ventricular ejection fraction, heart failure score, and NYHA functional class. Finally, intent-to-treat analysis showed that carvedilol significantly decreased all cause mortality (0.9% vs 4.0% with placebo, p = 0.048).

● In the **MOCHA** study (*Circulation* 1996;94:2807-2816), conducted in 345 subjects with mild-to-moderate chronic heart failure (secondary to ischemic or nonischemic heart disease), essentially NYHA class II-III, carvedilol used at 3 different dosages (6.25 mg bid, 12.5 mg bid or 25 mg bid), vs placebo, with a follow-up of 6 months, had no detectable effect on the submaximal stress test; however, it was accompanied by a significant, dose-dependent improvement of left ventricular function (p < 0.001) and survival (p < 0.001). Overall, when the 3 treatment groups were combined, carvedilol, which was generally well tolerated, significantly decreased overall actuarial mortality by 73% (p < 0.001) and hospitalization rate by 58% to 64% (p = 0.01).

● In the **PRECISE** study (*Circulation* 1996;94:2793-2799), conducted in 278 patients with moderate-to-severe NYHA class II-IV heart failure, carvedilol, at the dosage of 25 to 50 mg bid, vs placebo, induced a greater improvement of symptoms and was associated with a lower incidence of clinical deterioration evaluated in terms of modifications of the NYHA functional class (p = 0.014) or the patient's (p = 0.002) or physician's assessment (p < 0.001). Carvedilol also significantly increased left ventricular ejection fraction (p < 0.001) and significantly decreased the combined risk of morbidity and mortality (p = 0.029), but had little effect on exercise capacity or quality of life scores.

● In the **severe heart failure study** (*J Card Fail* 1997;3:173-179), carvedilol (6.25 to 25 mg bid) vs placebo, administered to 105 patients with class NYHA III-IV heart failure and a follow-up of 6 months, significantly increased left ventricular ejection fraction (+0.09 vs +0.02 with placebo, p = 0.004) and decreased the risk of clinical deterioration evaluated by the patients and their physician. These results confirm the clinical and hemodynamic efficacy already observed with carvedilol in less severe forms of heart failure.

● In the **Australian and New Zealand** study (**ANZ-HeFT**) (*Lancet* 1997;349:375-380), conducted in 415 patients with chronic stable NYHA class II-III heart failure, secondary to ischemic heart disease, with an isotope left ventricular ejection fraction < 0.45, carvedilol, prescribed in addition to conventional treatment [ACE-inhibitors (86% cases), diuretics (75% of cases), digoxin (38% of cases)], at the dosage of 6.25 to 25 mg bid vs placebo:

  ● after 12 months, increased left ventricular ejection fraction by 0.053 ($2p < 0.0001$) and decreased end-diastolic (by 1.7 mm, $2p = 0.06$) and end-systolic (by 3.2 mm, $2p = 0.0001$) dimensions without modifying treadmill exercise duration, 6-minute walk distance and NYHA class;

  ● after 19 months, significantly decreased the combined rate of death or hospital admission without modifying the frequency of episodes of worsening heart failure.

● According to **Chatterjee** (*Circulation* 1996;94:2689-2693), carvedilol, prescribed in addition to ACE-inhibitor in patients with left ventricular systolic dysfunction, can delay deterioration of heart failure. It should be considered to be a drug able to slow progression of heart failure rather than a treatment for refractory heart failure.

Beta-blockers: meta-analyses

● A recent meta-analysis by **Doughty** (*Eur Heart J* 1997;18:560-565), based on 24 randomized trials including a total of 3,141 patients with stable congestive heart failure, with a follow-up of 13 months, showed that beta-blockers vs placebo, prescribed in addition to conventional treatment (comprising ACE-inhibitor in 83% of cases), significantly decreased the risk of death by 31% ($2p = 0.0035$), as the mean annual mortality rate decreased from 9.7% to 7.5%.

● In a meta-analysis by **Heidenreich** (*J Am Coll Cardiol* 1997;30:27-34), based on 17 trials evaluating their effects on mortality in 3,039 patients with congestive heart failure, with a follow-up of 3 months to 2 years, beta-blockers significantly decreased all cause mortality (odds ratio [OR]: 0.69, 95% CI: 0.54 to 0.88) with a tendency towards a more marked reduction (OR: 0.58, 95% CI: 0.40 to 0.83) of non-sudden deaths (to a comparable degree regardless of the ischemic or nonischemic etiology of the heart disease) compared to sudden deaths (OR: 0.84, 95% CI: 0.59 to 1.12). The survival benefit was greater with carvedilol, but the difference was not statistically significant (p = 0.10) vs the other beta-blockers.

 In a meta-analysis by Lechat (*Circulation* 1998;98:1184-1191), based on 18 trials which evaluated their effect in 3,023 patients with heart failure, beta-blockers appeared to significantly increase left ventricular ejection fraction by 0.29 ($p < 10^{-9}$) and decreased the combined risk of death and hospitalization for heart failure by 37% (p < 0.001); they probably also increased survival, but the relatively small number of fatal events and the possibility of a different effect of selective and non-selective beta-blockers on this parameter, prevented any definitive conclusions on this last point.

State of knowledge before CIBIS II and MERIT HF studies

 Beta-blocker treatment improves left ventricular ejection fraction.

This improvement is essentially due to an increase of the stroke volume secondary to a marked reduction of left ventricular end-systolic volume.

 The results of beta-blocker treatment on symptoms, functional class, and submaximal exercise capacity are contradictory.

3 It had not yet been formally demonstrated by a large-scale trial that the improvement of left ventricular ejection fraction and the reduction of the number of hospitalizations observed with beta-blockers were accompanied by improvement of survival.

CIBIS II and MERIT HF studies

In the absence of formal proof that beta-adrenergic receptor blockade improved survival, the **CIBIS II** study (*Lancet* 1999;353:9-13) was conducted in 2,647 patients with ischemic or non-ischemic chronic heart failure (NYHA class III-IV; left ventricular ejection fraction ≤ 0.35). In these patients, addition of gradually increasing doses (1.25 mg to 10 mg daily) of bisoprolol (n = 1327) vs placebo (n = 1320) to conventional treatment, with a mean follow-up of 1.3 year, decreased all cause mortality (primary endpoint) by 34 % [156 (11.8 %) vs 228 (17.3 %) deaths, with a hazard ratio of 0.66 (95 % CI: 0.54 to 0.81), $p < 0.0001$], the number of sudden deaths by 44% [48 (3.6%) vs 83 (6.3%) deaths, with a hazard ratio of 0.56 (95% CI: 0.39 to 0.80), $p = 0.0011$]. Treatment effects were independent of the severity or cause of heart failure.

The results of the **CIBIS II** study were confirmed by those of the **MERIT-HF** study (Lancet 1999;353:2001-2007)which was stopped early on the recommendation of the independent safety committee (mean follow-up time: one year). In this international study (14 countries), conducted in 3,991 patients with moderate-to-severe heart failure (NYHA II-IV class; left ventricular ejection fraction ≤ 0.40), addition of gradually increasing doses of metoprolol CR/XL (12.5 to 200 mg daily) vs placebo to conventional treatment, significantly decreased all cause mortality by 34% [145(7.2% per patient-years of follow-up) vs 217 deaths (11.0%), RR 0.66(95% CI:0.53 to 0.81), p=0.00009 or adjusted for interim analyses p=0.0062], sudden deaths by 41% [79 vs 132, RR:0.59 (95% CI:0.45 to 0.78), p=0.0002] and deaths from worsening heart failure by 42% [30 vs 58, RR:0.51 (95% CI:0,33 to 0.79), p=0.0023].

Unresolved questions

 Should beta-blockers be considered as a treatment for refractory severe heart failure, or on the contrary, as a preventive treatment able to delay progression of the disease?

Should beta-blockers be used (at what stage of the disease?), which one, at what dosage and for how long?

Does the effect of beta-blockers depend on the etiology of heart failure (cardiomyopathy, ischemic or hypertensive heart disease)?

Do beta-blockers with vasodilator properties (bucindolol, carvedilol, nebivolol) provide a greater survival advantage over so-called first generation beta-blockers?

The results of ongoing studies conducted with bucindolol (**BEST** (*Am J Cardiol* 1995;75:1220-1223) and carvedilol (**CAPRICORN, CARMEN, COMET, COPERNICUS**) (see p. 275) are eagerly awaited.

● Which specific causes of death (worsening of heart failure, fatal myocardial infarction, sudden death) are decreased by beta-blocker treatment?

● What is the effect of beta-blocker treatment in patients with NYHA class IV heart failure?

These patients were practically always excluded from published therapeutic trials; for example, they constituted only 3% of the population of the **US Carvedilol Heart Failure Study**.

● What will be the place of new medications for heart failure, especially ET_A and ET_B endothelin receptor antagonists (endothelin is a vasoconstrictor substance involved in neuroendocrine reactions in the same way as catecholamines and angiotensin II)?

The **REACH 1** study (*Circulation* 1998;98 suppl. I:I-3) evaluated the effect of bosentan, an endothelin receptor antagonist, administered in addition to conventional treatment at gradually increasing dosages to reach 500 mg bid vs placebo in 370 patients with chronic heart failure (NYHA class IIIb-IV; left ventricular ejection fraction < 0.35). The study, intended to last 6 months, was stopped prematurely because of elevation of hepatic transaminases > 3 times normal with bosentan. Analysis of the results for the overall population did not reveal any difference of efficacy between bosentan and placebo. However, analysis of the 47% of patients who completed the 6 months of the trial showed that bosentan significantly improved clinical parameters [reduction of symptoms and number of acute episodes of heart failure: 26.5% vs 9% ($p = 0.045$) with placebo].

Basis for the use of beta-blockers in the treatment of heart failure

● Chronic heart failure increases sympathetic tone, resulting in elevation of plasma adrenaline concentrations and urinary catecholamine excretion, proportional to the degree of left ventricular dysfunction.

● Catecholamines are harmful, because they increase myocardial oxygen consumption (tachycardia and vasoconstriction) and sodium retention (stimulation of renin secretion and accentuation of tubular resorption of sodium); they alter left ventricular filling and decrease myocardial perfusion; finally, they have proarrhythmic effects and have a direct toxic effect on myocardial cells.

● The level of sympathetic hyperactivity has a prognostic significance because it is correlated with the mortality of heart failure.

● Beta-blockers could theoretically improve heart failure by:

  • decreasing energy expenditure (reduction of heart rate at rest and on effort; inhibition of positive inotropic stimulation; reduction of renin secretion);

  • improving left ventricular filling (lengthening of diastole secondary to bradycardia and improvement of relaxation);

  • protecting against the direct myocardial toxicity of high levels of catecholamines;

  • improving perfusion of the subendocardial layers of the myocardium;

  • counteracting the proarrhythmic effect of catecholamines;

  • protecting myocardial beta receptors from excess circulating catecholamines; they fully restore these beta receptors, thereby increasing their capacity to be stimulated (*upregulation*).

Ongoing trials with carvedilol

● The **CAPRICORN** study is evaluating the effect of carvedilol on the all cause mortality of patients presenting left ventricular dysfunction after myocardial infarction, either isolated or accompanied by clinical signs of heart failure and already treated with ACE-inhibitor.

● The **CARMEN** study, in patients with mild heart failure, is comparing the effect of carvedilol prescribed alone and the combination of carvedilol-enalapril vs enalapril on echocardiographic left ventricular end-systolic volume.

● The **COMET** study is comparing the effects of carvedilol and metoprolol on mortality and morbidity in patients with moderate-to-severe congestive heart failure (NYHA class II-IV).

● The **COPERNICUS** study is evaluating the effects of carvedilol on the mortality of patients with severe congestive heart failure (NYHA class III-IV).

Atrial fibrillation

*With the regression of rheumatic heart disease in industrialized countries, the incidence of atrial fibrillation has decreased from 18% to 4% (in the SPAF study, the presence of mitral stenosis represented only 4% of all reasons for exclusion). Atrial fibrillation unrelated to rheumatic heart disease has therefore now become the main preoccupation of practitioners (*Lancet *1997;350:943-950).*

Atrial fibrillation, either permanent or in the form of frequent episodes, usually develops around the age of 65 years; it affects 2 to 5% of the general population over the age of 60 and more than one million people in the United States. According to the **Framingham** *study (*N Engl J Med *1982;306: 1018-1022), the prevalence of atrial fibrillation increases exponentially with age: < 1% between 50 and 65 years, 2 to 3% between 70 and 80 years, > 5% after the age of 80. However, these figures do not accurately reflect the prevalence of atrial fibrillation, which often passes unnoticed, inasmuch as silent episodes are 12 times more frequent than symptomatic episodes. The European Society of Cardiology has recently published its recommendations on this subject (*Eur Heart J *1998;19:1294-1320).*

Antiarrhythmic treatment

Although atrial fibrillation is the arrhythmia most frequently encountered in clinical cardiology, it is rather surprising that no large-scale trial defining the choice or even the value of antiarrhythmic treatment has yet been published. The major difficulty of conducting such a study and interpreting the results is due to the multiplicity of the clinical features of atrial fibrillation: permanent or paroxysmal, triggered by vagal or catecholaminergic influences, presence or absence of associated heart disease, duration of arrhythmia, and degree of atrial dilatation and left ventricular dysfunction.

However, many small trials have defined some of the principles of antiarrhythmic treatment.

Pharmacological cardioversion

Current state of knowledge

 Pharmacological cardioversion is less effective than electrical cardioversion.

However, it has a success rate of about 80% in the case of recent-onset atrial fibrillation (< 8 days), with a minimally dilated left atrium, in the absence of any underlying heart disease. Cardioversion uses amiodarone and class Ic antiarrhythmic drugs (flecainide, propafenone), either orally or by IV, with the usual precautions concerning these antiarrhythmic drugs (in the case of conduction disorders or left ventricular dysfunction).

According to the DAAF study (*Eur Heart J* 1997;18:649-654), conducted in 239 patients with atrial fibrillation present for less than 7 days, IV digoxin, at the dosage of 0.5 mg x 3 injected at H0, H2 and H6 after inclusion, did not increase the sinus rhythm conversion rate at the 16th hour (51% vs 46% with placebo), and did not shorten the time to sinus rhythm vs placebo. However, it must be stressed that digoxin had a pronounced and rapid effect on heart rate, which was already significant at 2 hours [104.6 ± 20.9 vs 116.8 ± 22.5 b.p.m. ($p = 0.0001$)], improving functional tolerance.

2 **Cardioversion, either pharmacological or electrical, must be preceded by effective anticoagulation for at least 3 weeks, except when atrial fibrillation is very recent (present for less than 48 hours) or when transesophageal echocardiography has confirmed the absence of left intra-atrial thrombosis.**

The ACUTE study (*Am J Cardiol* 1998;81:877-883) is designed to include 3,000 patients in order to compare conventional anticoagulation vs brief anticoagulation associated with transesophageal echocardiography performed before electrical cardioversion.

Cardioversion, either pharmacological or electrical, must be followed by effective anticoagulation for at least 3 weeks.

Loss of mechanical contractile activity of the atrial myocardium is usually observed for the first few days, or even weeks following restoration of sinus rhythm. This period therefore predisposes to the formation of intra-atrial thrombosis.

Prevention of recurrence

Prevention is based on the use of class Ia, Ic and III antiarrhythmic drugs.

 Current state of knowledge

1 Antiarrhythmic drugs are superior to placebo, but maintenance of sinus rhythm does not exceed 50 to 70% after one year.

Amiodarone appears to be the most effective and best tolerated antiarrhythmic drug in patients with heart failure, but it is usually reserved for patients with refractory and symptomatic arrhythmia because of its extracardiac adverse effects. The ongoing CTAF study (*Am J Cardiol* 1997;80:464-468) is comparing two therapeutic strategies to maintain sinus rhythm: low-dose amiodarone vs conventional antiarrhythmic treatment (sotalol or propafenone).

Sotalol and class Ic antiarrhythmic drugs can give good results after failure of class Ia antiarrhythmic drugs. Some combinations (amiodarone-flecainide) appear to be particularly effective, but have not been extensively evaluated. Dofetilide, a new class III antiarrhythmic drug and a selective potassium channel blocker, appears to be promising. In the EMERALD study (71st session of the American Heart Association, 1998), which included 671 patients, maintenance of sinus rhythm one year after cardioversion was more frequent with dofetilide (66%) than with sotalol (50%) or placebo (21%). The DIAMOND-MI (see p. 303) and DIAMOND-CHF (see p. 258) studies also demonstrated the safety of use of this antiarrhythmic drug in patients with post-myocardial infarction left ventricular dysfunction and congestive heart failure.

Beta-blockers are useful in combination with class I antiarrhythmic drugs, especially to prevent the risk of atrial flutter with 1:1 conduction, and whenever a catecholaminergic triggering factor is clearly identified.

② **Class I antiarrhythmic drugs could be responsible for excess mortality, especially because of their proarrhythmic effects.**

The meta-analysis by **Coplen** (*Circulation* 1990;82:1106-1116), based on 6 trials including 727 patients, suggested that quinidine, compared to absence of antiarrhythmic treatment, was more effective to maintain sinus rhythm (50% vs 25% at one year), but increased all cause mortality (2.9% vs 0.8%, $p < 0.05$). However, cause of death analysis failed to attribute this excess mortality to antiarrhythmic treatment alone.

The **SPAF** study (*J Am Coll Cardiol* 1992;20:527-532), a retrospective analysis, and consequently subject to criticism, also revealed an excess of cardiac mortality (3.3-fold increased) and sudden death (5.8-fold increased risk) in patients treated with class I antiarrhythmic drugs, only when they had a history of heart failure. Despite the absence of any formal proof, it is tempting to see a parallel between these observations and the results of the **CAST** study (see p. 300).

Class I antiarrhythmic drugs must therefore be avoided in the presence of ischemic heart disease or left ventricular dysfunction or intraventricular conduction disorders.

Control of ventricular rate

This was evaluated in permanent or multi-recurrent atrial fibrillation.

Current state of knowledge

 Digitalis glucosides are generally sufficient to slow resting heart rate.

However, they poorly control tachycardia accompanying effort and hyperadrenergic states.

 Heart-rate-lowering calcium channel blockers (verapamil, diltiazem) and beta-blockers decrease atrioventricular node conduction and effectively control heart rate, even during effort.

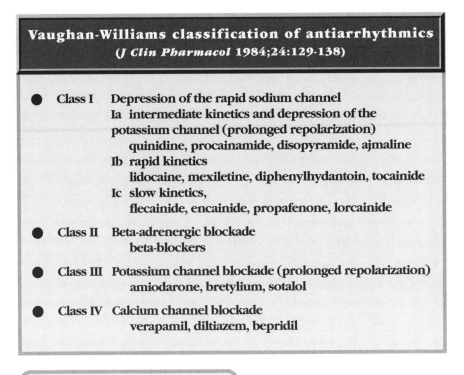

Vaughan-Williams classification of antiarrhythmics
(J Clin Pharmacol 1984;24:129-138)

- **Class I** Depression of the rapid sodium channel
  Ia intermediate kinetics and depression of the
  potassium channel (prolonged repolarization)
  quinidine, procainamide, disopyramide, ajmaline
  Ib rapid kinetics
  lidocaine, mexiletine, diphenylhydantoin, tocainide
  Ic slow kinetics,
  flecainide, encainide, propafenone, lorcainide
- **Class II** Beta-adrenergic blockade
  beta-blockers
- **Class III** Potassium channel blockade (prolonged repolarization)
  amiodarone, bretylium, sotalol
- **Class IV** Calcium channel blockade
  verapamil, diltiazem, bepridil

Unresolved questions

 Must sinus rhythm be maintained at all costs, or is it sufficient to control ventricular rate?

Maintenance of sinus rhythm is designed to eliminate symptoms, prevent the hemodynamic consequences of arrhythmia (including the development of cardiomyopathy), prevent thromboembolic complications and consequently reduce mortality. However, antiarrhythmic treatment is accompanied by an atrial fibrillation recurrence rate of almost 50% at one year and can be harmful, especially in the elderly and in the presence of left ventricular dysfunction. Their very relative efficacy also does not always allow discontinuation of anticoagulant therapy. Simple control of the ventricular rate, despite persistence of atrial fibrillation, could therefore represent a valid alternative.

Several ongoing trials, such as the **AFFIRM** study (*Am J Cardiol* 1997;79:1198-1202) and the **PIAF** study, are designed to answer this question.

Antithrombotic treatment

Atrial fibrillation unrelated to valvular heart disease is associated with an increased thromboembolic risk. Atrial fibrillation induces a 5-fold (or even 17.5-fold in the case of rheumatic heart disease) increase of the risk of ischemic cerebrovascular accident (more than 75,000 new cases per year in the United States, half of which are secondary to a cardiac thrombus), which increases annually by 5 to 7% (*Arch Mal Cœur Vaiss* 1994;87 suppl. III:17-23). It considerably increases the risk of asymptomatic cerebral myocardial infarction, which can be responsible for behavioral disorders in the elderly. CT scan has demonstrated the presence of asymptomatic cerebral infarcts in one quarter of patients with atrial fibrillation. From the neurologist's point of view, atrial fibrillation is also the leading cause of cerebral embolism and accounts for 15% of all cerebrovascular accidents: the frequency of this pathological association increases with age, from 6.7% between the ages of 50 and 59 to 32.2% between the ages of 80 and 89.

The presence of heart disease increases the risk of thromboembolic accidents, estimated to be 3.5% per annum in dilated cardiomyopathies and 18% in hypertensive heart disease. Chronic ischemic heart disease is certainly statistically correlated with atrial fibrillation, but this correlation is less marked than with other types of heart disease: only 0.6% of 18,343 coronary patients of the **CASS** study (*Am J Cardiol* 1988;61:714-717) presented atrial fibrillation.

In a certain number of cases, no etiology is detected and permanent atrial fibrillation appears to be isolated (lone atrial fibrillation) (*Br Heart J* 1954;16:189-194). The prevalence of idiopathic atrial fibrillation varies greatly from one series to another, depending on the extent of the etiological assessment: about 7% in the case of very thorough investigation (*N Engl J Med* 1987;317:669-674), but its real prevalence is difficult to assess. This type of arrhythmia has a good prognosis, as lone atrial fibrillation is associated with a very low risk of cerebral embolism (approximately 0.5% patient-years), comparable to that of the general population.

Current state of knowledge

1 Long-term anticoagulant treatment decreases the frequency of thromboembolic complications of rheumatic atrial fibrillation.

The thromboembolic risk associated with atrial fibrillation is maximum in the case of mitral valve disease, but is lower for aortic valve disease.

2 Long-term anticoagulant treatment decreases the frequency of thromboembolic complications, especially cerebral complications, of non-rheumatic atrial fibrillation (see p. 292).

This was demonstrated by 8 trials and confirmed in 2 meta-analyses.

● The Atrial Fibrillation Investigators meta-analysis (*Arch Intern Med* 1994;154:1449-1457), based on 5 studies (AFASAK, BAATAF, CAFA, SPAF 1, SPINAF) conducted in patients with a mean age of 69 years at the time of randomization, compared warfarin (INR: 1.2-1.5 to 2.8-4.2), on 1,889 patient-years vs a placebo group of 1,802 patient-years, or aspirin (AFASAK: 75 mg daily; SPAF: 325 mg daily), i.e. 1,132 patient-years vs a placebo group of 1,133 patient-years.

Warfarin vs placebo globally and significantly (95% CI: 50 to 79%) decreased the risk of any form of cerebrovascular accident by 68% and decreased the absolute annual risk by 3.1% ($p < 0.001$). This decreased risk was more marked in females (-84%) than in males (-60%). Warfarin decreased mortality by 33% ($p = 0.010$) and the combined incidence of cerebrovascular accident, systemic embolism, or death by 48% ($p < 0.001$).

The efficacy of aspirin vs placebo was not as constant. It significantly reduced the risk of cerebrovascular accident by 36% ($p = 0.03$) and the combined incidence of cerebrovascular accident, systemic embolism, or death by 28% ($p = 0.02$).

The annual major bleeding rate was 1.3% with warfarin, 1.0% with aspirin and 1.0% with placebo.

Multivariate analysis identified several factors predictive of the development of a cerebrovascular accident in the control group: advanced age, history of hypertension, transient ischemic attack, or cerebrovascular accident, and diabetes mellitus.

Finally, patients under the age of 65 presenting with lone atrial fibrillation and no other risk factors had a very low probability of cerebrovascular accident, even when they were not treated. However, the annual risk increased with age: 0 cerebrovascular accident in 112 patients under the age of 60 vs 3 cerebrovascular accidents in 44 patients over the age of 80.

● These conclusions are in line with those of the multivariate analysis by **Morley** (*Am J Cardiol* 1996;77:38A-44A), based on 7 large-scale trials (**AFASAK, BAATAF, SPINAF, SPAF** 1 and 2, **CAFA,** and **EAFT** trials). This analysis identified 3 factors increasing the risk of cerebrovascular accident in patients with chronic atrial fibrillation: hypertension, advanced age, history of ischemic cerebrovascular accident. In the absence of anticoagulant treatment, patients presenting one of these factors had an annual risk of cerebrovascular accident of 4%. Heart failure or coronary heart disease multiplied the risk of cerebrovascular accident by a factor of 3. In the absence of these factors, patients with an apparently normal heart appeared to have a low risk of cerebrovascular accident. In this meta-analysis, warfarin vs placebo reduced the risk of cerebrovascular accident by 64%. The beneficial effect of this treatment was less obvious after the age of 75 years, because of the high risk of hemorrhagic complications.

 Anticoagulants are just as effective in primary prevention as in secondary prevention.

Most of the major trials were primary prevention trials, although most of them included a small percentage (6.0% to 8.0%) of patients with a history of transient ischemic attacks or cerebrovascular accident.

The **EAFT** study (*N Engl J Med* 1995;333:5-10), the only real secondary prevention study, was conducted in patients with a history of transient ischemic attack or minor cerebrovascular accident during the previous 3 months.

 Anticoagulants moderately, but significantly increase the risk of hemorrhagic complications.

In the **Atrial Fibrillation Investigators** meta-analysis (see p. 283), the major bleeding rate (intracranial bleeding or hemorrhage requiring hospitalization or infusion of two units of packed cells) was 1.3% with warfarin, 1.0% with aspirin, and 1.0% with placebo.

The bleeding rate increases with the intensity of anticoagulation. Retrospective analysis of the results of the **EAFT** study showed that hemorrhagic complications increased considerably when INR was > 4.

In practice, in unselected patients, the essential problem consists of choosing a treatment that is able to prevent thromboembolic accidents without inducing major bleeding: the risk of major hemorrhage with long-term anticoagulants is 2 to 4% patient-years of treatment; almost 25% of these accidents are fatal and the risk of intracranial bleeding, already increased 8-fold, is even higher in patients with a history of ischemic cerebrovascular accident or hypertension.

5 **The optimum level of anticoagulation has not yet been determined.**

In a recent case-control study (method ensuring a high statistical power despite the inclusion of a relatively small number of patients), **Hilek** (*N Engl J Med* 1996;335:540-546) analysed 74 consecutive patients with atrial fibrillation (64% of whom were older than 75), hospitalized for ischemic cerebrovascular accident (fatal in 20% of cases, complicated by serious neurological sequelae in 19% of cases), occurring during treatment with warfarin. The level of anticoagulation of these patients was compared to that of a random sample of 222 patients (49% over the age of 75), in whom atrial fibrillation was treated with anticoagulants, but who did not develop a cerebrovascular accident.

The risk of ischemic cerebrovascular accident increased dramatically when INR was < 2.0; it doubled when INR decreased from 2.0 to 1.7 and more than doubled again when INR decreased from 1.7 to 1.4. In contrast, this risk was minimal when INR was ≥ 2.0.

This study demonstrates that it is unreasonable to propose low-level anticoagulation to patients with atrial fibrillation, as it does not provide sufficient protection against ischemic cerebrovascular accidents. Moreover, the **SPAF** 3 study (*Lancet* 1996;348:633-638), which set the objective of an INR between 1.2 and 1.5, had to be prematurely discontinued because of the insufficient efficacy of this treatment.

In practice, the first-line treatment in patients with atrial fibrillation must be an oral anticoagulant that maintains the INR between 2 and 3-4, while avoiding an INR < 2, which may be ineffective, and an INR between 4 and 5, which considerably increases the bleeding rate, especially in the elderly.

 Aspirin is less effective than oral anticoagulants in prevention of thromboembolic accidents, especially cerebrovascular accidents.

This was demonstrated by the results of primary prevention (**AFASAK**, **SPAF 2**) or secondary prevention (**EAFT**) studies comparing aspirin and warfarin. All studies reported that aspirin was less effective than oral anticoagulants in the prevention of thromboembolic accidents secondary to atrial fibrillation (aspirin reduced the thromboembolic risk by 14% in **AFASAK**, 42% in **SPAF 1**, and 17% in **EAFT**). A meta-analysis of these 3 trials by the **Atrial Fibrillation Investigators** (*Arch Intern Med* 1997; 157:1237-1240) reported a 21% (95% CI: 0% to 38%, $p = 0.05$) reduction of the relative risk of ischemic cerebrovascular accident with aspirin.

Despite its ease of prescription and the fact that it carries a lower risk of hemorrhagic complications than warfarin, aspirin is less effective and should therefore only be reserved to patients in whom the use of anticoagulants is contraindicated.

 In patients with atrial fibrillation not secondary to valvular heart disease and presenting a relatively low risk of thromboembolism, aspirin (325 mg daily) is accompanied by a low short-term risk of ischemic cerebrovascular accident.

This was demonstrated by a prospective study (*JAMA* 1998;279: 1273-1277) conducted in 892 patients (with a mean age of 67 ± 10 years, 78% of whom were males, followed for 2 years) with atrial fibrillation categorized as low risk based on the absence of 5 pre-specified thromboembolic risk factors: history of thromboembolism, systolic blood pressure > 160 mm Hg, female sex at age > 75 years, recent congestive heart failure or left ventricular shortening fraction ≤ 0.25. The annual risk of ischemic stroke in this population was about 2% (in contrast, the presence of one or several of these exclusion criteria considerably increased the risk, which was approximately 8% in the **SPAF III** study). It is impossible to say whether aspirin contributed to this low event rate due to the absence of a control group comprising nontreated patients. At the dosage of 325 mg daily, the annual major bleeding rate with aspirin was 0.5%.

The combination of low-dose warfarin and low-dose aspirin is less effective than more intense anticoagulation ensuring an INR of 2 to 3.

This was shown by the **SPAF 3** study (see p. 296), conducted in 1,044 patients, in whom a fixed low-dose warfarin ensuring a low level of anticoagulation (INR: 1.2 to 1.5) combined with aspirin (325 mg daily), was found to be insufficient to prevent cerebrovascular accidents, while a higher dosage of warfarin (INR: 2.0 to 3.0) was able to significantly reduce this risk, especially in patients with a history of thromboembolic disease.

In the final analysis, the choice of antithrombotic treatment, oral anticoagulant, or aspirin, must be personalized as a function of the emboligenic risk and the hemorrhagic risk.

In the **SPAF 2** study (see p. 295), in patients over the age of 75, warfarin (INR: 2 to 4.5) vs aspirin, decreased the number of thromboembolic accidents. However, it is precisely in these elderly patients that the physician is more reticent to use anticoagulants because of the increased risk of hemorrhagic complications.

In the **AFASAK** (see p. 292) and **SPINAF** (see p. 294) trials, which included patients of the same age as those included in **SPAF 2**, the hemorrhagic complication rate with anticoagulants was lower, probably because the target INR was lower (1.4 to 2.8) in **SPINAF** than in **AFASAK** (2.8 to 4.2).

Unresolved questions

● **Does the permanent or paroxysmal type of atrial fibrillation affect the annual risk of thromboembolic accidents?**

In the **Atrial Fibrillation Investigators** meta-analysis (*Arch Intern Med* 1994;154:1449-1457), paroxysmal atrial fibrillation and chronic atrial fibrillation were associated with a similar risk of embolic cerebrovascular accidents, regardless of how long atrial fibrillation had been present.

These recent data are in contradiction with studies showing that the thromboembolic risk of paroxysmal atrial fibrillation is lower than that of permanent atrial fibrillation. In the **Framingham** study (*Am J Med* 1984;27:4-12), the annual cerebrovascular accident rate was 5.4% in men with permanent atrial fibrillation, but only 1.3% in subjects presenting paroxysmal episodes of atrial fibrillation. Three other studies (*Am J Cardiol* 1996;77:38A-44A) also showed that the cerebrovascular accident rate was considerably lower in paroxysmal atrial fibrillation.

● **When should anticoagulant treatment be started after an embolic cerebrovascular accident?**

The most appropriate time for introduction of treatment remains controversial. This problem is dominated by the high risk of recurrent embolism during the first month, in favor of rapid anticoagulation followed by oral anticoagulants, and by the risk of hemorrhagic transformation and aggravation of cerebral lesions, which occurs in the majority of cases during the 48 hours after embolism. After excluding a hemorrhagic cerebral infarction by early computed tomography (24th hour), it seems reasonable to propose: immediate anticoagulation of small and medium-sized cerebral infarcts, and delayed anticoagulation (after the 7th day, following another CT scan) of large cerebral infarcts or associated with poorly controlled hypertension.

● **For how long should anticoagulants be continued after a cerebrovascular accident?**

Probably for as long as possible, for three reasons: firstly, because of the high annual recurrence rate, of the order of 15 to 20%; secondly, because, in the **EAFT** study (see p. 294), the beneficial effect persisted at 2 and 3 years; and finally, because the presence of a first ischemic cerebrovascular accident is a risk factor for the development of another embolic accident.

Reduction of the thromboembolic risk with anticoagulants was obtained with different INRs

AFASAK	BAATAF	SPAF 1 et 2	CAFA	SPINAF	EAFT	SPAF 3
2.8-4.2	1.5-2.7	2.0-4.5	2.0-3.0	1.4-2.8	2.5-4.0	2.0-3.0

Ischemic cerebrovascular accidents and nonrheumatic atrial fibrillation

● The development of an ischemic cerebrovascular accident in a patient with atrial fibrillation not related to rheumatic heart disease, does not automatically mean that it is due to cardiac embolism related to the presence of left atrial or ventricular thrombus.

● An ischemic cerebrovascular accident can be due to:

- migration of thrombi derived from ulcerated atheromatous plaques in the ascending aorta (particularly well demonstrated by transesophageal echocardiography) or large intracranial or extracranial arteries supplying the brain;

- a lacunar type of cerebrovascular accident related to hypertensive arteriolar disease.

● In practice, although a certain number of factors argue in favor of embolic occlusion arising from cardiac thrombi, and although, according to anatomical studies, approximately 2/3 of ischemic cerebrovascular accidents associated with nonrheumatic atrial fibrillation are probably due to emboli derived from the heart, it must not be forgotten that, in a given patient, the mechanism of the cerebrovascular accident often remains uncertain and it is this uncertainty which sometimes makes it difficult to choose preventive treatment.

Atrial fibrillation: ongoing studies

● The multicenter, randomized, double-blind **FFAACS** study of aspirin vs placebo is evaluating:

- the preventive efficacy of aspirin 100 mg daily combined with fluindione (INR: 2 to 2.6) on complications and vascular mortality in high-risk patients with nonvalvular atrial fibrillation, i.e. with a history of cerebrovascular accident regardless of age and, in the absence of such a history and in subjects > 65 years, presence of one of the following risk factors: hypertension, episode of heart failure during the previous 3 months, left ventricular shortening fraction < 25%;

- the correlation between the level of thromboembolic risk, the presence of intra-atrial contrasts and left atrial function assessed on transesophageal echocardiography. Mean duration of follow-up: 3 years.

● The **ACUTE** study is designed to evaluate the feasibility, safety, and cost of systematically performing transesophageal echocardiography before electrical cardioversion in a population of 3,000 patients.

Thromboembolic accident prevention trials

The results of 8 prospective, randomized trials of the prevention of thromboembolic accidents, conducted in patients with atrial fibrillation unrelated to rheumatic heart disease, have been available since 1989.

- In the **AFASAK** study (*Lancet* 1989;1:175-179), 1,007 patients with a mean age of 74.2 years, presenting nonrheumatic chronic atrial fibrillation, were randomized to receive placebo, aspirin (75 mg daily), or warfarin (INR: 2.8 to 4.2). With a 2-year follow-up, warfarin vs aspirin and vs placebo significantly reduced the global incidence of thromboembolic complications by 59% ($p < 0.05$), and decreased the cardiovascular and cerebrovascular mortality ($p < 0.02$) at the price of a significant increase of the number of nonfatal hemorrhagic accidents. In contrast, in this study, aspirin, prescribed at the dosage of 75 mg daily, provided similar results to placebo and did not significantly modify the number of thromboembolic accidents and the cardiovascular and cerebrovascular mortality.

- In the **BAATAF** study (*N Engl J Med* 1990;323:1505-1511), 420 patients with a mean age of 68 years, presenting nonrheumatic atrial fibrillation, either permanent (83% of cases) or intermittent (17% of cases), 6% of whom had history of cerebrovascular accident, were randomized to the low-dose warfarin group (INR: 1.7 to 2.7) or to the control group, which did not receive anticoagulant, but possibly aspirin. With a mean follow-up of 2.2 years, warfarin vs the control group significantly decreased the annual cerebrovascular accident rate by 86% (0.41% vs 2.98%, $p = 0.0022$) and also significantly decreased the annual mortality rate (2.25% vs 5.97%, $p = 0.005$), without modifying the major hemorrhage rate, but at the price of a 60% increase of the number of minor hemorrhages.

- In the **SPAF 1** study (*Circulation* 1991;84:527-539), 1,330 patients with a mean age of 67 years, suffering from nonrheumatic atrial fibrillation (permanent in 66% of cases), 7% of whom had already experienced a transient ischemic attack, were randomized to two groups:

● in group 1 (no contraindication to oral anticoagulants), the patients were randomized to receive warfarin (INR: 2 to 4.5), in an open-label study, or aspirin (325 mg daily) or placebo, in a double-blind study;

● in group 2 (contraindications to oral anticoagulants), the patients were randomized to receive aspirin 325 mg daily or placebo.

With a mean follow-up of 1.3 year, warfarin, vs placebo, significantly decreased the annual risk of major events by 67% (p = 0.01), i.e. ischemic cerebrovascular accidents and peripheral embolism (2.3% vs 7.4%) and the annual risk of major events or death by 58% (p = 0.01) (3.8% vs 9.8%). Aspirin (combined results of groups 1 and 2) vs placebo also significantly decreased the annual rate of major events by 42% (3.6% vs 6.3%, p = 0.02), the annual rate of death or major events by 32% (7.9% vs 11.8%, p = 0.02) and the annual rate of cerebrovascular accidents, transient ischemic attacks and systemic embolism by 44% (p < 0.01). The annual risk of serious bleeding was 1.5% with warfarin, 1.4% with aspirin and 1.6% with placebo. In this study, the two medications, at recommended dosages, were well tolerated and demonstrated their safety. With warfarin, the amplitude of the annual reduction of the number of ischemic cerebrovascular accidents and systemic embolisms (-5.1%) and the number of moderate-to-severe cerebrovascular accidents (-2.1%) largely counterbalanced the increased annual risk of serious hemorrhagic complications, estimated to be +0.8%. It must be remembered that, in this study, the serious bleeding rate was low in these highly selected, closely monitored patients, who usually did not receive warfarin over the age of 75 years. Aspirin and warfarin were therefore both effective to reduce the incidence of ischemic cerebrovascular accidents and systemic embolism in patients with atrial fibrillation. However, the amplitude of reduction of the event rate obtained with warfarin cannot be compared to that observed with aspirin because patients eligible to receive warfarin constituted a subgroup of all patients eligible to receive aspirin and also presented a low event rate.

● In the CAFA study (*J Am Coll Cardiol* 1991;18:349-355), 388 patients with a mean age of 67.7 years, presenting permanent (86.3 of cases) or paroxysmal (13.7% of cases) atrial fibrillation, with a history of cerebrovascular accident or transient ischemic attack in 7.4% of cases, were randomized to received warfarin (INR: 2 to 3) or placebo. The study was prematurely discontinued in the light of the results of the AFASAK and SPAF studies. With a follow-up of 15.2 months, warfarin vs placebo tended to reduce the annual rate of major events [ischemic cerebrovascular accidents, peripheral embolism, fatal or intracranial hemorrhages (3.5% vs 5.2%)] by 37% (p = 0.17) at the price of an increased annual rate of fatal or major hemorrhages (2.5% vs 0.5%).

● In the **SPINAF** study (*N Engl J Med* 1992;327:1406-1412), 571 male patients with a mean age of 67 years, presenting nonrheumatic chronic atrial fibrillation, 46 (8.0%) of whom had a history of ischemic cerebrovascular accident, while 525 had no such history, were randomized to receive warfarin (INR: 1.4 to 2.8) or placebo. The study was prematurely discontinued following the publication of the favorable results of **AFASAK, BAATAF**, and **SPAF**. However, with a mean follow-up of 1.7 year, warfarin vs placebo:

● in 525 subjects with no history of ischemic cerebrovascular accident, significantly decreased the annual rate of ischemic cerebrovascular accidents by 79% (0.9% vs 4.3%, p = 0.001) and significantly reduced the annual rate of ischemic cerebrovascular accidents in 228 patients over the age of 70 by 79% (0.9% vs 4.8%, p = 0.02), without increasing the annual risk of major hemorrhage (1.3% vs 0.9%);

● in 46 subjects with a history of ischemic cerebrovascular accident, the annual recurrence rate was higher (6.1% vs 9.3%) and was not significantly modified by warfarin (p = 0.63).

In this study, low-dose warfarin effectively prevented a first ischemic cerebrovascular accident (primary prevention), even in subjects over the age of 70, without increasing the risk of major hemorrhage. It seems reasonable to extend these results to the prevention of recurrent ischemic cerebrovascular accidents (secondary prevention), but with certain reservations due to the small number of patients in this group.

● In the **EAFT** study (*Lancet* 1993;342:1255-1262), 1,007 patients with a mean age of 72 years, presenting nonrheumatic atrial fibrillation and a transient ischemic attack or minor cerebrovascular accident during the previous 3 months, were randomized to 2 groups:

● in group 1 (no contraindication to oral anticoagulants), the patients were randomized to receive an anticoagulant (INR: 2.5 to 4) in an open-label study, or aspirin (300 mg daily) or placebo, in a double-blind study;

● in group 2 (contraindication to oral anticoagulants), the patients were randomized to receive aspirin (300 mg daily) or placebo.

In this secondary prevention study, with a follow-up of 2.3 years:

● oral anticoagulants vs placebo significantly decreased the combined annual rate of major events by 47% (95% CI: 0.36 to 0.79), i.e. cardiovascular deaths, nonfatal cerebrovascular accidents (including intracerebral hemorrhages), nonfatal myocardial infarction, or systemic embolism (8% vs 17%, combined $p = 0.001$); they significantly decreased the annual rate of disabling or fatal cerebrovascular accidents by 66% (95% CI: 0.20 to 0.57) (4% vs 12%, $p < 0.001$);

● aspirin (combined results of groups 1 and 2) vs placebo tended to reduce the annual risk of major events by 17% (95% CI: 0.65 to 1.05) (15% vs 19%; NS);

● oral anticoagulants vs aspirin were significantly more effective in the prevention of major events, which were decreased by 40% ($p = 0.008$), especially due to a 62% reduction of fatal or nonfatal cerebrovascular accidents ($p < 0.001$);

● this result was obtained at the price of a low annual serious bleeding rate with either oral anticoagulants (2.8%) or aspirin (0.9%), but oral anticoagulants were responsible for more frequent minor and serious hemorrhages than aspirin ($p < 0.001$), which also tended to slightly increase the frequency of these events vs placebo ($p = 0.39$, NS).

In this study, conducted in patients with nonrheumatic atrial fibrillation and a recent history ($\leq$ 3 months) of transient ischemic attack or minor cerebrovascular accident, oral anticoagulants prevented 90 vascular events (essentially cerebrovascular accidents) per 1,000 patients treated for one year. Aspirin, which can be used safely, was found to be less effective and prevented only 40 vascular events per 1,000 patients treated for one year.

● The **SPAF 2** study (*Lancet* 1994;343:687-691), conducted in 1,100 patients with nonrheumatic atrial fibrillation, compared the efficacy of warfarin (INR: 2 to 4.5) and aspirin (325 mg daily) on the prevention of major events: ischemic cerebrovascular accidents and systemic embolism (this direct comparison was not possible in the **SPAF 1** study because of the small number of thromboembolic events) and the effects of these two treatments were evaluated according to age. Patients were divided into 2 groups according to age $\leq$ 75 years or > 75 years. The mean follow-up was 3.1 years and 2 years in each of the 2 groups, respectively:

● in patients ≤ 75 years, warfarin vs aspirin tended to decrease the annual rate of major events by 0.7% (1.3% vs 1.9%). In the absence of any embolic risk factors (hypertension, recent heart failure, or history of thromboembolic accident), the absolute annual rate of major events was low, of the order of 0.5%, with aspirin. Warfarin was responsible for an annual serious hemorrhage rate of 1.7% vs 0.9% with aspirin (p = 0.17);

● in patients > 75 years, warfarin vs aspirin tended to decrease the annual rate of major events by 1.2% (3.6% vs 4.8%, p = 0.39), and significantly increased the annual serious bleeding rate, especially cerebral hemorrhages (4.2% vs 1.6%, p = 0.04), despite an INR within the therapeutic zone.

This study therefore appears to show that the reduction of the ischemic cerebrovascular accident rate obtained with warfarin was only moderate, regardless of age, compared to that obtained with aspirin. In patients ≤ 75 years, in the absence of any predisposing factors, the risk of ischemic cerebrovascular accident was low (0.5% per year) and the additional reduction of this risk did not justify the risks, cost and disadvantages of long-term oral anticoagulant treatment. Regardless of the preventive treatment used, the incidence of ischemic and hemorrhagic cerebrovascular accidents was considerable in patients over the age of 75.

Age and potential thromboembolic risk must be taken into account in the choice of prophylactic antithrombotic treatment. Schematically, according to the authors of the **SPAF 2** study, in patients ≤ 75 years, in the absence of any risk factors, aspirin is recommended because of the low probability of thromboembolic events. In the presence of risk factors, warfarin may be indicated in patients of this age-group. No definitive conclusions have been reached for patients over the age of 75.

● In the **SPAF 3** study (*Lancet* 1996;348:633-638), 1,044 patients with a mean age of 72 years, presenting nonrheumatic atrial fibrillation (permanent in 84% of cases) and at least one of the following thromboembolic risk factors: congestive heart failure or echocardiographic left ventricular shortening fraction ≤ 25% (45% of cases), thromboembolic history (38% of cases), SBP ≥ 160 mm Hg (32% of cases), were randomized to receive open-label low-dose warfarin (INR: 1.2 to 1.5) combined with aspirin (325 mg daily) or warfarin alone at a slightly higher dosage (INR: 2.0 to 3.0).

After a mean follow-up of 1.1 year, the trial was stopped because the low-dose warfarin-aspirin combination vs warfarin prescribed alone:

● was accompanied by a high annual rate of major events: ischemic cerebrovascular accidents and systemic embolism (7.9% vs 1.9%, p < 0.0001, which represents an absolute reduction of 60% in favor of warfarin prescribed alone), disabling cerebrovascular accidents (5.6% vs 1.7%, p = 0.0007), and major events or vascular deaths (11.8% vs 6.4%, p = 0.002);

● considerably increased the annual rate of major events in patients with a history of thromboembolic disease (11.9% vs 3.4%, p = 0.02); in comparison, in high-risk patients with no history of thromboembolic disease, the annual rate of these events was 5.3% vs 1.1% (p = 0.01), respectively

● was responsible for a similar annual major bleeding rate (2.4% vs 2.1%; NS).

In this study, the combination of fixed low-dose warfarin, ensuring low-level anticoagulation (INR: 1.2 to 1.5), and aspirin (325 mg daily) proved to be insufficient to prevent ischemic cerebrovascular accidents, while, on the contrary, a higher dosage of warfarin, adapted to the INR (2.0 to 3.0), considerably and significantly decreased this risk, especially in patients with a history of thromboembolic disease.

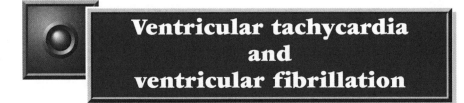

Ventricular tachycardia and ventricular fibrillation

Cardiac sudden death constitutes a major public health problem, with approximately 50,000 cases per year in France. One half of all deaths from coronary heart disease are sudden deaths (death in less than one hour after onset of the first symptoms) and the main mechanism is ventricular fibrillation, either primary or secondary to ventricular tachycardia.

Primary prevention measures must include detection of markers predictive of malignant ventricular arrhythmias, especially in patients with coronary heart disease with recent myocardial infarction or severe left ventricular dysfunction. However, antiarrhythmic treatment remains poorly defined in these patients.

Secondary prevention is addressed to subjects who have survived an episode of ventricular fibrillation or tolerated poorly ventricular tachycardia, occurring in the absence of an acute coronary event. The management of these patients is now more clearly defined with the advent of the implantable cardioverter-defibrillator.

Primary prevention in high-risk patients with coronary heart disease

The risk of sudden death is maximal during the first year following myocardial infarction. Noninvasive investigations designed to assess the risk of arrhythmia include 24-hour Holter ECG monitoring, high amplification signal-averaged ECG, sinus variability, and baroreflex sensitivity studies. Although the negative predictive value of these various tests is high, their positive predictive value remains less than 30%. However, the positive predictive value increases when several tests are positive, which may then lead to electrophysiological studies, especially in the presence of severe left ventricular dysfunction (ejection fraction < 35%), as left ventricular dysfunction, together with occlusion of the myocardial infarction-related artery, constitutes the main predictive factor of mortality.

Current state of knowledge

1 Class I antiarrhythmic drugs are effective to decrease the number of post-myocardial infarction ventricular premature depolarizations.

The **IMPACT** study (*J Am Coll Cardiol* 1984;4:1148-1163), conducted in 630 patients, demonstrated that the sustained-release form of mexiletine, vs placebo, significantly reduced the incidence of frequent post-myocardial infarction premature ventricular complexes.

In the **CAPS** study (*Am J Cardiol* 1988;61:501-509), which included 502 patients, flecainide and encainide gave the best results with 79% and 83% of responding patients, respectively (70% reduction of the total number of ventricular premature complexes) vs 37% with placebo.

2 Despite a "cosmetic effect" on ventricular premature depolarizations, class I antiarrhythmic drugs can be harmful, especially in the case of left ventricular dysfunction. They are responsible for increased morbidity and mortality, attributed to their negative inotropic and proarrhythmic effects.

The **IMPACT** study already showed a tendency to excess mortality with mexiletine, but the results of the **CAST I** and **CAST II** studies led to contraindication of class Ic antiarrhythmic drugs in the treatment of asymptomatic or minimally symptomatic ventricular premature depolarizations. The **CAST I** study (*N Engl J Med* 1989; 321:401-412), conducted in 1,727 patients, was interrupted at the 10th month in the light of the excess mortality observed with encainide or flecainide vs placebo: 7.7% vs 3.0% for all cause mortality and 4.5% vs 1.2% for deaths from arrhythmia. In the **CAST II** study (*N Engl J Med* 1992;327:227-233), which included 2,700 patients with left ventricular ejection fraction ≤ 0.40, moricizine increased the mortality at 2 weeks without modifying the long-term prognosis (18 months), with however an accentuation of nonfatal events, especially cardiovascular events (15.7% vs 8.2% with placebo).

Finally, the meta-analysis by **Teo** (*JAMA* 1993;270:1589-1595), based on 51 trials and 23,000 patients, confirmed that, overall, class I antiarrhythmic drugs significantly increased post-myocardial infarction mortality [odds ratio (OR) 1.14, $p = 0.03$]. However, the harmful effects vary according to the subclass considered: a simple unfavorable tendency for classes Ia and Ib, but significant excess mortality for class Ic antiarrhythmic drugs (OR 1.82, p = 0.02).

 Beta-blockers are the only antiarrhythmic drugs able to decrease both all cause mortality and sudden death (see p. 208).

The results of several meta-analyses are perfectly concordant: **Beta-Blocker Pooling Project** (9 trials, 14,000 patients; *Eur Heart J* 1988;9:8-16), meta-analysis by **Yusuf** (25 trials, 23,000 patients, *JAMA* 1988;260:2088-2093), meta-analysis by **Teo** (55 trials, 53,000 patients, *JAMA* 1993;270:1589-1595). Beta-blockers decrease all cause mortality by about 20% at one year and more markedly reduce (by 32%) the risk of sudden death. Beta-blockers appear to be more effective when they are prescribed in high-risk patients with arrhythmia, moderate heart failure, or a history of myocardial infarction.

It should be noted that these results were obtained before the age of thrombolysis. The exact place of beta-blockers after a coronary reperfusion strategy for acute myocardial infarction has yet to be defined.

4 **Amiodarone decreases the incidence of sudden death, but has not been shown to modify total post-myocardial infarction mortality.**

This beneficial effect is attributed to class III antiarrhythmic properties, combined with a non-competitive alpha- and beta-adrenergic antagonist activity, while the proarrhythmic and negative inotropic effects are considered to be negligible.

● Two small studies, the **BASIS** study (*J Am Coll Cardiol* 1990;16:1711-1718) and a **Polish** study (*J Am Coll Cardiol* 1992;20:1056-1062) concluded on a reduction of mortality, especially due to sudden death, when amiodarone was prescribed for asymptomatic complex ventricular ectopic activity (**BASIS** study) or when beta-blockers were contraindicated (**Polish** study). This was confirmed by the meta-analysis by **Teo** (*JAMA* 1993;270:1589-1595), which revealed a significant reduction of mortality with amiodarone (OR: 0.71, p = 0.003), but based on data limited to a sample of 1,500 patients recruited by 8 trials.

● Two large-scale trials have recently tempered these results.

The **EMIAT** study (*Lancet* 1997;349:667-674) included 1,486 high-risk patients with left ventricular ejection fraction ≤ 0.40. Amiodarone, vs placebo, did not modify all cause mortality after a mean follow-up of 21 months, but significantly decreased arrhythmic deaths by 35%. However, many patients discontinued treatment with amiodarone: 40% at 2 years.

The **CAMIAT** study (*Lancet* 1997;349:675-682) was conducted in 1,202 patients, also at risk because of frequent (≥ 10/hour) or repeated ventricular premature depolarizations (≥ one run of 3 to 10 premature depolarizations) on 24-hour Holter monitoring. After a mean follow-up of 1.8 year, amiodarone, vs placebo, decreased arrhythmic deaths or resuscitated ventricular fibrillation by 48% (p = 0.016) (3.3% vs 6%), but cardiac mortality and all cause mortality were not significantly decreased. The beneficial effect of amiodarone was more marked, in absolute values, in patients with congestive heart failure or a history of myocardial infarction.

On the basis of these studies, we can conclude that amiodarone is the only antiarrhythmic drug, with the exception of beta-blockers, able to decrease the incidence of sudden death after myocardial infarction, in the presence or absence of ventricular premature depolarizations or left ventricular dysfunction. However, it should not be prescribed systematically due to the absence of any obvious beneficial effect on total and cardiac mortality. Other studies are therefore necessary to determine the patient groups likely to obtain a real benefit from this treatment.

Unresolved questions

● **Should quinidine be used in preference to class Ic antiarrhythmics?**

Following publication of the **CAST** study, many practitioners have modified their prescribing habits by replacing class Ic antiarrhythmic drugs by a class Ia drug to treat ventricular arrhythmias. This approach does not appear to be supported by the meta-analysis by **Morganroth** (*Circulation* 1991;84:1977-1983), based on 4 trials including 1,009 patients with benign or potentially lethal ventricular arrhythmias. Although these studies were not specifically devoted to post-myocardial infarction, the majority of patients suffered from ischemic heart disease. Compared to the other antiarrhythmic drugs tested (classes Ib and Ic), quinidine sulphate accentuated the mortality over a period of 2 to 12 weeks, with a tendency to an increased incidence of early proarrhythmic effects.

● **Do class Ic antiarrhythmic drugs still have a place in post-myocardial infarction?**

The results of the **CAST** study theoretically only concern the treatment of unsustained, asymptomatic ventricular premature depolarizations. Although no studies have been specifically devoted to sustained ventricular arrhythmias after myocardial infarction, it must be remembered that class I antiarrhythmic drugs were shown to be harmful and less effective than amiodarone or sotalol in the treatment of malignant ventricular arrhythmias (**CASCADE, ESVEM, CASH** studies, see pp. 305 and 306).

● **Class III antiarrhythmic drugs other than amiodarone have variable effects.**

d-sotalol, a selective antagonist of potassium channels, was not marketed due to the negative results of the **SWORD** study (*Lancet* 1996;348:7-12). This trial, which included 3,121 patients with myocardial infarction complicated by left ventricular dysfunction, was suspended due to a significant excess mortality with d-sotalol (5.0% vs 3.1% with placebo), mainly due to an excess of arrhythmic deaths. d-sotalol, devoid of any beta-blocking properties, must not be confused with sotalol which, in an already old trial (*Lancet* 1982;1:1142-1147), non-significantly decreased all cause mortality.

Dofetilide, another selective antagonist of potassium channels, did not worsen total or arrhythmic mortality in 1,500 patients included 2 to 7 days after myocardial infarction and presenting a left ventricular ejection fraction ≤ 0.35 (**DIAMOND-MI** study; 70th Scientific Session of the American Heart Association, 1997). This study, providing a 3-day telemetric electrocardiographic monitoring during introduction of treatment, demonstrated the safety of use of dofetilide in a high-risk population, as the mortality was 22% at one year.

Azimilide blocks both Ikr and Iks potassium channels. This antiarrhythmic is currently being evaluated in the **ALIVE** mortality study, designed to include 5,900 patients with recent myocardial infarction (6 to 21 days) complicated by left ventricular dysfunction and decreased sinus variability (*Am J Cardiol* 1998;81 suppl.6A:35D-39D).

● An implantable cardioverter-defibrillator (ICD) probably constitutes the treatment of choice in asymptomatic patients at high risk of sudden death, but these patients are difficult to identify.

For example, patient selection of the **MADIT** study (*N Engl J Med* 1996;335:1933-1940) was based on the presence of inducible sustained ventricular tachyarrhythmia on electrophysiological testing, not suppressed by procainamide, in patients with a documented episode of unsustained ventricular tachyarrhythmia and left ventricular ejection fraction < 0.35 following myocardial infarction. The study was discontinued after inclusion of the first 196 patients due to the superiority of the ICD, which reduced all cause mortality by 54% (p = 0.009) compared to antiarrhythmic treatment, consisting of amiodarone in 3/4 of cases. In addition to the numerous criticisms raised by this trial (small sample size, empirical antiarrhythmic treatment, and almost complete absence of beta-blockers), these results were obtained in a highly selected population. Economic analyses performed in the **MADIT** study also showed a cost-effectiveness ratio in favor of the implantable cardioverter-defibrillator (*Circulation* 1998;97:2129-2135).

The ongoing **MUSTT** study (*Prog Cardiovasc Dis* 1993;36:215-226) is designed to compare ICD and antiarrhythmic treatment with a control group, in patients with coronary heart disease, with or without a history of myocardial infarction, but presenting left ventricular dysfunction and episodes of non-sustained ventricular tachycardia.

Apart from the post-myocardial infarction setting, ICD was also evaluated in the **CABG-Patch** study (*N Engl J Med* 1997;337: 1569-1575), which randomized 900 patients with coronary heart disease scheduled for elective coronary artery bypass grafting. These patients were at high risk because of a left ventricular ejection fraction ≤ 0.35 and the presence of late potentials. Compared to the control group, the ICD did not improve survival with a mean follow-up of 32 months. The benefit of ICD may have been masked by a lower than expected mortality (18% at 2 years) and by favorable modification of the proarrhythmic substrate induced by myocardial revascularization.

The **MADIT II** study is designed to evaluate ICD in patients with coronary heart disease and a left ventricular ejection fraction < 0.30, with no rhythmic inclusion criterion.

Secondary prevention

The prognosis of patients with a history of cardiac arrest not related to acute myocardial infarction is very poor. The risk of recurrence, in the absence of treatment or following prescription of empirical treatment, is generally considered to be as high as 40% at 2 years.

Current state of knowledge

 Class III antiarrhythmic drugs, amiodarone and sotalol, are better tolerated and more effective than class I antiarrhythmic drugs, which should not be prescribed as first-line treatment.

In the **CASCADE** study (*Am J Cardiol* 1993;72:280-287), which included 228 survivors of out-of-hospital ventricular fibrillation, empirical treatment with amiodarone (100 to 400 mg daily) was superior to treatment with a class I antiarrhythmic drug, guided by electrophysiological testing or Holter recording. Amiodarone improved survival without sustained ventricular arrhythmia: 78% vs 52% at 2 years, 52% vs 36% at 4 years and 41% vs 20% at 6 years (*p* < 0.001). In patients treated by implantable defibrillator during the study (46% of cases), amiodarone significantly reduced the incidence of syncopal defibrillator shock.

The **ESVEM** study (*N Engl J Med* 1993;329:445-451 and 452-458) compared sotalol and 6 class I antiarrhythmic drugs in the prevention of recurrent ventricular tachycardia-fibrillation in 296 patients. The choice of antiarrhythmic drug was determined by predicting its efficacy by electrophysiological testing or Holter monitoring. Sotalol, compared to class I antiarrhythmic drugs, significantly reduced recurrences of ventricular tachyarrhythmia, all cause mortality, deaths from cardiac causes, and deaths from arrhythmic causes. However, this trial was not designed to detect a difference in mortality.

In the **CASH** study (*Pace* 1993;16:552-558), which included 230 survivors of cardiac arrest due to ventricular tachycardia-fibrillation, deterioration of the prognosis during treatment with propafenone led to premature interruption of the evaluation of this class Ic antiarrhythmic drug, which was compared to amiodarone, metoprolol, and implantable defibrillator.

The implantable cardioverter-defibrillator (ICD) reduces the mortality compared to class III antiarrhythmic treatment, especially in the presence of left ventricular dysfunction.

This was demonstrated by the **AVID** study (*N Engl J Med*, 1997; 337:1576-1583), which was prematurely discontinued in the light of the results of interim analysis. Approximately 1,000 patients with poorly tolerated sustained ventricular tachycardia or ventricular fibrillation, were randomized to receive either an ICD, or a class III antiarrhythmic drug, usually amiodarone prescribed empirically (a small number of patients were treated with sotalol after electrophysiological testing). The ICD improved the survival at 3 years (75.4% vs 64.1%), i.e. a significant 31% reduction of mortality, and this result appeared to be independent of age and initial type of arrhythmia. Although the proportion of patients receiving beta-blocker was higher in the ICD group (42% vs 17%), this bias is unlikely to be responsible for the superior results observed with implantable defibrillator. In this study, the ICD did not decrease 2-year mortality in 396 patients with left ventricular ejection fraction ≥ 0.35 (71st session of the American Heart Association, 1998).

Two other studies, **CIDS** and **CASH** (47th session of the American College of Cardiology, 1998) tended to temper the enthusiasm aroused by the **AVID** study.

In the Canadian **CIDS** study, which included 642 patients, mostly suffering from ventricular fibrillation or syncopal ventricular tachycardia, the benefit of ICD compared to amiodarone appeared to be more modest, as it non-significantly ($p = 0.07$) reduced the total 5-year mortality by 20%. As in the **AVID** study, the prognosis was improved by ICD only in the most severely ill patients (advanced age, NYHA functional class III or IV, and left ventricular ejection fraction ≤ 0.35).

After discontinuation of the propafenone arm (see above), the German **CASH** study was continued by comparing ICD (99 patients) vs antiarrhythmic treatment by metoprolol or amiodarone (189 patients). Reduction of the 2-year mortality by ICD (12.1% vs 19.6%) was at the limit of significance ($p = 0.047$).

The results of studies evaluating ICD led to the elaboration of recommendations by the American College of Cardiology/American Heart Association (*J Am Coll Cardiol* 1998;31:1175-1209) and European Society of Cardiology (*Arch Mal Cœur Vaiss* 1993;86:491-498).

Unresolved questions

 Antiarrhythmic drugs have not been demonstrated to improve the prognosis of malignant ventricular tachyarrhythmia.

Randomized trials have compared various antiarrhythmic drugs, but without a placebo group.

 The superiority of implantable cardioverter defibrillators compared to antiarrhythmic drugs may raise a public health problem because of their high cost.

The cost-efficacy ratio is being analysed in the **AVID**, **CASH**, and **CIDS** studies. Hopefully these economic analyses will lead to a change in health policies in France, where, in 1997, only 9 implantable cardioverter-defibrillators were implanted per million inhabitants vs 125 in the USA and 38 in Germany.

Proarrhythmic effects of antiarrhythmic drugs

- Atrial flutter with 1:1 conduction with classes Ia and Ic

- Torsades de pointes, especially with class Ia and much more rarely with class III

- Ventricular tachycardia-fibrillation with all antiarrhythmic drugs

- Aggravation of sick sinus syndrome with all antiarrhythmic drugs

- High degree atrioventricular block with digitalis glucosides, and class Ia and Ic

- Acceleration of heart rate and risk of ventricular fibrillation in the case of atrial fibrillation in a context of Wolff-Parkinson-White syndrome, with verapamil and digitalis glucosides which shorten the anterograde refractory period of the accessory pathway.

Ventricular premature depolarizations: Lown and Wolff classification
(*Circulation* 1971;44:130)

- Degree 0   No ventricular premature depolarization (VPD)

- Degree 1   Less than 30 VPDs/hour

- Degree 2   30 or more VPDs/hour

- Degree 3   Polymorphous VPDs

- Degree 4a   Doublets (2 consecutive VPDs)

          4b   Triplets (3 consecutive VPDs)

- Degree 5   R/T phenomenon (short coupling)

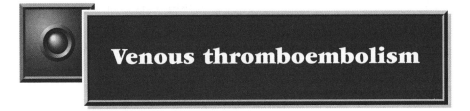

Venous thromboembolism

Venous thromboembolism is one of the commonest cardiovascular diseases, immediately after ischemic heart disease and cerebrovascular accidents, in terms of frequency. The precise diagnosis of venous thromboembolism has been considerably improved by the development of modern invasive and noninvasive techniques.

Deep vein thrombosis

In urban settings, the annual incidence of deep vein thrombosis is 48 per 100,000 inhabitants (*Arch Intern Med* 1991;151:933-938). In western countries, 2 to 4 per 1,000 inhabitants each year require anti-coagulants to treat symptomatic deep vein thrombosis or pulmonary embolism (*J Intern Med* 1992;232:155-160).

The diagnosis of a venous thromboembolic accident is now based on a whole series of objective examinations (venous Duplex ultrasound, phlebography, Iodine 125-labeled fibrinogen scintigraphy), which have allowed determination of the real frequency of deep vein thrombosis. In patients over the age of 40 years, deep vein thrombosis complicates 20 to 30% of all general surgical operations and approximately 50% of major orthopedic operations (*BMJ* 1992;305:913-920 and *Lancet* 1992; 340:152-156). In the absence of prophylactic treatment, it occurs in 40 to 60% of cases after total hip replacement and 60 to 70% of cases after total knee replacement (*N Engl J Med* 1993;329:1370-1376). It occurs in 58% of cases after trauma and is located proximally in 18% of cases (*N Engl J Med* 1994;331:1601-1606). Deep vein thrombosis was observed during the month following general surgery in 25% patients not presenting any signs of deep vein thrombosis on discharge from hospital (*BMJ* 1988;297:28-32).

Finally, it must be stressed that, in the absence of adequate treatment, proximal deep vein thromboses is associated with an approximately

50% risk of recurrent thromboembolism (*N Engl J Med* 1992;326:975-982).

Randomized trials have demonstrated the efficacy of unfractionated heparin (standard heparin) and low molecular weight heparins (LMWHs) in the prevention and treatment of venous thromboembolism.

Prophylactic treatment

Current state of knowledge

 Prophylaxis with unfractionated heparin decreases the incidence of postoperative venous thromboembolism.

The meta-analysis by **Collins** (*N Engl J Med* 1988;318:1162-1173) showed that systematic prescription of SC heparin after general, orthopedic or urological surgery significantly decreased the frequency of asymptomatic deep vein thrombosis and the incidence of fatal pulmonary embolism.

2 **LMWH is as effective as unfractionated heparin in the prevention of deep vein thrombosis.**

The meta-analysis by **Nurmohamed** (*Lancet* 1992;340:152-156), based on 23 trials of prevention of venous thromboembolism, with 17 trials performed in general surgery and 6 trials in orthopedic surgery, including a total of 8,172 patients, failed to formally demonstrate that LMWH vs unfractionated heparin significantly improves the benefit/risk ratio in general surgery, but it may be more effective in orthopedic surgery.

In the meta-analysis by **Leizorovicz** (*BMJ* 1992;305:913-920), based on 52 trials (29 in general surgery and 23 in orthopedic surgery), including a total of 18,543 patients, LMWH, administered as a daily SC injection, appeared to be significantly more effective than placebo ($p < 0.001$), dextran ($p < 0.001$), and unfrac-tionated heparin. Compared to unfractionated heparin, LMWH significantly reduced the risk of deep vein thrombosis by 15% ($p = 0.02$) and the risk of pulmonary embolism by 41% ($p = 0.02$), and tended to reduce mortality by 5% ($p = 0.55$; NS). The results of this meta-analysis show that LMWHs appear to have a higher benefit/risk ratio than unfractionated heparin in the prevention of perioperative deep vein thrombosis.

● Four subsequent studies confirmed the efficacy and safety of use of LMWHs.

In the **North-American** study (*N Engl J Med* 1993;329:1370-1376), conducted in 1,436 patients after total hip or knee replacement, logiparin, at the dosage of a daily SC injection of 75 anti-Xa U/kg, was at least as effective as warfarin in the prevention of deep vein thromboses, at the price of a slight, but significant, elevation of the major bleeding and wound hematoma rates, which nevertheless remained low in both groups.

In the **English** study (*Lancet* 1993;341:259-265), conducted in 3,809 patients undergoing major abdominal surgery, dalteparin, started 1 to 4 hours before the operation and continued for at least 5 days at the dosage of a single SC injection of 2,500 U, had an identical efficacy to that of unfractionated heparin administered by SC injection at the dosage of 5,000 U bid, but with greater safety of use by significantly reducing the minor bleeding and wound hematoma rates.

In the study by **Bergqvist** (*N Engl J Med* 1996;335:696-700), conducted in 262 patients after total hip replacement, enoxaparin, administered as a single daily SC injection of 4,000 U, vs placebo, significantly reduced the number of venous thromboembolic complications (18% vs 39%, $p < 0.001$) and the incidence of proximal deep vein thrombosis (7% vs 24%, $p < 0.001$), especially when it was prescribed for a whole month and not only while the patient was in hospital.

In the study by **Geerts** (*N Engl J Med* 1996;335:701-707), conducted in 344 patients following major trauma (excluding intracranial bleeding), enoxaparin, administered by SC injection at the dosage of 1500 AXaU/mg bid, was more effective (significantly superior reduction of the proximal deep vein thrombosis rate) and just as safe (no significant difference of the major bleeding rate between the two groups) as SC calcium heparin (2,500 U bid).

③ Aspirin ensures effective prophylaxis of deep vein thrombosis and pulmonary embolism.

In the **Antiplatelet Trialists' Collaboration** (*BMJ* 1994;308:235-246), which analysed 80 studies, 53 of which were conducted in a surgical setting, including almost 10,000 patients, platelet aggregation inhibitor treatment (aspirin, aspirin and dipyridamole, ticlopidine), prescribed for an average of 2 weeks after the operation, very significantly decreased the incidence of deep vein thrombosis (25% vs 34% in the control group, i.e. effective prevention in 90 per 1,000 treated patients, $2p < 0.00001$) and pulmonary embolism (1.9% vs 2.7% in the control group, i.e. effective prevention in 17 per 1,000 treated patients, $2p < 0.00001$).

4 **Hirudin (specific inhibitor of thrombin) has been successfully used in deep vein thrombosis prevention.**

In the study by **Eriksson** (*N Engl J Med* 1997;337:1329-1335), conducted in 2,079 patients following total hip replacement and therefore presenting a high thromboembolic risk, the efficacy and safety of preventive administration of recombinant hirudin (desirudin) was compared to those of enoxaparin. Desirudin was started 30 minutes before surgery by SC injection and continued at the dosage of 15 mg bid for 8 to 12 days. Enoxaparin was administered by SC injection on the evening before the operation at a dose of 40 mg and was then continued daily for 8 to 12 days.

Compared to enoxaparin, desirudin significantly decreased the relative risk of proximal deep vein thrombosis by 40.3% (4.5% of cases vs 7.5%, $p = 0.01$), and the overall relative risk of deep vein thrombosis regardless of site by 28% (18.4% of cases vs 25.5%, $p = 0.01$). The safety of use of the two medications was similar. It should be noted that the use of desirudin does not require any particular laboratory surveillance.

Curative treatment

Current state of knowledge

 LMWHs are safe and effective in the treatment of deep vein thrombosis.

This has been demonstrated by numerous therapeutic trials conducted in proximal deep vein thrombosis, either isolated or associated with pulmonary embolism, in the presence or absence of a history of thromboembolism.

It was confirmed by the **Colombus** study (*N Engl J Med* 1997; 337:657-662), based on 1,021 patients treated with a fixed dose of SC reviparin.

2 **LMWHs administered by two, or even one SC injection, are safer and more effective than unfractionated heparin administered by continuous infusion.**

In the meta-analysis by **Leizorovicz** (*BMJ* 1994;309:299-303), based on 16 trials including 2,045 patients with documented deep vein thrombosis, LMWH, vs unfractionated heparin, very significantly decreased cases of phlebographic thrombus extension by 49% (*p* = 0.006) and tended to reduce recurrent thromboembolism by 34% (NS) (either recurrent deep vein thrombosis or fatal or nonfatal pulmonary embolism), the number of major hemorrhagic accidents by 35% (NS), and mortality by 28% (NS).

In the meta-analysis by **Lensing** (*Arch Intern Med* 1995;155:601-607), based on 10 strictly selected randomized trials, SC LMWH at fixed doses adjusted to the patient's body weight and without laboratory surveillance, as initial treatment for deep vein thrombosis, appeared to be safer and more effective than unfractionated heparin prescribed at dosages adapted to the results of clotting tests. With a follow-up of 3 to 6 months (which was able to be evaluated in 5 of the 10 studies), the LMWH therefore significantly reduced the risk of thromboembolic complications by 53% (95% CI:, 18% to 73%), the mortality by 47% (95% CI: 10% to 69%), and the major bleeding rate by 68% (95% CI: 31% to 85%). This result was obtained with dalteparin, nadroparin, logiparin, and clexane. According to the authors, the significant results concerning efficacy and safety of use of LMWHs compared to unfractionated heparin were demonstrated by a more drastic selection of the studies included in this meta-analysis.

In the meta-analysis by **Siragusa** (*Am J Med* 1996;100:269-277), LMWHs prescribed for the treatment of acute venous thromboembolism, were significantly safer and more effective than unfractionated heparin: the LMWH decreased the relative risk of recurrent venous thromboembolism [RR: 0.24 (95% CI: 0.06 to 0.80, p = 0.02)] and death from any cause [RR: 0.51 (95% CI: 0.2 to 0.9, p = 0.01)], particularly in the subgroup of cancer patients [RR: 0.33 (95% CI: 0.1 to 0.8, p = 0.01)]. It was also safer, inducing fewer episodes of major bleeding [RR: 0.42 (95% CI: 0.2 to 0.9, p = 0.01)].

❸ Except in particular cases, LMWH treatment does not require regular surveillance of clotting parameters.

In the studies in which this parameter was measured (*Circulation* 1992;185:1380-1389 and *Thromb Haemost* 1994;71:698-702), no correlation was demonstrated between mean anti-Xa activity and angiographic improvement. As emphasized by **Kher** and **Fiessinger** (*Sang Thromb Vaiss* 1998;110:431-438), the Agence du Médicament (French Drug Agency) has eliminated the obligation to monitor treatment by anti-Xa activity, which is now reserved for patients with renal failure, bleeding, or no clinical response.

❹ Even proximal deep vein thromboses can now be treated at home with LMWHs.

Outpatient treatment is now possible due to the simple administration and ease of use of LMWHs, which usually do not require repeated monitoring of clotting parameters, as recently confirmed by two clinical trials.

In the study by **Koopman** (*N Engl J Med* 1996;334:682-687), conducted in 400 patients with recent, symptomatic, proximal deep vein thrombosis (thrombosis of the popliteal vein or a more proximal vein), nadroparin, administered by SC injection twice a day for an average of 6 days at home, at a dosage adapted to body weight, appeared to be as effective and as safe as IV heparin administered in hospital, as it was associated with a comparable rate of recurrent thromboembolism and serious hemorrhagic complications (no significant difference between the two groups).

In the study by **Levine** (*N Engl J Med* 1996;334:671-681), conducted in 500 patients with recent proximal deep vein thrombosis, enoxaparin essentially administered at home by SC injection at the dosage of 1 mg/kg daily x 2, was as safe and as effective as unfractionated heparin administered in hospital by IV injection: no significant difference was observed in terms of thromboembolic recurrence and serious hemorrhagic complication rates.

 LMWH treatment is not necessarily more expensive than unfractionated heparin treatment, which requires surveillance of clotting parameters.

 Following proximal deep vein thrombosis, compression stockings are effective and decrease the incidence of post-thrombotic syndrome.

This was demonstrated by a randomized trial (*Lancet* 1997;349: 759-762) conducted in 194 patients with proximal deep vein thrombosis documented by phlebography.

Unresolved questions

● **The optimal duration of anticoagulant treatment after venous thromboembolism is still unknown.**

In the **English** study (*Lancet* 1992;340:873-876), conducted in 712 patients following deep vein thrombosis and/or pulmonary embolism, warfarin anticoagulant treatment continued for 3 months gave better overall results than treatment for only 4 weeks, although the difference was not statistically significant.

In the Swedish **DURAC** study (*N Engl J Med* 1995;332:1661-1665), conducted in 902 patients followed for 2 years after a first episode of venous thromboembolism (deep vein thrombosis or pulmonary embolism), prophylactic anticoagulant treatment with warfarin or dicoumarol (INR: 2 to 2.85) continued for 6 months vs treatment administered for only 6 weeks, was accompanied by a lower recurrence rate and no fatal hemorrhages occurred in 282 patient-years of anticoagulant treatment.

Although the optimal duration of prophylactic oral anticoagulant treatment therefore remains controversial, it is obvious that the risk of recurrence after discontinuation of treatment is intimately related to the presence or absence of a predisposing cause.

In practice, according to the Société Française de Cardiologie **recommendations** (*Arch Mal Cœur Vaiss* 1997;90:1289-1305), the following guidelines can be proposed:

● short-term anticoagulant treatment (6 weeks to 3 months) whenever the thromboembolic accident is clearly related to a transient epiphenomenon, for example a surgical operation;

● longer treatment (3 to 6 months) when the thromboembolic accident appears to be idiopathic;

● treatment continued indefinitely in the case of recurrent deep vein thrombosis or pulmonary embolism. A multicenter, randomized trial by **Schulman** (*N Engl J Med* 1997;336:393-398), demonstrated that oral anticoagulant treatment, continued indefinitely, ensured clearly more effective prevention of long-term recurrences than treatment continued for only 6 months (2.6% vs 20.7% after 4 years), at the price of a moderate elevation of the bleeding rate.

Origin and characteristics of LMWHs

LMWHs were discovered in the 1970s; they are prepared by depolymerization of standard heparin. Administered by SC injection at fixed doses adjusted to body weight, LMWHs differ from standard unfractionated heparin by a higher anti-factor Xa/anti-factor IIa activity ratio, a greater bioavailability, a longer half-life, and a more predictable anticoagulant response. LMWHs are distinct compounds that differ by their pharmacological profile and their dosage. They are therefore not strictly interchangeable and the favorable results obtained with one compound in a particular clinical trial cannot be directly extrapolated to all other heparins of this class (*Sang Thromb Vaiss* 1996;8 special issue:5-13).

Heparin-induced thrombocytopenia

The diagnosis of heparin-induced thrombocytopenia should be considered in any case of sudden or progressive marked reduction of the platelet count. Two types are distinguished (*Drug Saf* 1997;17:325-341 and *J Am Coll Cardiol* 1998;31:1449-1459):

● a benign, early form (before the 5th day), with no thrombotic complications, reversible and non-immunological. It is attributed to a direct interaction between heparin and platelets. It affects 10 to 20% of patients treated with heparin and resolves without sequelae, even when heparin is continued. The platelet count rarely falls below 100,000/mm³.

● a late (5th to 10th day; mean: 7th-8th day), potentially serious form, induced by curative or preventive treatment regardless of the dosage of heparin used. It is caused by heparin-dependent IgG antibodies, which activate platelets, and is generally due to immunization against a heparin-platelet factor IV complex. Paradoxically, this thrombocytopenia is sometimes responsible for thrombotic complications (*N Engl J Med* 1995;332:1330-1335). It occurs more frequently during standard IV heparin therapy at the usual doses (as high as 30% in some studies), but less frequently (2.7%) when heparin is administered by SC injection and is virtually non-existent with LMWH. The diagnosis must be confirmed retrospectively by platelet activation tests or preferably by the more specific ELISA method.

In practice, thrombocytopenia must be detected systematically by monitoring the platelet count twice a week until the 21st day. The total duration of heparin therapy must be reduced to a minimum, hence the growing tendency to coprescribe oral anticoagulants with heparin from the first day of treatment of venous thromboembolism.

The treatment of heparin-induced thrombocytopenia consists of discontinuation of heparin; it is preferable to avoid using LMWHs because of the very high frequency of cross-reactions, but to use danaparoid, with a low risk of cross-reactions (10 to 20%) and a response rate exceeding 90%.

Pulmonary embolism

50,000 to 75,000 cases of pulmonary embolism are observed in France each year and about 10% of cases are fatal. **Goldhaber** devoted a recent review to this frequent disease (*N Engl J Med* 1998;339: 93-104). The mortality at 3 months was 17.5% in 2,454 patients of the **ICOPER** register (*Circulation* 1997;96 suppl. I:I-159 and 20th session of the European Society of Cardiology, 1998), and half of these deaths occurred during the first 48 hours. In this register, the two main factors of poor prognosis were the presence of initial right ventricular hypokinesia and recurrent pulmonary embolism.

Heparin

Current state of knowledge

1 Conventional heparin therapy inhibits extension of venous thrombosis and prevents recurrent embolism.

> However, pulmonary revascularization with this treatment is exclusively due to physiological fibrinolysis, which remains negligible for the first 24 hours (**UPET** study: *Circulation* 1973;47 suppl. II:II-108).

2 The efficacy of unfractionated heparin has been clearly demonstrated, as it has decreased the hospital mortality of pulmonary embolism to less than 10% vs 25 to 30% prior to heparin.

> However, it should be noted that this statement is exclusively based on a single, already old, randomized, placebo-controlled trial with a small sample size (**Barritt**, *Lancet* 1960;1:1309-1312).

Unresolved questions

 Low molecular weight heparins (LMWHs) will probably replace unfractionated heparin in non-massive pulmonary embolism.

> Few studies have been conducted in pulmonary embolism. Two small trials, by **Thery** (*Circulation* 1992;85:1380-1389) with sodi-

um dalteparin and **Meyer** (*Thromb Haemost* 1995;74:1432-1435) with calcium nadroparin, showed equivalent results to those of unfractionated heparin.

The French **THESEE** multicenter trial (*N Engl J Med* 1997;337: 663-669) suggested that tinzaparin (a single daily SC injection for at least 5 days with early introduction of oral anticoagulants) can be used in the treatment of non-massive acute pulmonary embolism. In this study, which included 612 patients, the combined rate of recurrent thromboembolism, major hemorrhage, or death was identical with LMWH and unfractionated heparin: 3.0% vs 2.9% on the 8th day and 5.9% vs 7.1% on the 90th day.

In the **Colombus** study (*N Engl J Med* 1997;337:657-662), which randomized 1,021 patients, reviparin was shown to be as effective and as safe as unfractionated heparin in the treatment of patients with isolated thrombophlebitis or complicated by pulmonary embolism (present in one third of patients).

Thrombolytic agents

Current state of knowledge

1 **A consensus has been reached in favor of thrombolysis in the treatment of massive pulmonary embolism (pulmonary arterial obstruction > 50%) associated with shock.**

The mortality of these patients exceeds 30% with heparin therapy and intravenous thrombolysis has been found to be superior to heparin to ensure early pulmonary revascularization (40 to 50% relative gain in 12 to 24 hours) and a rapid reduction of pulmonary artery resistance (30 to 40% reduction in less than 6 hours).

However, 7 prospective trials failed to demonstrate a reduction of mortality after thrombolysis. The small sample sizes of these trials (total of 420 patients) and the heterogeneity of the patient population could explain these disappointing results.

2 **In contrast, thrombolysis is not justified in non-massive pulmonary embolism with no severity criteria.**

This was the conclusion reached by the **PAIMS 2** study (*J Am Coll Cardiol* 1992;20:520-526). The thrombolysis-induced bleeding rate is higher than that induced by heparin, with about 10% of major hemorrhages (half of which are life-threatening) and 1.7% of cerebral hemorrhages. The improvement of pulmonary perfusion and hemodynamic parameters after several days of heparin therapy also becomes identical to that observed after thrombolysis, which explains why the benefit/risk ratio is not in favor of thrombolysis in this indication.

Unresolved questions

● **Thrombolysis could be indicated in massive pulmonary embolism without associated shock in the presence of signs of poor clinical (systemic hypotension), hemodynamic (cardiac index < 2.5 L/minute/m²) or echocardiographic tolerance (dilatation of right cavities).**

This appears to be suggested by the recent German **MAPPET** register (*Circulation* 1997;96:882-888), which prospectively compared the outcome of 550 patients treated with heparin and 169 patients treated with thrombolysis for serious pulmonary embolism without shock. Compared to heparin, thrombolysis significantly decreased mortality at the 30th day (4.7% vs 11.1%) and the embolic recurrence rate (7.7% vs 18.7%). However, these results need to be confirmed by a large-scale randomized trial.

● **Which thrombolytic agent?**

Three thrombolytic agents are currently authorized for the treatment of pulmonary embolism: streptokinase, urokinase, and tissue plasminogen activator (tPA) (see p. 323).

tPA, at the dose of 100 mg by 2-hour infusion, was found to be more effective on hemodynamic and angiographic parameters (**ECSG-PE:** *J Am Coll Cardiol* 1992;19:239-245) than urokinase administered at the usual dose of 4,400 IU/kg/hour for 12 to 24 hours, the protocol most widely used since the **UPET** and **USPET** trials (*JAMA* 1974;229:1606-1613). However, a study conducted by **Goldhaber** (*J Am Coll Cardiol* 1992;20:24-30) showed that urokinase was equivalent to tPA when prescribed at the dose of 3 million IU over 2 hours. Similarly, in a **French** multicenter study (*J Am Coll Cardiol* 1998;31:1057-1063), streptokinase, at the dose of 1.5 million IU over 2 hours, was found to be as effective as tPA in terms of improvement of hemodynamic parameters at the end of the 2nd hour.

Single boluses of thrombolytic agent (urokinase 15,000 IU/kg over 5 to 10 minutes or tPA 0.6 mg/kg over 15 minutes) appear to give equivalent results to prolonged infusions, without increasing the bleeding rate and with a lower cost of treatment.

Vena cava filters

Current state of knowledge

1 **Vena cava filters should be reserved for patients in whom anticoagulant treatment is contraindicated and in those who present recurrent pulmonary embolism despite well conducted anticoagulation.**

The presence of a proximal deep vein thrombosis with a high emboligenic potential does not constitute an indication for vena cava filter. This was demonstrated by the French **PREPIC** study (*N Engl J Med* 1998;338:409-415), which randomized 400 patients. Vena cava filter associated with anticoagulation, compared to anticoagulation alone, decreased the pulmonary embolism rate on the 12th day (1.1% vs 4.8%, p = 0.03), but did not modify mortality and increased the 2-year deep vein thrombosis recurrence rate (20.8% vs 11.6%, p = 0.02).

Pulmonary embolism: Miller's index
(*BMJ* 1971;2:681-687)

Miller's index is used to evaluate the severity of pulmonary embolism by estimating the percentage of pulmonary vascular obstruction. It is calculated by attributing:

● A peripheral pulmonary perfusion coefficient to each of the six pulmonary territories according to the following score:
  • normal blood supply = 0
  • moderately decreased blood supply = 1
  • severely decreased blood supply = 2
  • total absence of blood supply = 3.
The left and right perfusion coefficient therefore varies between 0 and 9.

● A pulmonary artery obstruction coefficient, which increases with the calibre of the artery blocked by the thrombus:
  • pulmonary artery trunk = 16
  • right pulmonary artery = 9
  • left pulmonary artery = 7
  • right upper lobe artery = 3
  • culmen = 2
  • middle lobe artery = 2
  • lingula = 2
  • right lower lobe artery = 4
  • left lower lobe artery = 3
  • segmental artery = 1 (9 arteries on the right and 7 on the left)

The maximum obstruction coefficient is 9 on the right and 7 on the left. The total score (perfusion coefficient + obstruction coefficient) therefore varies between 0 and 18 on the right and 0 and 16 on the left.

Miller's index (%): $\dfrac{\text{perfusion coefficient + obstruction coefficient}}{34}$

Miller's index is commonly used in Europe. It can overestimate the extent of pulmonary vascular obstruction in the case of massive embolism. Walsh's score (*Circulation* 1973;47 suppl. II:II-101) is more widely used in the United States. It does not take into account the alteration of peripheral perfusion.

Thrombolytic agent administration protocols in pulmonary embolism

● **STREPTOKINASE**

Loading dose of 250,000 IU over 15 to 30 minutes followed by continuous IV infusion of 100,000 IU/hour for 12 to 24 hours, with heparin therapy deferred until the end of thrombolysis (when fibrinogen is > 1 g/L).

Other protocol:
• infusion of 1.5 million IU over 2 hours.

● **UROKINASE**

Loading dose of 4,400 IU/kg over 10 minutes followed by continuous IV infusion of 4,400 IU/kg/hour for 12 to 24 hours, with heparin therapy started at the end of thrombolysis.

Other protocol:
• continuous infusion of 2,000 IU/kg/hour for 24 to 48 hours with simultaneous heparin therapy
• infusion of 3 million IU over 2 hours
• bolus of 15,000 IU/kg over 10 minutes

● **TISSUE PLASMINOGEN ACTIVATOR**

Initial bolus of 10 mg followed by continuous IV infusion of 90 mg over 2 hours (if weight ≤ 65 kg: bolus of 7 mg followed by continuous IV infusion of 63 mg).

Other protocol:
• bolus of 0.6 mg/kg over 10 minutes without exceeding 50 mg.

Heart valve prostheses and anticoagulants

Despite anticoagulation, there is a persistent risk of valve thrombosis and major embolism, which is twofold higher for mechanical prostheses in the mitral position (1.8 vs 0.9 per 100 patient-years for prostheses in the aortic position), and also higher for caged ball valves compared to tilting disk valves and bileaflet disk valves (Circulation 1994;89:635-641).

Current state of knowledge

 The only exception to permanent anticoagulant therapy is valvular bioprostheses in the absence of any associated thromboembolic risk factors (especially atrial fibrillation).

Anticoagulant treatment is nevertheless required during the postoperative period (for 3 months), maintaining the INR between 2.5 and 3.5.

 In patients with mechanical heart valves, oral anticoagulants are unavoidable and cannot be replaced by platelet aggregation inhibitors alone.

In the meta-analysis by **Cannegieter** (*Circulation* 1994;89:635-641), based on 13,088 patients recruited by 46 studies with a total follow-up of 53,647 patient-years, anticoagulant treatment reduced the risk of major embolism by 75%, which decreased from 4 (in the absence of treatment) to 1 per 100 patient-years. This benefit largely outweighed the risk of major bleeding, which was 1.4 per 100 patient-years. Compared to the absence of any treatment, aspirin reduced the risk of major embolism by 40%, but was only half as effective as oral anticoagulation.

The bleeding rate with oral anticoagulants is dose-dependent.

In 214 patients of the **EAFT** study (*N Engl J Med* 1995;333:5-10) treated for atrial fibrillation, the risk of major bleeding was 1 per 100 patient-years when INR was between 2 and 2.9, 3 per 100 patient-years for INR between 3 and 3.9, 4 per 100 patient-years for INR between 4 and 4.9 and as high as 50 per 100 patient-years when INR exceeded 5.

 Marked anticoagulation (INR: 2.5 to 3.5) is required in the presence of a high thromboembolic risk.

● This is the case in all of the following situations: any type of mitral valve prosthesis, multiple valve prostheses; first generation aortic valve prostheses (Starr, Bjork standard, Omniscience), history of thromboembolism, or presence of another embolic factor (atrial fibrillation, heart failure, severe left ventricular dysfunction). The optimal INR range (2.5 to 3.5) corresponds to the latest American College of Cardiology/American Heart Association recommendations (*Circulation* 1998;98:1949-1984). A higher INR value (3 to 4.5) is recommended by the Société Française de Cardiologie in this indication (*Arch Mal Cœur Vaiss* 1998;91 suppl. 1:63-79).

● It is useless to try to achieve more intense anticoagulation: in the **Saudi Arabian** study (*N Engl J Med* 1990;322:428-432), which included 247 patients followed for an average of 3.5 years, maintenance of INR close to 9 did not decrease the thromboembolic risk compared to moderate anticoagulation (INR close to 2.65), but doubled the bleeding rate.

5 **Moderate anticoagulation (INR: 2 to 3) can be applied to patients with a bileaflet disk valve prosthesis in the aortic position, in the absence of any other associated embolic factors.**

This was demonstrated by the French **AREVA** study (*Circulation* 1996;94:2107-2112), which included 380 patients with a low thromboembolic risk (sinus rhythm, no thromboembolic history, no severe left atrial dilatation or intracavitary thrombus), undergoing single-valve replacement, essentially in the aortic position (364 patients), with a bileaflet disk valve prosthesis (mainly Saint-Jude). With a mean follow-up of 2.2 years, moderate anticoagulation (INR: 2 to 3), compared to classical anticoagulation (INR: 3 to 4.5), did not increase the incidence of thromboembolic accidents, but significantly reduced minor hemorrhagic events.

Unresolved questions

 Should aspirin be coprescribed with oral anticoagulants?

Two meta-analyses evaluating the coprescription of aspirin and oral anticoagulants reported discordant results. The meta-analysis by **Cannegieter** (*Circulation* 1994;89:635-641), based on 4 studies including 820 patients, concluded on an accentuation of the bleeding rate without any reduction of the thromboembolic risk. In contrast, the meta-analysis by **Cappeleri** (*Am Heart J* 1995; 130:547-552), based on 5 trials, revealed a benefit-risk ratio in favor of platelet aggregation inhibitor treatment. However, many aspects of these meta-analyses are open to criticism: based on old studies, heterogeneous and limited sample sizes, aspirin dosage varying from 100 to 1000 mg daily, varying degrees of oral anticoagulation.

The **Canadian** study by **Turpie** (*N Engl J Med* 1993;329:524-529) is more interesting. It evaluated the combination of low-dose aspirin (100 mg daily in the enteric-coated sustained-release form) with usual anticoagulation (INR: 3 to 4.5) in 370 patients with valve prosthesis followed for an average of 2.5 years. Compared to isolated anticoagulation, the addition of aspirin decreased the combined rate of cardiovascular mortality and major embolism by 77% (1.9% vs 8.5% per year, $p < 0.001$), but slightly increased the bleeding rate. This study has nevertheless been criticized because of the high proportion of atheromatous patients (especially ischemic heart disease in one third of cases), in whom the favorable impact of aspirin on the prognosis was probably not related exclusively to the antithrombotic action on the prosthesis.

Systematic coprescription of aspirin and oral anticoagulants cannot be recommended on the basis of all of the published results. However, low-dose aspirin (100 mg daily) must be considered in 2 groups of patients: patients with a valve prosthesis and documented atheromatous disease (coronary, carotid or other arteries) and those presenting recurrent embolism despite satisfactory anticoagulation and in the absence of indication for reoperation. Aspirin at the dose of 500 to 1000 mg daily must be abandoned because of the unacceptable bleeding rate.

● **Should dipyridamole be coprescribed with oral anticoagulants?**

The meta-analysis by **Pouleur** (*J Thorac Cardiovasc Surg* 1995; 110:463-472) reviewed 6 trials which had randomized a total of 1,141 patients followed for 12 to 30 months, depending on the trial. The addition of dipyridamole (225 to 400 mg daily) compared to isolated oral anticoagulation, significantly decreased the thromboembolic risk by 56% and all cause mortality by 40%, without increasing the bleeding rate. Despite the usual criticisms related to this type of meta-analysis, these results are sufficiently encouraging to justify the setting up of a large-scale clinical trial.

List of boxes

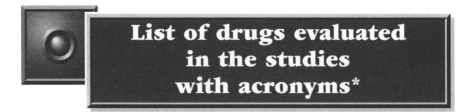

List of drugs evaluated in the studies with acronyms*

Ongoing studies are shown in brackets

Abciximab	**CAPTURE; EPIC; EPILOG; EPISTENT; (GUSTO IV)**
Acebutolol	**APSI**
Acenocoumarol	**EPSIM**
Amiloride	**(STOP Hypertension 2)**
Amiodarone	**ATMA; AVID; CAMIAT; CASCADE; CASH; CIDS; EMIAT; GESICA; MADIT; STAT-CHF**
Amlodipine	**PRAISE; PREVENT; (ALLHAT; ASCOT; CAMELOT; PRAISE 2; VALUE)**
Anistreplase (APSAC)	**AIMS; EMIP; ISIS 3**
Aspirin	**AFASAK; CABADAS; CAPRIE; CARS; EPSIM; HOT; ISIS 2; RISC; SAPAT; SPAF 1; (FFAACS; HELAS)**
Atenolol	**ACIP; ASIST; ISIS 1; TIBET; UKPDS; (INVEST; LIFE; STOP Hypertension 2)**
Atorvastatin	**AVERT; CURVES; (MIRACL)**
Azimilide	**ALIVE**
Bezafibrate	**BECAIT; BIP**
Bisoprolol	**CIBIS I et II; TIBBS**
Bucindolol	**(BEST)**
Candesartan	**RESOLVD; (CHARM; SCOPE)**
Captopril	**CAPPP; CATS; CCS-1; ISIS 4; PRACTICAL; SAVE; UKPDS; (ELITE; OPTIMAAL; VALIANT)**
Carvedilol	**ANZ-HeFT; MOCHA; PRECISE; (CAPRICORN; CARMEN; COMET; COPERNICUS)**
Cerivastatine	**(ENCORE)**
Chlortalidone	**VHAS; (ALLHAT)**
Clopidogrel	**CAPRIE; (CLASSICS; CREDO; CURE)**
Cholestyramine	**LRC-CPPT; STARS**
Colestipol	**CLAS I et II; FATS**

Dalteparin	FRAMI; FRIC; FRISC
Dicoumarol	DURAC
Digoxin	DAAF; DIG; PROVED; RADIANCE
Dihydralazine	VheFT I
Diltiazem	ACIP; DRS; INTERCEPT; MDPIT; (NORDIL)
Dofetilide	DIAMOND-CHF; DIAMOND-MI; EMERALD
Doxazosin	(ALLHAT)
Enalapril	ABCD; CAMELOT; CONSENSUS; CONSENSUS II; ENAI; LIVE; NETWORK; PRACTICAL; SOLVD; SYST-EUR; VHeFT II; (CARMEN; RESOLVD; STOP Hypertension 2;)
Encainide	CAPS; CAST I
Enoxaparine	ESSENCE; TIMI 11B
Eptifibatide	IMPACT II; PURSUIT
Felodipine	HOT; VHeFT III; (STOP Hypertension 2)
Fenofibrate	(DAIS; FIELD)
Flecainide	CAPS; CAST I
Fluvastatin	CURVES; LCAS; (FAME)
Gemfibrozil	VA-HIT
Heparin	ATACS; RISC
Hirudin	GUSTO IIb; HIT IV; OASIS; TIMI 9B
Hirulog	HASI; HERO
Hydralazine	VHeFT I et II
Hydrochlorothiazide	MIDAS; (STOP Hypertension 2)
Ibopamine	PRIME II
Indapamide	HYVET; PATS; PROGRESS
Inogatran	TRIM
Irbesartan	(CSG)
Isosorbide dinitrate	VHeFT I et II
Isradipine	MIDAS; (STOP Hypertension 2)
Lacidipine	(SHELL)
Lamifiban	PARADIGM; PARAGON
Lanoteplase (n-PA)	In-TIME I; (In-TIME II)
Lepirudin	OASIS II
Lisinopril	ATLAS; GISSI 3; (ALLHAT; STOP Hypertension 2)
Losartan	ELITE; (ELITE II; LIFE)

Lovastatin	**ACAPS; AFCAPS-TexCAPS; CCAIT; CURVES; MARS; Post-CABGT**
Magnesium (sulfate)	**ISIS 4; LIMIT 2**
Metoprolol	**APSIS; CASH; HINT; LIT; MDC; MERIT-HF; MIAMI; TIMI IIB; (COMET; STOP Hypertension 2;)**
Mexiletine	**IMPACT**
Mibefradil	**MACH 1**
Milrinone	**PROMISE**
Molsidomine	**ESPRIM**
Moricizine	**CAST II**
Nadroparin	**FRAXIS**
Nicardipine	**MHIS**
Nicorandil	**(IONA)**
Nifedipine	**ACTION; HINT; INTACT; PRESERVE; STONE; TIBBS; TIBET; TRENT; (ENCORE; INSIGHT)**
Nisoldipine	**ABCD**
Nitrendipine	**SYST-China; SYST-EUR**
Orbofiban	**OPUS TIMI 16**
Oxprenolol	**EIS**
Perindopril	**ASCOT; (EUROPA; PREDICT Coversyl; PROGRESS)**
Pimobendan	**PICO**
Pindolol	**ASPS; (STOP Hypertension 2)**
Practolol	**MIS**
Pravastatin	**CARE; CURVES; HARP; KAPS; LIPID; PLAC I et II; REGRESS; WOSCOPS; (ALLHAT; PRESERVE = PROSPER)**
Prazosin	**VHeFT I**
Probucol	**MVP; PART; PQRST**
Propafenone	**CASH; (CTAF)**
Propranolol	**BHAT; MILIS**
Quinapril	**QUIET; TREND**
Ramipril	**AIRE; (HOPE)**
Reteplase (rPA)	**GUSTO III; INJECT; RAPID II; SPEED; (GUSTO IV)**

Saruplase (pro-urokinase)	BIRD; COMPASS
Simvastatin	CIS; CURVES; MAAS; 4S; (HPS)
Sotalol	EMERALD; Sotalol trial; (CTAF)
d-Sotalol	SWORD
Spironolactone	RALES
Staphylokinase	STAR
Streptokinase	COMPASS; GISSI 1 et 2; GUSTO I; INJECT; ISAM; ISIS 2 et 3;
Sulodexide	IPO-V2
Ticlopidine	FANTASTIC; ISAR; STARS; (CLASSICS; CREDO)
Tinzaparin	THESEE
Tirofiban	PRISM; PRISM PLUS; RESTORE
TNK-tPA	ASSENT 1; TIMI 10B; (ASSENT 2)
tPA (alteplase)	ASSET; COBALT; ECSG-PE; ECSG 6; GISSI 2; GUSTO I et III; HART; ISIS 3; LATE; PACT; RAAMI; TIMI IIIB; (In-TIME II)
Trandolapril	TRACE; (PEACE)
Trimetazidine	TEMS
Urokinase	TAUSA; UPET; USPET
Valsartan	VALIANT; (VAL-HeFT; VALUE)
Verapamil	APSIS; CRIS; DAVIT II; VHAS; (CONVINCE; INVEST)
Warfarin	ACAPS; AFASAK; APRICOT; BAATAF; CAFA; CARS; DURAC; EAFT; OASIS; SPAF 1, 2 et 3; SPINAF; WARIS; (HELAS)
Xemilofiban	EXCITE; ORBIT
Zofenopril	SMILE

Index of acronyms